RESIDENTIAL
SEGREGATION

RESIDENTIAL SEGREGATION

Karl E. Taeuber
Alma F. Taeuber

 Routledge
Taylor & Francis Group

LONDON AND NEW YORK

First published 1965 by Transaction Publishers

Published 2017 by Routledge
2 Park Square, Milton Park, Abingdon, Oxon OX14 4RN
711 Third Avenue, New York, NY 10017, USA

Routledge is an imprint of the Taylor & Francis Group, an informa business

Library of Congress Catalog Number: 2008039941

Library of Congress Cataloging-in-Publication Data

Taeuber, Karl E.
    [Negroes in cities]
    Residential segregation and neighborhood change / Karl E. Taeuber and Alma F. Taeuber.
        p. cm.
    Includes bibliographical references and index.
    Reprint. Originally published under title: Negroes in cities. Chicago : Aldine Pub. Co., 1965.
    ISBN 978-0-202-36279-3 (acid-free paper)
        1. African Americans--Housing. 2. Discrimination in housing--United States. 3. Housing--United States--Statistics. I. Taeuber, Alma F. II. Title.

HD7293.T33 2008
307.3'36208996073--dc22

                                                                    2008039941

ISBN 13: 978-0-202-36279-3 (pbk)

FOREWORD

The program of Comparative Urban Research undertaken at the Population Research and Training Center had its rationale in the need for urban sociology to move beyond case studies to a systematic delineation of the nature and causes of intercity variations.

The study on which this monograph is based is one of a number made possible by a Ford Foundation grant for a program of Comparative Urban Research. Other publications to date coming wholly or partially from this program include *Ethnic Patterns in American Cities,* by Stanley Lieberson (New York: The Free Press of Glencoe, 1963); *Metropolis and Region,* by Otis Dudley Duncan *et al.* (Baltimore: The Johns Hopkins Press, 1960); *Journey to Labor: A Study of Births in Hospitals and Technology,* by Donnell M. Pappenfort (Chicago: Population Research and Training Center, University of Chicago, 1964); *On the Impact of Population and Community Changes on Local Government,* by Philip M. Hauser (Pittsburgh: Institute of Local Government, University of Pittsburgh, 1961); some eighteen articles in various journals or as chapters in books, a full listing of which is available in the *Summary Report, 1947–63* of the Population Research and Training Center.

All these studies represent the continuation of a series of urban studies conducted at the University of Chicago since the 1920's, including the four monographs previously published by the Center; namely, *The Daytime Population of the Central Business District of Chicago,* by Gerald William Breese (1949); *Recent Migration to Chicago,* by Ronald Freedman (1950); *The Negro Population of Chicago,* by Otis Dudley Duncan and Beverly Duncan (1957); and *Housing a Metropolis — Chicago,* by Beverly Duncan and Philip M. Hauser (1960).

The research of the Taeubers follows the tradition of earlier researches in utilizing quantitative methods to achieve a better understanding of a significant social problem. It contributes to the objective of the Comparative Urban Research program in moving beyond case studies of individual cities to a systematic delineation of the nature

v

and causes of intercity variations. The present monograph is ample testimony to the fact that even the most careful case study of an individual city, such as the Duncan study of *The Negro Population of Chicago*, cannot be generalized to other cities. Patterns of residential segregation and neighborhood change vary from city to city, and only comparative research can elucidate some of the underlying sources of this variation. Another interesting methodological feature of the study is its emphasis on pattern as well as process, for it includes both detailed analyses of the contemporary situation and longitudinal data extending back more than a century.

By bringing empirical data to bear on an important and timely social problem, this monograph should help the search for reasonable solutions. Residential segregation is shown to be a prominent and enduring feature of American urban society. Southern cities as well as Northern, large cities as well as small, are beset with the difficulties that residential segregation imposes not only on harmonious race relations but also on the solution of most pressing city problems. Residential segregation is a problem that must be faced directly; an intricate statistical analysis demonstrates that even very rapid Negro economic advances are unlikely to have much effect on patterns of residential segregation.

Many stereotypes still present in discussions of race relations would be laid to rest if the authors' monograph were widely read. Negroes in cities resemble whites in cities. Both racial groups are highly urbanized, and most of the in-migrants of either race to a city are former residents of another city. The rural Negro sharecropper is disappearing from the American scene, and no longer makes up a significant share of the Negro in-migrants to cities. Within cities, both Negroes and whites display similar patterns of residential behavior, with those of higher incomes seeking out newer and better housing. Both Negroes and whites respond similarly to national social and economic factors which set the context within which local changes occur. The authors' comparisons of residential change in the 1940's with that in the 1950's, for example, demonstrate that general housing market conditions are the chief factor in determining the type and amount of change in racial residential patterns in individual cities throughout the country.

It is appropriate to observe that this volume is a melding of the doctoral dissertations of its authors together with the findings of continued joint research. This work may well be the beginning of a series of distinguished monographs by a promising new husband-wife team.

PHILIP M. HAUSER, *Director*
Population Research and Training Center
University of Chicago

ACKNOWLEDGMENTS

Portions of this research were initially undertaken in connection with the authors' doctoral dissertations. At Harvard University, Professors Sanford Dornbusch and Samuel A. Stouffer, successive chairmen of Mr. Taeuber's thesis committee, were particularly helpful. The completion of Mrs. Taeuber's thesis was made easier by Professor G. Franklin Edwards, who arranged for office space and clerical assistance at Howard University, and gave generously of his own time. Most of the work of updating and reworking the material for publication was performed at the Population Research and Training Center, University of Chicago. Professor Philip M. Hauser, Director of the Center, is responsible for providing the facilities and encouragement permitting completion of the research.

We are indebted to Professor Otis Dudley Duncan and Dr. Beverly Duncan for frequent advice and intellectual stimulation.

Principal financial support during all stages of the research was provided by the Comparative Urban Research program at the Population Research and Training Center, under a grant from the Ford Foundation. Additional funds were provided by the Laboratory of Social Relations at Harvard University and by the Field Foundation.

We appreciate the contributions of the following students who assisted on the project:

At Howard University: Shirley Broderick, Paul Chen Young, Ida Smith, Leroy Stone, and Martha Stone.
At the University of Chicago: Harold Abramson, Pirhiya Beck, Walter Bernhardt, Lee Jay Cho, Judith Field, Clyde Franklin, Sultan Hashmi, Howard Hill, Kenneth Kessin, Philip Lehpamer, Noel Oakley, Joyce Richardson, Judith Spiegler, Erwin Stein, and Mark Warden.

KARL E. TAEUBER
ALMA F. TAEUBER

CONTENTS

ix

PART TWO □ THE PROCESS OF NEIGHBORHOOD CHANGE

FIGURES

TABLES

NEGROES IN CITIES

If, for instance, Boston in the East, Chicago and perhaps Kansas City in the West, and Atlanta, New Orleans and Galveston in the South, were studied in a similar way, we should have a trustworthy picture of Negro city life.

—W. E. B. DuBois,
The Philadelphia Negro, 1899

1

PREVIEW OF PRINCIPAL FINDINGS

Residential segregation occupies a key position in patterns of race relations in the urban United States. It not only inhibits the development of informal, neighborly relations between whites and Negroes, but ensures the segregation of a variety of public and private facilities. The clientele of schools, hospitals, libraries, parks, and stores is determined in large part by the racial composition of the neighborhood in which they are located.

It is sometimes argued that personal contact between whites and Negroes is more common in the South than in the North, and that a mutually agreed-upon etiquette of race relations permits whites and Negroes to live side by side without overt conflict. In recent years, however, the rapid downfall of legal barriers to desegregation of schools and other public facilities has led whites in many Southern communities to a recognition that residential segregation can accomplish *de facto* what can no longer be accomplished *de jure*. In the North, too, residential segregation is a major focus of racial controversy and conflict. In both regions, residential segregation is not only a vital social issue in itself, but is closely intertwined with most of the problems confronting urban society.

In 1910, 73 per cent of the Negro population of the United States were rural; in 1960, 73 per cent were urban. Negroes have moved from farms and villages to cities within the South, and in even greater numbers to the large industrial cities of the North and West. In the course of this massive redistribution of Negro population, many Negro families moved from an isolated rural society to the heart of contemporary urban society. Like the European immigrants of earlier days, Negroes initially were fitted into the lowest status positions in the urban social structure, and were restricted in their housing opportunities. In sharp contrast to the immigrants, however, the social position of Negroes has remained at the bottom, and Negro ghettos are expanding rather than disappearing. Residential segregation persists as a major barrier to equality in race relations.

Our approach to the analysis of Negro residential segregation and processes of neighborhood change is comparative and statistical. By quantitative comparison of the situation in many different cities, we attempt to assess those patterns and processes which are common to all communities and those which vary. Much of the text presents documentation of our conclusions. As a preliminary guide to the reader, therefore, we preview here our major findings, free of the technical details and qualifications with which they are presented in later chapters. However, the conclusions from a research undertaking such as this cannot stand alone, independent of their methodological underpinnings. Hence, this preview is intended to be a guide to the subsequent material, an annotated table of contents, rather than an independent summary. In addition to the discussions in succeeding chapters, we call attention in particular to the overview of segregation index methodology in the final section of Appendix A.

□ PATTERNS OF RESIDENTIAL SEGREGATION

Negro protest groups often seek publicity with claims that their city is the most segregated in the nation, and Southerners often allege that residential segregation is greater in Northern than in Southern cities. However, systematic study of the block-by-block patterns of residential segregation reveals little difference among cities. A high degree of racial residential segregation is universal in American cities. Whether a city is a metropolitan center or a suburb; whether it is in the North or South; whether the Negro population is large or small — in every case, white and Negro households are highly segregated from each other. Negroes are more segregated residentially than are Orientals, Mexican Americans, Puerto Ricans, or any nationality group. In fact, Negroes are by far the most residentially segregated urban minority group in recent American history. This is evident in the virtually complete exclusion of Negro residents from most new suburban developments of the past fifty years as well as in the block-by-block expansion of Negro residential areas in the central portions of many large cities.

The poverty of urban Negroes is often regarded as contributory to their residential segregation. Because low-cost housing tends to be segregated from high-cost housing, any low-income group within the city will be residentially segregated to some extent from those with higher incomes. Economic factors, however, cannot account for more than a small portion of observed levels of racial residential segregation. Regardless of their economic status, Negroes rarely live in "white" residential areas, while whites, no matter how poor, rarely live in "Negro" residential areas. In recent decades, Negroes have been much more successful in securing improvements in economic status than in obtaining housing on a less segregated basis. Continued economic gains by Negroes are not likely to alter substantially the prevalent patterns of racial residential segregation.

For many Northern cities, the first rapid in-migration of Negroes occurred between 1910 and 1930, and this period witnessed the initial development of large, racially homogeneous areas of Negro residence. In Southern cities, residential segregation between Negroes and whites has been increasing ever since the Civil War, as less segregated residential patterns which originated during slavery have been gradually obliterated. Those cities whose principal growth has occurred since the Civil War probably began with a greater degree of residential segregation than older Southern cities, but differences diminished as time passed. For both Northern and Southern cities, therefore, levels of segregation have been increasing for many decades up to 1940. By then, a high degree of residential segregation typified every city with a sizable Negro population, although average levels of segregation were slightly lower in Southern than in Northern cities.

During the 1940's, wartime restrictions on new construction caused the housing supply to lag behind population growth. In a tight housing market, housing alternatives for both whites and Negroes were limited, and prevailing patterns of segregation narrowed the choice even more for Negroes. Under these circumstances, neither the pressures of rapidly growing Negro populations in many cities, nor improvement among Negroes in levels of occupational status and income had much effect on patterns of residential segregation. Because most of the new housing that was built between 1940 and 1950 was occupied on a segregated basis, small increases in levels of residential segregation were typical during the decade. Larger increases in segregation were most prevalent in the South, where many of the cities were new, small cities which still had vacant land within the city limits suitable for residential development.

During the period following World War II, the housing supply increased rapidly, and by the mid-1950's much of the "tightness" had gone out of the housing market. New residential developments were predominantly in the suburbs, and the rate of suburbanization increased rapidly, especially for whites. Many central cities lost white population, so that Negroes, as a result, had a much greater range of housing available within the city than during the previous decade. Substantial expansion in Negro residential areas occurred, in contrast to the crowding and congestion of the preceding decade. In this more permissive housing market situation, the pressure of a growing Negro population and the economic gains among Negroes were able to counteract some of the forces producing increases in segregation. In most Northern and Western cities, the historical trend toward increasing segregation was halted or reversed. Declines in segregation were common, although many decades of such declines would be necessary to reduce racial residential segregation to truly low levels. In Southern cities, by contrast, Negro economic gains and population growth were insufficient to overcome the long-term trend toward increasing segregation, and levels of residential segregation generally increased. By 1960, average levels of residential segregation were somewhat higher in Southern than in Northern cities.

□ PROCESSES OF NEIGHBORHOOD CHANGE

A high degree of residential segregation in a city is maintained by the creation of additional all-Negro and all-white neighborhoods. The typical process is assumed to be residential succession, in which a neighborhood "turns" from white to Negro as the dwellings left by white families moving out are occupied by incoming Negro families. Although an aura of inevitability is often attributed to this process, as in the popular notion of a "tipping point," processes of change in the racial composition of neighborhoods do not always follow such simple patterns.

Whether or not a city's neighborhoods increase in Negro proportion, as well as the rate at which such racial transition proceeds, is largely dependent on the rate of increase in Negro and white populations. The greater the rate of Negro population growth relative to white population growth in a city, the more likely an increase in proportion Negro in neighborhoods, and the faster the rate of racial change. A high growth rate of white population relative to Negro population, on the other hand, is accompanied by declines in the proportion Negro in many neighborhoods and a slow rate of racial change. Any "tipping point" would thus seem to have less to do with levels of racial tolerance among whites than with the levels of supply and demand for housing in areas that will accept Negro residents. In some Southern cities with low rates of Negro population growth, neighborhoods of both high and low proportions Negro have experienced little change in racial composition over several decades.

Most accounts of residential succession have been based on the experiences of Northern and border cities during periods of very rapid growth of Negro population coupled with a stable or declining white population. These cities have a substantial stock of older housing, much of which is difficult and expensive to rehabilitate and unattractive in comparison with newer housing. For cities in these circumstances, the conventional type of racial residential succession — Negroes taking up residence in homes formerly occupied by whites — has indeed been the prevalent pattern of neighborhood change in racial composition. Racial homogeneity of neighborhoods may, however, be fostered by other processes, such as new construction designed for occupancy on a segregated basis, or selective demolition of dwellings in racially mixed areas. In many Southern cities, new housing is built for both Negroes and whites, but in separate neighborhoods. An unusual example of racial change is provided by Memphis during the 1940's, a decade in which the rate of growth of the white population exceeded that of the Negro population. Most neighborhoods declined in proportion Negro, not as a result of white families taking over housing previously occupied by Negroes, but primarily as a result of the construction of additional housing to accommodate the growing population.

Because of the lesser volume of Negro in-migration and the alternative offered by new construction, there appears to be less pressure for Negroes to take over white-occupied housing in Southern cities than in Northern cities. In Northern cities, on the other hand, vacant land is at a premium and Negro residential areas are already densely built-up. A rapidly growing Negro population must either crowd into existing Negro-occupied units or move into white-occupied dwellings on the periphery of Negro areas. This, then, represents a basic difference between Northern and Southern cities. In most Southern cities, Negroes have continuously been housed in areas set aside for them, whereas in the North, most areas now inhabited by Negroes were formerly occupied by whites.

This regional difference in settlement pattern is reflected in the residential locations of persons of differing social status. In Northern cities, Negroes and whites respond in similar fashion to the social and economic forces producing a general differentiation of residential neighborhoods: whites and Negroes living in racially mixed areas tend to be of rather similar socioeconomic status, and areas undergoing substantial changes in racial composition have nonetheless retained their general socioeconomic character. High-status neighborhoods tend to remain high-status, and low-status neighborhoods remain low-status.

In Southern cities, on the other hand, there is little relationship between the characteristics of whites and Negroes living in the same neighborhoods—high-status Negroes are as likely to live near low-status whites as near high-status whites. Furthermore, there is a tendency for high-status Negroes to live in predominantly Negro areas, whereas in the North high-status Negroes are more likely to live outside of the core of the ghetto, in recently invaded neighborhoods or other neighborhoods of low proportion Negro. The Northern Negro community was superimposed upon a pre-existing pattern of urban residential differentiation, whereas in Southern cities the initial pattern of residential differentiation already included an adaptation to the presence of a large Negro population. Race is therefore an important factor in the residential structure of Southern cities, but in Northern cities residential structure is in large measure independent of the racial composition of the community's inhabitants.

Some of these patterns of neighborhood racial change may be altered in coming decades. Land suitable for residential use is becoming increasingly scarce in Southern cities, many of which are now experiencing the net losses of white population so common in Northern cities in recent decades. Continued growth of Southern cities is likely to result in a greater frequency of the patterns of residential succession typical in the North. At the same time, changes are occurring in processes of racial change in Northern cities. Urban renewal and rehabilitation programs, legal barriers to housing discrimination, rising socioeconomic levels among Negroes, and wider experience with successful examples of racially mixed neighborhoods portend gradual declines in levels of residential segregation.

Change is already evident in patterns of Negro migration. The picture of illiterate Negro peasants settling in congested slums is clearly inapplicable to the present scene. The high level of urbanization of the Negro population and the rising socioeconomic status of Negroes are reflected in changes in the characteristics of Negro migrants to cities and in the spatial distribution of migrants within cities. An increasing number of Negro migrants to cities are coming from other cities rather than farms; they are of higher average educational and occupational status than the resident Negro population in the cities to which they move. In-migrant Negroes seek housing corresponding to their socioeconomic status, and are distributed throughout the city much like the Negro non-migrant population. There is no evidence that the average Negro migrant faces housing problems any more severe than those faced by other Negroes.

Changing conditions within the Negro community reflect to a large extent changes occurring throughout the metropolitan area and the nation. With the decline in residential construction during World War II, the pace of suburbanization of the white population was retarded, and Negro population in many cities grew at a much faster rate than additional housing could be obtained. During the 1940's, therefore, Negro residential areas expanded only slowly, there was frequent conversion of existing dwellings into larger numbers of units, and pronounced increases occurred in the degree of congestion and overcrowding. In the 1950's, with the resumption of residential construction and a rapid rate of suburbanization among whites, there were substantial additions to Negro residential areas in many cities. The increase in the housing alternatives available to Negroes not only lessened overcrowding as many predominantly Negro areas lost population, but also provided Negroes greater opportunity to seek housing appropriate to their socioeconomic status. As compared with the previous decade, there were sharp increases in the degree of residential segregation within the Negro community of persons holding white-collar jobs from those holding blue-collar jobs.

It is virtually impossible to isolate neighborhood changes due to racial transition from those changes reflecting broader trends at work throughout the metropolitan area and the nation. As the position of the Negro in the national economy and the national social structure changes, accompanying alterations in processes of neighborhood change become inevitable. Traditional accounts of the process of racial residential succession, which stress the low socioeconomic status of the Negro population entering a new neighborhood, the overcrowding and deterioration of housing, the declines in property values, and the flight of whites from the neighborhood are outdated oversimplifications. Expansion of Negro residential areas in recent years has been led by Negroes of high socioeconomic status – not only higher than the rest of the Negro population, but often higher than the white residents of the "invaded" neighborhood. The invaded areas tend to be occupied by whites of moderately high socioeconomic status, and the housing is predominantly in good rather than substandard condition. To attribute the processes of racial transition primarily to racial attitudes – to whites fleeing incoming Negro population – is an exaggeration. Given the favorable conditions in the housing market since the late 1940's, and the prevalent tendency of high-status whites to seek newer housing on the periphery of the urbanized area, suburbanization has affected a disproportionate number of those whites in the central city who lived in higher-status neighborhoods. Similarly, higher-status Negroes have been seeking better housing, but within the segregated housing market they find their chief opportunities in those nearby neighborhoods being abandoned by whites. Among both Negroes and whites, the search for better housing is led by those who can best afford it. Patterns of racial transition reflect such general processes of urban change as well as the racial attitudes prevalent in the national society.

With the Civil Rights Act of 1964, steady progress in outlawing segregation in public places seems assured. Negroes have made rapid gains in economic welfare in recent decades, and although full equality is not in sight, further progress is likely. Patterns of residential segregation, however, have yet to show signs of significant weakening. Continuing conflict over residential segregation thus seems inevitable, not only because of Negro dissatisfactions over housing, but because residential segregation is a particularly tenacious barrier to the full participation of Negroes in the general society.

Part One

THE PATTERN OF NEGRO RESIDENTIAL
SEGREGATION

2

□

THE DEVELOPMENT OF AN URBAN
NEGRO POPULATION

A century ago, the majority of the population of the United States depended on agriculture for a livelihood. Cities, although growing rapidly, contained only 20 per cent of the national population in 1860. Of the 4.5 million Negroes in the country, 89 per cent were slaves. More than 90 per cent of Negroes lived in the South, nearly all in rural areas. For the North the decades after the Civil War were a period of rapid industrialization and urbanization, while the South retained its rural character and dependence upon agriculture.

Despite extensive political and social changes in the South during Reconstruction and its aftermath, change for the great bulk of the Negro population was relatively slight. The exodus of Negroes from the South which had been expected to accompany emancipation did not occur. There was little alteration in the social and economic opportunities in rural agriculture, and the various forms of tenancy which replaced slavery kept most Negroes tied to the soil and under white domination. By the turn of the century, forty years after the war, 90 per cent of Negroes still lived in the South. The westward spread of cotton and agriculture was reflected in an increasing population, both white and Negro, in the Gulf states, but stability rather than change was the outstanding demographic fact during this period.

In the decades before the Civil War, the small Negro population of the North had been comprised mainly of free men, not slaves. In 1860, there were in the North and West 230,000 free Negroes, but only 115,000 Negro slaves (nearly all of whom were in Missouri). Almost half the nation's free Negro population was in the North. These free Negroes were concentrated in cities, where they depended on domestic work and other services and on jobs for unskilled labor and craftsmen. Their situation changed little in the first few decades after the Civil War.

A movement of Negroes toward the North and the cities was developing early in the twentieth century, but events of the second decade of the century gave impetus to the movement and transformed

11

it into one of the major migration streams in the nation's history. Large-scale migrations are usually interpreted in terms of a combination of "push" and "pull" factors—the push of limited social and economic opportunities at the place of origin, and the pull of promised opportunities at the place of destination. For Southern Negroes, the boll weevil's devastation of cotton farming added a significant new "push" to the generally worsening rural opportunities in an era of agricultural as well as industrial mechanization.

The significant new elements in the "pull" exerted by cities, especially Northern cities, grew out of World War I. Although Northern industry was expanding in response to the war effort and general prosperity, the international conflict had brought to a halt the flow of immigrants from Europe. Some of the Northern industries which had depended upon the steady influx of immigrants to fill their needs for unskilled labor now turned to the Southern Negro. Labor recruiters, newspapers, letters, and personal contacts all played a part in stimulating many Negroes to seek new opportunities in Northern cities.

This population movement, accelerated by the coincidence of the boll weevil and the war, continued at a high level for perhaps ten years. The war was followed by continued industrial prosperity and legal restrictions on European immigration, and the circumstances of Negroes in the South continued difficult. Data are lacking to specify the dimensions or timing of the Negro migrations during this period, and there has been no definitive assessment of the nature and causes of the movements. The available demographic data suffice to demonstrate that the impact of these migrations was great in both North and South. New York, Detroit, Chicago, Philadelphia, and other Northern cities experienced very rapid increases in their Negro populations between the censuses of 1910 and 1930. The social upheavals of these changes are shown dramatically in the race riots of the period, and less spectacularly in the developing flood of literature on the position of Negroes in Northern cities.

The in-migrations to Northern cities were very large, particularly in relation to the small Negro populations resident there in 1910. The out-migrations from the South, however, were also proportionately very large, despite the large base population from which the migrants were drawn. Between 1920 and 1930, Georgia, for instance, had a net out-migration amounting to one-fourth of its Negro population over ten years of age.

Most migrations, and these were no exception, are highly selective of young adults. It is the young who are both less bound to a former place of residence and more ready to respond to new opportunities. These Negro migrations, which rapidly altered the character of race relations in American society, were undertaken principally by young men and women seeking a new way of life.

The national economic depression of the 1930's caused a further deterioration in the economic circumstances of Southern Negroes, but it also cut off their opportunities for employment in Northern cities. Negro interstate migration slowed to a low level. The lull, however, was only temporary, for channels of communication between Northern and Southern Negroes were well-established, and knowledge of opportunities and circumstances flowed rapidly. With the wartime resurgence of Northern industry in the early 1940's, Negro migration to Northern cities resumed at very high levels. Again the rapid shifts of population were accompanied by intensified racial conflicts, but accommodations were reached and Negro migration continued at a rapid pace during the ensuing prosperity of the late 1940's and 1950's.

Between 1950 and 1960, every Southern state, with the exception of Florida, Maryland, and Delaware, had a net out-migration of Negro population. Migration losses were particularly heavy in the young adult age group. At the same time, every Northern state except North and South Dakota had a net in-migration of Negro population. Altogether during this single decade the North and West gained one and one-half million non-whites in the exchange of migrants with the South. For the first time, the westward movement reached major proportions, with California gaining nearly one-third of a million non-whites by migration. Most of the large cities in the North and West experienced rapid rates of Negro population growth.

Because of a high rate of natural increase — the excess of births over deaths — the actual Negro population of the South has not been depleted by sustained high rates of out-migration. However, much of the *potential* Negro population growth has been moved from the South to the North. Between 1940 and 1960, for example, the Negro population of the South increased by 1.4 million, while that of the North increased by 4.6 million.

Out-migrations of such high magnitude have had myriad social and economic effects on Southern states. On one hand these migrations have tended to ease the economic plight of Southern Negroes, especially in agriculture. Without Negro out-migration, the Southern states would have had up to twice as many young Negro men seeking jobs. Up to twice as many families would have been forming, seeking housing, raising children and sending them to schools which were already underfinanced. By lessening the piling-up of additional population in depressed agricultural areas, out-migration has eased the Malthusian problems posed by high rates of natural increase among rural Negroes. On the other hand, these out-migrations have had numerous deleterious effects on the South. Large numbers of young adults in the prime working ages have left, leaving behind large numbers of children and older persons to be supported by the diminished numbers of working men. The Negroes who were in their late teens and early twenties when they left the South had already been the recipients of heavy investments in their upbringing and education by their parents, communities, and states. On becoming adults, they have left the South, to make their productive contributions to the labor force of other regions.

The migration of Southern Negroes has not been solely away from the South. Particularly during the last twenty years, there has been an accompanying movement within the South from rural areas to cities. Within the South, Negroes have always been about as urbanized as whites, and thus they have participated in the rapid growth of Southern cities. In the ten years from 1950 to 1960, despite a large natural increase, the number of Negroes living in rural areas of the South decreased from 5.4 to 4.8 million. In 1960, more than 6.5 million Negroes were living in Southern cities, and more than 7 million in Northern cities.

The continuing changes in patterns of Negro population distribution have profoundly altered the character of race relations in the United States. As late as 1900, more than half the Negro population lived in a group of overwhelmingly rural Southern counties, where they outnumbered whites. In 1910, no city in the United States had as many as 100,000 Negro residents, and 73 per cent of Negroes were rural. In 1960, 73 per cent of Negroes were urban—five large cities contained more than one of every six Negroes, and more than one-third of the nation's Negroes lived in 25 large cities. When Myrdal's An American Dilemma was published in the early 1940's, the focus of national concern with problems of the Negro's position in American society was largely on Negroes in the rural South. But by the mid-1950's, national attention was centered on Negro problems in Birmingham, Little Rock, Detroit, Chicago, New York, Los Angeles, and other cities throughout the country. In discussing urban residential patterns, we are discussing the circumstances of more than two-thirds of the nation's population, Negro and white.

□ THE LITERATURE ON RESIDENTIAL SEGREGATION

As the number of Negroes and whites exposed to urban racial residential segregation has increased, so has the literature touching on various aspects of this facet of race relations. Reuter's comment on the general race relations literature applies equally to the subcategory of works concerned with residential segregation:

> The body of literature concerned with the Negro in America is very large but its quality is not high: in large measure it is polemic, and for the most part it proceeds from unanalyzed assumptions. It has value chiefly as an exemplification of the historic and current attitudes.[1]

The great bulk of this literature is explicitly problem-oriented, and its perspective is far different from our concern with Negro-white residential segregation as an aspect of general processes of urban residential differentiation. Nonetheless a study of Negro-white relations from whatever perspective can hardly avoid drawing on the race relations literature for insight and understanding of the distinctive relationships between these two groups in America.

By the late 1930's when Reuter wrote, there were already some notable exceptions to his criticism, and in recent years there have appeared many valuable discussions from a variety of viewpoints. Those works directly relevant to our own approach will be mentioned in the course of the later analysis. At this point we want to sketch a number of different approaches that can contribute to the understanding of residential segregation. This sketch will serve the dual purpose of indicating more explicitly the distinctive features of our approach, and of providing a core of background knowledge and perspectives on which we must draw in interpreting our statistical findings. What follows is not a comprehensive review of the literature, but an introductory overview of perspectives on the understanding of contemporary residential segregation in the United States.

Any complex phenomenon may be examined from a variety of viewpoints, each of which can make a legitimate contribution to our understanding. Three broad approaches to the interpretation of residential segregation may be distinguished. One approach emphasizes the historical genesis of contemporary patterns and the lingering residues of the past which tend, if unrecognized, to obscure the present. A second approach considers the social behavior that may be regarded as the immediate cause of residential segregation, and focuses on the attitudes, motivations, and actions of persons involved in building, trading, and living in housing. A third approach views the social behavior of individuals within the context of the general sociological setting, emphasizing the position of the segregated groups in the social structure, as well as broader aspects of social organization, such as demographic trends and urban land use patterns.

1. Edward Byron Reuter, *The American Race Problem* (rev. ed.; New York: Thomas Crowell, 1938), p. 17.

Historical Approaches. — Historically, residential segregation between whites and Negroes may be viewed in two ways. (1) It may be considered as a case of residential segregation of a minority group. In particular, Negroes may be considered as yet another immigrant group, experiencing the patterns of discrimination accorded immigrants and other newcomers to cities, and reacting to a similar set of factors concerning residential patterns. (2) Or, contemporary Negro segregation may be viewed as one facet of the distinctive history of the relationships between whites and Negroes in the United States. Current patterns may be interpreted in terms of their continuity with race relations under slavery, with emphasis on the factors distinguishing Negroes from immigrants and all other minority groups.

1. Assuming underlying similarities between the original Jewish ghettos and the more recent ethnic colonies in cities, we may look to Wirth's study of *The Ghetto* to provide historical depth to a sociological interpretation.

> The ghetto, as it is here conceived, owes its existence not to legal enactment, but to the fact that it meets a need and performs a social function. The ghetto is, in short, one of the so-called "natural areas" of the city.[2]

Wirth traced the processes of accommodation between Jews and gentiles that gave rise to various patterns of residential segregation which were sustained through many centuries. The connections and similarities between the ghettos of Europe and the immigrant Jewish ghettos in New York and Chicago were appraised.

The notion of the ghetto has been readily adopted for the characterization of the urban concentrations of various ethnic groups and of Negroes. Whether the term *ghetto* is restricted to its original usage or given a more general meaning, it is apparent that the residential patterns of Jews and of other immigrant groups in this country were more than simple extensions of traditional Jewish ghettos. Ethnic colonies developed in the cities of the United States both before and after the main periods of Jewish immigration. New migrants to the United States in the nineteenth and early twentieth centuries were, in the main, poorly educated as well as financially poor. No matter what their language, country, or creed, many of the new migrants inevitably tended at first to crowd into low-rent areas with their relatives or friends and others of similar language and cultural background. As the original immigrants or their children accumulated money and knowledge of opportunities, many left the ethnic colonies, to be replaced by more recent arrivals. This pattern has been repeated at many times and in many places. This type of residential segregation

2. Louis Wirth, *The Ghetto* (Chicago: University of Chicago Press, 1928), p. x.

and gradual residential dispersion is neither a new phenomenon nor one occurring exclusively with any particular group.

During and after World War I, immigration from abroad was reduced sharply at the same time that industrial growth in Northern cities required large supplies of unskilled labor. The migration of Negroes from the rural and urban South to the metropolitan North, which became extensive at that time, may be interpreted as supplementing the labor supplied previously by the great transoceanic migrations. Many of the Negro migrants were illiterate; nearly all of them started in jobs at the bottom of the socioeconomic scale, with little chance of economic advancement. These similarities between the immigrants from abroad and the Negro migrants to cities were accompanied by broad similarities in patterns of residence. Negro residential areas quickly developed in many Northern cities, although previously the few Negro residents had been allowed much greater freedom of residence. As Negro migrants continued to move to the cities, Negro residential areas expanded, but within the tightly segregated pattern.[3]

Unlike the European immigrant before him, the Negro encountered nearly impenetrable barriers both to occupational and economic advancement and to residential movement outside the Negro areas. European immigrants or their children or grandchildren were often able to overcome prejudice and discrimination, and for most immigrant groups the handicap of ethnic background diminished over time. The Negro migrant to a Northern city is already a native American, but he and his children and grandchildren still encounter the handicaps imposed upon Negroes. The perpetuation of minority group identity, combined with the persistence of patterns of discrimination and segregation against Negroes, sharply differentiates the situation of urban Negroes from that of the European immigrant groups. Although a comparison of Negroes with immigrants is a useful approach for understanding the early experience of Negroes in Northern cities, it gives no clear guide to recent conditions. The original immigrant colonies have disappeared or undergone radical transformations, while the urban Negro concentrations continue to grow.[4]

2. Consideration of the history of the Negro and Negro-white relations in the United States provides insight into some of the distinctive features of the Negro experience. From the beginning of the

3. The works of Oscar Handlin have emphasized this approach; see *The Newcomers: Negroes and Puerto Ricans in a Changing Metropolis* (Cambridge: Harvard University Press, 1959).

4. Historical evidence is given in Stanley Lieberson, *Ethnic Patterns in American Cities* (New York: The Free Press of Glencoe, 1963). See also Karl E. Taeuber and Alma F. Taeuber, "The Negro as an Immigrant Group," *American Journal of Sociology,* LXIX, No. 4 (January, 1964).

eighteenth century to the Civil War, most of the Negroes in the United States were slaves. Despite the close personal relationships sometimes found between master and servant working together in the fields or between household slave and members of the white family, there was no question of equality of status.

Current patterns of discrimination and segregation were not necessary in slave society. The low status of Negroes was maintained by rigid economic and political repression, and by an elaborate "etiquette of race relations."[5] Following the Civil War there was a period of relative chaos in race relations. It was not until the closing years of the nineteenth century that the current "Jim Crow" patterns of public discrimination and segregation emerged in the South. In the North, on the other hand, legal discrimination was rapidly eliminated following the Civil War.[6]

In contrast to this, residential segregation and various other means of defining and maintaining the low status of Negroes have been the usual *social* pattern in North and South alike since long before the Civil War. Although most Southern cities have never had any large-scale immigration of low-status European immigrants, they developed Negro residential areas similar to those that arose in the North as an extension of the segregation of immigrant groups.

The distinctive history of Negroes in the North and the South leads to frequent emphasis on regional differences in patterns of race relations. Residential segregation is often seen as serving different functions in the North than in the South:

> The taboo against social equality and intimate association apparently takes care of the problem of residential propinquity in southern communities, where there have always been Negroes and their place is so well defined in social space that their location in ecological space does not loom as a great issue. In the North, however, where their social status is more anomalous and where they have no customary place in the community, the residential location of Negroes becomes an issue.[7]

The "etiquette of race relations" prescribes rituals of behavior for both whites and Negroes in the South which continually demonstrate and reinforce the differential statuses of the groups. In Northern cities, according to Drake and Cayton, Negro migrants from the South gradually lose their "caste mentality" and take advantage of the greater degree of social and economic freedom. A "color line," how-

5. Bertram W. Doyle, *The Etiquette of Race Relations in the South* (Chicago: University of Chicago Press, 1937).

6. C. Vann Woodward, *The Strange Career of Jim Crow* (New York: Oxford University Press, 1955).

7. Doyle, *op. cit.*, p. 172.

ever, still exists, and its "strongest visual evidence . . . is the existence of a Black Belt."[8]

In addition to these two major historical approaches to interpretation of residential segregation, the value of local historical knowledge for any individual city may be emphasized. Whatever the general factors, the particular residential patterns of a given city are also influenced by a variety of factors peculiar to that city and its growth. For example, the alley dwellings which developed in Washington, and to a lesser extent in Baltimore and Philadelphia, created a distribution of the Negro population in small clusters intermixed with clusters of better dwellings of whites. In Charleston (S. C.), an old pattern of having Negro servant quarters in the back yards of town houses persisted until recently, although with time, increasing proportions of these Negroes no longer maintained any servant relationship with the white families on whose land they lived. The persistence of early patterns of land use and the influence of topographical features may also affect the residential configuration of a city.

Behavioral Approaches. — The actual buying, selling, and renting of housing depends upon the actions of individuals. The understanding of Negro residential segregation can therefore be furthered through a social-psychological analysis of the behavior associated with the allocation of dwelling space. Individual behavior, however, is so much a function of the person's position in the social structure and the groups to which he belongs that this approach must also take account of the organizations which are involved in the housing market, and how they structure and limit the alternatives open to any individual buyer or seller.

The sale or lease of any particular housing space can be seen to only a limited extent as a transaction involving only one seller and one buyer. To be sure, the confrontation of individual personalities and the manifestation of personal prejudices may affect the course of a particular transaction. In general, however, the housing market functions in a highly organized way, and both buyer and seller behave with a measure of impersonality according to various socially prescribed rules. The person selling or renting dwelling space is usually an agent, whose business behavior depends not only on his personality, but also on his training, on his informal contacts with other sales agents, and on the advice and support of a series of more formal organizations, including realty boards, neighborhood improvement associations, banks, mortgagors, other financial institutions, and legal and regulatory agencies. The real estate agent is, as he would

8. St. Clair Drake and Horace R. Cayton, *Black Metropolis: A Study of Negro Life in a Northern City* (New York: Harcourt, Brace, 1945), pp. 759, 174.

insist, representing the owner of the house or apartment, but this does not eliminate his own importance, as a professional or expert businessman, in structuring the situation.[9]

As in any business, so in the real estate business there are many formal and informal rules defining good business practices. The maintenance of the "character" of neighborhoods and the avoidance of introducing into a neighborhood types of land use which might hurt the value of sales or rental property have long been among the basic tenets of good real estate practice. Particularly in the past, this policy often included explicit rules against allowing Negroes to occupy dwellings in "white areas." For instance, in 1938 the Federal Housing Administration, in its *Underwriting Manual*, specifically sanctioned such segregation.

More recently, especially in Northern cities, explicit rules against "mixed" neighborhoods have become less common, but racial residential segregation continues to be defended in various indirect ways. Residential segregation is seen as a result of essential aspects of good business practice, and as reflecting the preferences of the general public who still view the possibility of Negro neighbors as threatening the welfare and stability of the neighborhood.

This situation is a complex one, and it is clear that racial segregation is so much a part of our society that it is indeed impossible to pin responsibility for residential segregation on the prejudice or discriminatory behavior of any particular agency or group. Nonetheless, as the Civil Rights Commission has emphasized in its recommendations, the diffusion of responsibility does not mean a lack of responsibility. Rather there is much that each agency and group involved in the housing market could do to combat the perpetuation and maintenance of racial residential segregation, but which they do not do within the current pattern of social roles and rules. Explicit actions to discourage residential segregation are not only possible, but are becoming more common at all levels, from the federal agencies which have so much power over the basic financial structure of the housing market, the various financial agencies themselves, which underwrite so much of the market, and the realtors and others who own and manage real estate, to the individuals seeking to buy, sell, or rent living space.[10]

To illustrate that shared beliefs may outweigh facts in the deter-

9. Stuart H. Palmer, "The Role of the Real Estate Agent in the Structuring of Residential Areas: A Study in Social Control" (unpublished Ph. D. dissertation, Yale University, 1955).

10. United States Commission on Civil Rights, *1961 Report*, Part VI, *Housing* (Washington: Government Printing Office, 1961). See also the Report of the Commission on Race and Housing, *Where Shall We Live?* (Berkeley: University of California Press, 1958).

mination of residential behavior, two assumptions widely held both in the real estate business and among the general public may be briefly considered. First there is the argument that once Negroes gain access to a "white" neighborhood, the neighborhood will rapidly become all Negro; and second, the argument that Negro occupancy hurts property values, so that regardless of personal feelings, it is bad business to sell to Negroes in "white" neighborhoods.

It is not inevitable that a neighborhood will rapidly become all-Negro once a few Negroes move in. Yet rapid turnover of neighborhoods from predominantly white to predominantly Negro occupancy does occur. When it does, it is likely to be the result of a "self-fulfilling prophecy."

> When a few Negro families do come into a white neighborhood, some more white families move away. Other Negroes hasten to take their places, because the existing Negro neighborhoods are overcrowded due to segregation. This constant movement of Negroes into white neighborhoods makes the bulk of the white residents feel that their neighborhood is doomed to be predominantly Negro, and they move out—with their attitudes against the Negro reinforced. Yet if there were no segregation, this wholesale invasion would not have occurred. But because it does occur, segregational attitudes are increased, and the vigilant pressure to stall the Negroes at the borderline is kept up.[11]

The argument that Negro occupancy hurts property values in a neighborhood is a persistent myth. How often it is true, and to what extent this may also represent a self-fulfilling prophecy, is seldom considered. In addition, there is confusion arising from the fact that many Negroes live in deteriorating and blighted areas. Not considered is the fact that an area may have been deteriorating before Negro occupancy, and would be blighted whether occupied by whites or Negroes. A second self-fulfilling prophecy also operates if white owners lower their expenses and standards of property maintenance when Negroes move in, making it inevitable that deterioration will be accelerated.

None of the prevalent theories of the relationships between race and property values is based on an adequate assessment of the facts. It is widely acknowledged, for instance, that "block-busters" and others in the real estate business may profit from the willingness of non-whites to pay prices above fair market value for housing outside of predominantly Negro neighborhoods. The housing speculator may be able to sell to Negroes at prices above fair market value, and to induce sufficient panic or fear of falling prices among the white

11. Gunnar Myrdal, *An American Dilemma* (New York: Harper and Brothers, 1944), Vol. I, p. 623.

residents that he is able to buy from them at prices below fair market value. The fact that such a neighborhood turns from white to Negro occupancy is then a result of deliberate machinations. Whether housing values in such a neighborhood return to a normal pattern over the long run is seldom considered. If prices decrease and the neighborhood deteriorates, it may be the continuation of a trend that began prior to Negro occupancy, or it may result from the speculator's lack of concern with good real estate practice in matching housing to the ability of the family to pay for it, and in maintaining the property and the neighborhood.

Concern with maintaining property values is the major reason put forth in defense of barring Negroes from middle-class "white" suburbs. However, on the basis of the most comprehensive study yet made of actual price trends on house sales in middle-class home-owning neighborhoods undergoing non-white entry, as compared with price trends in comparable control neighborhoods without non-white entry, Laurenti reached two broad conclusions:

> First, price changes which can be connected with the fact of non-white entry are not uniform, as often alleged, but diverse. Depending on circumstances, racial change in a neighborhood may be depressing or it may be stimulating to real estate prices and in varying degrees. Second, considering all of the evidence, the odds are about four to one that house prices in a neighborhood entered by non-whites will keep up with or exceed prices in a comparable all-white area. These conclusions are chiefly based on observations of real estate markets in a period of generally rising prices. This period, moreover, was characterized by unusually strong demand for housing, particularly by non-whites who had been making relatively large gains in personal income. These conditions seem likely to continue into the foreseeable future, and therefore the main findings of the present study may be valid for many neighborhoods certain to experience the entry of non-whites.[12]

It has been argued that not only the attitudes of whites and the functioning of the white-dominated real estate business prescribe racial residential segregation, but that Negroes, too, prefer it. For most Negroes, to live near family and friends is to live near other Negroes; on a mass basis this will produce a high degree of residential segregation. Residential segregation may have other voluntary aspects. It is sometimes argued by both Negroes and whites that

12. Luigi Laurenti, *Property Values and Race. Studies in Seven Cities* (Berkeley: University of California Press, 1960), pp. 52–53. For discussions of beliefs prevalent in the real estate industry, see Laurenti, ch. 2; Palmer, *op. cit.*; and Rose Helper, "The Racial Practices of Real Estate Institutions in Selected Areas of Chicago" (unpublished Ph. D. dissertation, University of Chicago, 1958).

Negroes enjoy a greater measure of freedom in Negro areas where they need not be concerned about getting along in the face of continued slights and discriminatory acts.[13]

Although the relevance of "ethnic group attachment" to residential segregation is plausible, its importance has never been subjected to careful evaluation. In a society where white prejudice and discrimination against Negroes account for much of the attraction of living within an all-Negro community, and at the same time help account for the exclusion of Negroes from other neighborhoods, it seems impossible to separate coercive and voluntary components of residential segregation. To the extent that housing alternatives are not open to Negroes, of course, the coercive aspects would seem to be of primary importance.

The Negro's Position in the Social Structure. — In the early years of this century, large proportions of urban Negro workers were employed as domestic servants, and areas of Negro residence had to be accessible to white residential areas. Particularly in the South, this locational factor may account for the much lower degree of residential segregation in the past than at present. As industrial and commercial employment became more important — during and after World War I for Northern Negroes, more recently for Southern Negroes — Negroes no longer needed access to white residential areas. Access to their major employment centers was obtained by living in the central areas of cities, either near their work-places, or along the major transit lines permitting easy access to the major work-places. The changing occupational structure of the urban Negro population may thus help account for the gradual disappearance of the back-yard and other scattered residential patterns formerly existing in many cities.

The occupational structure of the Negro population is a complicating factor in assessing the degree to which Negro residential segregation is voluntary. Residential concentration of Negroes has permitted an accompanying development of services for Negroes in these areas. Some Negro businessmen, professionals, politicians, and others working in Negro areas have a vested interest in segregation:

> Residential segregation is not only supported by the attitudes of white people who object to Negro neighbors — it is also buttressed by the internal structure of the Negro community. Negro politicians and businessmen, preachers and civic leaders, all have a vested interest in maintaining a solid and homogeneous Negro community

13. Drake and Cayton, *op. cit.*, chs. 6–8; Nathan Glazer and Daniel Patrick Moynihan, *Beyond the Melting Pot: The Negroes, Puerto Ricans, Jews, Italians, and Irish of New York City* (Cambridge: The M.I.T. Press and Harvard University Press, 1963), chapter, "The Negroes."

among quality, size, and rent might be quite different in the two markets.[15]

The concept of the dual housing market is helpful in explaining certain facets of the relationship between race, residence, and income. It can be assumed that the supply of housing for non-whites is restricted in terms of both number of units and quality of units. For non-whites, then, demand is high relative to supply, and this situation is aggravated by the rapidly increasing urban Negro populations. Housing within Negro areas can command higher prices than comparable housing in white residential areas. Furthermore, there has been a continual need for Negro housing, which has been met by transferring property at the periphery of Negro areas from the white housing market to the Negro housing market. The high demand among Negroes for housing, combined with a relatively low demand among whites for housing in many of these peripheral areas, makes the transfer of housing from whites to Negroes profitable.

Certain broad features of the population of a city may be relevant to the processes of residential segregation within the city. While the size of the city, its growth, the size and growth of the Negro population, and the proportion of Negroes have all been discussed in the literature, particular stress has been given to the Negro component of the total city population. Several investigators have emphasized the rapid development of patterns of racial residential segregation in Northern cities that accompanied the rapid increase in numbers of Negroes during and following World War I. The assumption that increasing numbers or proportions of Negroes may increase discriminatory behavior has been interpreted in terms of a psychological relation between the "visibility," or perceived threat, of a minority group and the activation of prejudiced behavior among whites. In considering this hypothesis, Allport has indicated the need to distinguish between the causes of segregation and the causes of changes in segregation.

> The principles of relative size and gradient of density cannot stand alone. . . . Some ethnic groups seem more menacing than others — either because they have more points of difference or a higher visibility. Growing density, therefore, is not in itself a sufficient principle to explain prejudice. What it seems to accomplish is the aggravation of whatever prejudice exists.[16]

The relative size and rate of growth of Negro and white populations may affect residential segregation through their relationship to

---

15. Beverly Duncan and Philip M. Hauser, *Housing A Metropolis — Chicago* (Glencoe, Ill.: The Free Press, 1960), pp. 203–204.

16. Gordon W. Allport, *The Nature of Prejudice* (Cambridge: Addison-Wesley, 1954), pp. 228–229.

the character of the housing market. If population is increasing and housing is in short supply, as was generally true following World War II, real estate agents will generally have little difficulty in marketing housing, and will suffer little economic disadvantage by discriminating among potential buyers or renters in any way they or their customers wish. On the other hand, if the housing supply is large relative to the demand, the cost to the real estate agent of maintaining rigid residential segregation may become very high. A similar argument has been used by Lerner, who suggested that the necessity for a mass market for rapid selling of new housing in post-war suburban developments reduced the traditional barriers against Catholics and Jews.[17] Similarly, although the supply of new privately developed interracial housing is very small, much of that in existence came about through market factors—developments intended for whites only or Negroes only were unsuccessful, but were successful when the demand was enlarged by accepting both whites and Negroes.[18]

□ COMPARATIVE URBAN ANALYSIS OF NEGRO RESIDENTIAL SEGREGATION

Our approach to the analysis of Negro residential segregation and processes of neighborhood change differs from most of those enumerated in the review of the literature. This is not to say that the approach of this book is novel and without precedent, but that it derives from a tradition and body of literature rather separate from most of that concerned with race relations and segregation. This tradition stems from the urban sociology of Park and Burgess, and their use of Chicago and other cities as laboratories for investigating the nature and forms of contemporary social organization. Spatial patterns are the focus of our analysis, but these are examined because they are aspects of communal organization. Communities—cities and metropolitan areas—are the units in our analysis. The residential organization of social groups is viewed as an aspect of the communal adaptation of men not only to their environment but to the problems of living with each other.[19]

Within this theoretical framework, our analysis is comparative and statistical. It is comparative in its effort to seek general patterns

17. Max Lerner, *America as a Civilization* (New York: Simon and Schuster, 1957), pp. 178–179.

18. Eunice Grier and George Grier, *Privately Developed Interracial Housing. An Analysis of Experience* (Berkeley: University of California Press, 1960).

19. For a general theoretical discussion, see Amos Hawley, *Human Ecology* (New York: The Ronald Press, 1950).

by examining the situations in many cities. We draw extensively on prior case studies, but our aim is not so much detailed knowledge of any one community or neighborhood as an assessment of which patterns and processes are common to all communities, and which vary. The most distinctive feature of our analysis is its reliance upon quantitative data and statistical analysis. Existing data from recent United States censuses have not been fully exploited, and their analysis can shed light on many of the topics and approaches reviewed in the preceding section.

■

3

□

NEGRO RESIDENTIAL SEGREGATION
IN UNITED STATES CITIES

□ CONCEPT AND MEASUREMENT

That cities in the United States are characterized by a high degree of residential segregation between Negroes and whites is apparent from the most casual observation. Within almost any city with a sizable Negro population there are "Negro areas" where few whites reside, and "white areas" where no Negroes other than domestics reside. In few neighborhoods of any size are the residences of Negroes and whites interspersed more or less randomly.

The difference between the spatial distribution of dwellings occupied by Negroes and that of dwellings occupied by whites underlies the measure of residential segregation to be used in our analysis in this chapter and in Chapter 4. We view residential segregation, for the purposes of this analysis, as an existing *pattern*, observable at any given point in time. This usage must be clearly distinguished from use of the same term to describe behaviors and processes. Many types of behavior are involved in the processes of segregating whites from Negroes, all of which combine to produce a segregated residential distribution as an end result.

Focusing on existing residential patterns rather than on their genesis greatly narrows the range of problems to be considered in determining suitable metrics, but residential patterns still are complex and not susceptible to complete representation in any simple numerical index. Although racial residential patterns in Birmingham (Alabama) and Gary (Indiana) are both represented by a score of 92.8 on the "segregation index" to be explained shortly, these two cities differ nonetheless in residential patterns. It is likely that the more knowledge one had of each city, the more difficult it would be to accept their characterization as equivalent. Our use of a single numerical index to represent a complex phenomenon is defensible in the same way as the use of any average measure. Although no single measure can adequately reflect all the detailed differences between two patterns of residential distribution, a numerical segregation index, reflecting one basic aspect of a city's racial residential pattern, permits a variety of comparisons. Comparison of the index value for a city at one point in time with this value at a subsequent point in time permits some assessment of the impact of various intervening processes thought to encourage segregation or desegregation. Such an index is useful also for comparing different cities with each other. It lends objectivity to an effort to determine what features of the social organization of a city or what characteristics of the city's population are related to the degree of residential segregation. Are Northern or Southern cities more segregated residentially? Is the degree of residential segregation greatest in cities with many Negro residents or with few Negro residents? Is racial residential segregation increasing or decreasing in U. S. cities? Are the trends different in different kinds of cities? Once a suitable metric for residential segregation is chosen, these questions become subject to statistical investigation.

There has developed a considerable literature and several points of controversy concerning "segregation indexes" for measuring the degree of racial residential segregation. (Appendix A is given over to discussion of these issues and of the basis for reliance on one of the many possible measures.) Leaving methodological intricacies for the appendix, the nature of the index utilized in the remainder of this chapter and in Chapter 4 may be sketched.

Our segregation index is an index of dissimilarity, and its underlying rationale as a measure of residential segregation is simple: Suppose that whether a person was Negro or white made no difference in his choice of residence, and that his race was not related to any other factors affecting residential location (for instance, income level). Then no neighborhood would be all-Negro or all-white, but rather each race would be represented in each neighborhood in approximately the same proportion as in the city as a whole. Thus, in a city where Negroes constitute half the population, the residents of any city block would be about equally divided between Negroes and whites. In a city where Negroes constitute 10 per cent of the population, one of every ten households in each block might be expected to be Negro. This situation would represent a completely even distribution of Negroes and whites, with the same proportion Negro in each and every block. For this situation, the segregation index assumes a value of zero, indicating no racial residential segregation whatsoever.

The opposite situation, that of a completely uneven or segregated distribution, occurs if there is no residential intermixture of whites and Negroes. Operationally, this situation obtains if each city block contains only whites or only Negroes, but not both. For this situation, the segregation index assumes a value of 100, indicating a maximum degree of residential segregation.

The index of residential segregation can assume values between 0 and 100. The higher the value, the higher the degree of residential segregation, and the lower the value, the greater the degree of residential intermixture. The value of the index may be interpreted as showing the minimum percentage of non-whites who would have to change the block on which they live in order to produce an unsegregated distribution — one in which the percentage of non-whites living on each block is the same throughout the city (0 on the index). For instance, if some governing council had the power and the inclination to redistribute the population of Birmingham so as to obtain an unsegregated distribution of white and non-white residences, they would have to move 92.8 per cent of the non-whites from blocks now containing an above-average proportion of non-whites to blocks now disproportionately occupied by whites.[1] It is evident from this interpretation of the segregation index that values of 70, 80, and above indicate a residential pattern very far from the minimum possible degree of segregation.

A few comments may be made here on the usefulness and limitations of such an index. We have already emphasized that the index is an average measure representing the situation for an entire city, and thus intentionally glosses over the full complexity and detail of a residential pattern. Second, because of the nature of available data, the indexes have been computed in most cases for central cities only, excluding the suburban areas lying beyond the corporate limits. The political border of the city is seldom a meaningful barrier to the processes of growth and deterioration of urban neighborhoods and accompanying population movements. The political boundaries are relevant, however, in studying political and administrative programs such as urban renewal, public housing, open occupancy legislation, and other public actions. At least in Northern metropolitan areas, most Negroes live within central cities. Nonetheless, residential segregation within cities takes place within the larger context of segregation between the component parts of metropolitan areas.

1. Otis Dudley Duncan has pointed out, in correspondence, that a more efficient redistribution of the population to achieve desegregation could be made by having white and non-white households exchange residences. Without altering the existing distribution of housing units, desegregation could be accomplished by moving pD per cent of the city's non-white households and qD per cent of the city's white households, where p is the proportion of white households, q is the proportion of non-white households $(q = 1-p)$, and D is the index of dissimilarity. The percentage of those relocated in the total population would then be $2pq$D.

(Other techniques will be used for the analysis of some of these problems.)

The segregation index on which the bulk of this analysis is based is computed from data for city blocks. Characterization of the racial composition of blocks is made on the basis of color of household heads, which means that Negro domestics living-in with white households do not contribute to the measure of residential intermixture. From these census data, white and non-white households may be distinguished, but not Negroes and other non-whites. For most cities, Negroes constitute an overwhelming proportion of the non-white population, so that the difference between Negro and non-white can be ignored. However, separate attention will be given subsequently to those cities where large Chinese or Japanese populations, or sub-groups of the white population such as Puerto Ricans, obscure interpretation of white — non-white comparisons.

Although our basic intercity comparisons of the over-all degree of residential segregation depend on indexes computed from data for city blocks, various special topics must be analyzed with data for census tracts or wards. As discussed in Appendix A, segregation indexes computed from different sets of subareas are not strictly comparable. In particular, the smaller the subareas, the larger the index value. Where indexes are computed from tract or ward data, both the specific index values and, to some extent, the relative positions of specific cities, will differ from the patterns obtained with city block data.

□ NEGRO RESIDENTIAL SEGREGATION, 1960

Indexes of residential segregation for 207 cities are presented in Table 1. The table includes all cities in the coterminous United States for which the requisite census data for city blocks were published,[2] and which in 1960 had more than 1,000 occupied housing units with a non-white head. Among the 207 cities are virtually all the large cities of the country (those of more than 50,000 population), as well as a large but non-random selection of smaller cities.

2. "Statistics by blocks are published for each city or urban place which had a population of 50,000 or more in 1950 or in an interim census prior to 1960, and also had a population of 50,000 or more in 1960. In addition, a number of localities were included in the city block program through an agreement whereby the local government furnished satisfactory block maps and paid the Bureau of the Census for the incremental cost of collecting and publishing the information." U. S. Bureau of the Census, *U. S. Census of Housing: 1960, Vol. III, City Blocks*, Series HC(3), (Washington, D. C.: U. S. Government Printing Office, 1961), p. viii.

TABLE 1

INDEXES OF RESIDENTIAL SEGREGATION FOR 207 CITIES, 1960

City	Index	City	Index
Abilene, Tex	93.6	Decatur, Ill.	88.4
Akron, Ohio	88.1	Denver, Colo.	85.5
Albany, N.Y.	76.5	Des Moines, Iowa	87.9
Albuquerque, N.M.	76.5	Detroit, Mich.	84.5
Alexandria, Va.	87.8	Durham, N.C.	92.7
Amarillo, Tex.	88.6	East Chicago, Ill.	82.8
Ann Arbor, Mich.	64.3	East Orange, N.J.	71.2
Annapolis, Md.	80.9	East St. Louis, Ill.	92.0
Asheville, N.C.	92.3	Elizabeth, N.J.	75.2
Atlanta, Ga.	93.6	El Paso, Tex.	80.5
Atlantic City, N.J.	89.2	Englewood, N.J.	87.9
Augusta, Ga.	93.0	Erie, Pa.	86.9
Austin, Tex.	93.1	Evanston, Ill.	87.2
Bakersfield, Calif.	87.5	Evansville, Ind.	91.2
Baltimore, Md.	89.6	Fayetteville, N.C.	88.4
Baton Rouge, La.	92.2	Flint, Mich.	94.4
Battle Creek, Mich.	80.2	Fort Lauderdale, Fla.	98.1
Berkeley, Calif.	69.4	Fort Smith, Ark.	90.3
Bessemer, Ala.	87.9	Fort Wayne, Ind.	91.7
Beaumont, Tex.	92.3	Fort Worth, Tex.	94.3
Birmingham, Ala.	92.8	Fresno, Calif.	83.9
Boston, Mass.	83.9	Gadsden, Ala.	89.1
Bridgeport, Conn.	69.7	Galveston, Tex.	82.9
Buffalo, N.Y.	86.5	Gary, Ind.	92.8
Cambridge, Mass.	65.5	Grand Rapids, Mich.	90.1
Camden, N.J.	76.5	Greensboro, N.C.	93.3
Canton, Ohio	81.5	Greenville, S.C.	89.7
Centreville, Ill.	88.6	Hamilton, Ohio	91.7
Charleston, S.C.	79.5	Hampton, Va.	85.8
Charleston, W. Va.	79.0	Harrisburg, Pa.	85.7
Charlotte, N.C.	94.3	Hartford, Conn.	82.1
Chattanooga, Tenn.	91.5	Highland Park, Mich.	77.4
Chester, Pa.	87.4	High Point, N.C.	94.4
Chicago, Ill.	92.6	Houston, Tex.	93.7
Cincinnati, Ohio	89.0	Huntington, W. Va.	88.8
Cleveland, Ohio	91.3	Huntsville, Ala.	87.9
Columbia, S.C.	94.1	Indianapolis, Ind.	91.6
Columbus, Ga.	92.2	Inkster, Mich.	95.0
Columbus, Ohio	85.3	Jackson, Mich.	89.3
Compton, Calif.	84.4	Jackson, Miss.	94.2
Corpus Christi, Tex.	88.6	Jacksonville, Fla.	96.9
Covington, Ky.	87.8	Jersey City, N.J.	77.9
Dallas, Tex.	94.6	Joliet, Ill.	90.2
Dayton, Ohio	91.3	Kalamazoo, Mich.	82.8
Daytona Beach, Fla.	96.7	Kansas City, Kan.	91.5

City	Index	City	Index
Kansas City, Mo.	90.8	Paterson, N.J.	75.9
Knoxville, Tenn.	90.7	Pensacola, Fla.	90.7
Lakeland, Fla.	96.3	Peoria, Ill.	86.7
Lansing, Mich.	89.3	Philadelphia, Pa.	87.1
Las Vegas, Nev.	91.8	Phoenix, Ariz.	85.6
Lexington, Ky.	87.0	Pittsburgh, Pa.	84.6
Lima, Ohio	85.1	Pontiac, Mich.	90.5
Little Rock, Ark.	89.4	Port Arthur, Tex.	90.4
Long Beach, Calif.	84.0	Portland, Ore.	76.7
Lorain, Ohio	79.8	Portsmouth, Va.	94.0
Los Angeles, Calif.	81.8	Providence, R.I.	77.0
Louisville, Ky.	89.2	Racine, Wis.	87.8
Lubbock, Tex.	91.3	Raleigh, N.C.	92.8
Lynchburg, Va.	84.0	Reading, Pa.	76.2
Macon, Ga.	83.7	Richmond, Calif.	77.3
Memphis, Tenn.	92.0	Richmond, Va.	94.8
Miami, Fla.	97.9	Riverside, Calif.	85.5
Midland, Tex.	93.4	Roanoke, Va.	93.9
Milwaukee, Wis.	88.1	Rochester, N.Y.	82.4
Minneapolis, Minn.	79.3	Rockford, Ill.	89.4
Mobile, Ala.	91.9	Sacramento, Calif.	63.9
Monroe, La.	96.2	Saginaw, Mich.	87.5
Montclair, N.J.	80.3	St. Louis, Mo.	90.5
Montgomery, Ala.	94.7	St. Paul, Minn.	87.3
Mount Vernon, N.Y.	73.2	St. Petersburg, Fla.	97.1
Muncie, Ind.	92.1	Salisbury, N.C.	91.4
Nashville, Tenn.	91.7	Salt Lake City, Utah	68.9
Newark, N.J.	71.6	San Antonio, Tex.	90.1
Newburgh, N.Y.	84.2	San Bernardino, Calif.	84.0
New Haven, Conn.	70.9	San Diego, Calif.	81.3
New Orleans, La.	86.3	San Francisco, Calif.	69.3
Newport News, Va.	90.2	San Jose, Calif.	60.4
New Rochelle, N.Y.	79.5	San Mateo, Calif.	87.6
New York City, N.Y.	79.3	Santa Monica, Calif.	83.3
Niagara Falls, N.Y.	82.3	Savannah, Ga.	92.3
Norfolk, Va.	94.6	Seattle, Wash.	79.7
North Little Rock, Ark.	93.8	Shreveport, La.	95.9
Norwalk, Conn.	74.3	South Bend, Ind.	85.8
Oakland, Calif.	73.1	Spartanburg, S.C.	87.5
Odessa, Tex.	98.0	Spokane, Wash.	80.1
Oklahoma City, Okla.	87.1	Springfield, Ill.	86.9
Omaha, Neb.	92.0	Springfield, Mo.	81.2
Orlando, Fla.	98.0	Springfield, Ohio	84.7
Pasadena, Calif.	83.4	Stamford, Conn.	78.0
Passaic, N.J.	71.8	Statesville, N.C.	88.1

TABLE 1

INDEXES OF RESIDENTIAL SEGREGATION FOR 207 CITIES, 1960 (CONT.)

City	Index	City	Index
Stockton, Calif.	70.6	Washington, D. C.	79.7
Syracuse, N.Y.	81.1	Waterbury, Conn.	79.9
Tacoma, Wash.	80.4	Waterloo, Iowa	89.4
Tampa, Fla.	94.5	West Palm Beach, Fla.	97.7
Terre Haute, Ind.	90.1	White Plains, N.Y.	79.3
Toledo, Ohio	91.8		
Topeka, Kan.	83.5	Wichita, Kan.	91.9
Trenton, N.J.	79.6	Wichita Falls, Tex.	88.5
Tucson, Ariz.	81.1	Wilmington, Del.	79.8
Tulsa, Okla.	86.3	Wilmington, N.C.	92.3
Tuscaloosa, Ala.	89.7	Winston-Salem, N.C.	95.0
Vallejo, Calif.	83.1	Yonkers, N.Y.	78.1
Waco, Tex.	90.7	York, Pa.	78.1
Warren, Ohio	90.4	Youngstown, Ohio	78.5

The index values range from 60.4 to 98.1; the distribution of index values is plotted in Fig. 1. Only a few cities have values in the lower range of observed scores — 8 cities with values below 70, and 31 cities with values below 79. Half the cities have values above 87.8, and a fourth above 91.7.

Recall that the index value represents the percentage of non-whites that would have to shift from one block to another to effect an even, unsegregated distribution — it is apparent that these values are generally high. Similar indexes have been used in the study of various other (non-racial) types of residential segregation, and values of this high a magnitude are seldom observed. A study for ten cities, comparing the residential segregation of various ethnic and minority groups from each other and from whites, has demonstrated that current levels of Negro-white segregation are higher than those between any nationality group and native whites.[3] A study of the residential segregation between various occupational groups (in eight cities) permits us to conclude that racial residential segregation is also much greater than class segregation in American cities.[4] A study for Detroit showed that variability in racial composition among

3. Stanley Lieberson, *Ethnic Patterns in American Cities* (New York: Free Press of Glencoe, 1963), especially pp. 120–132.

4. Arthur H. Wilkins, "The Residential Distribution of Occupation Groups in Eight Middle-sized Cities of the United States in 1950" (unpublished Ph.D. dissertation, University of Chicago, 1956).

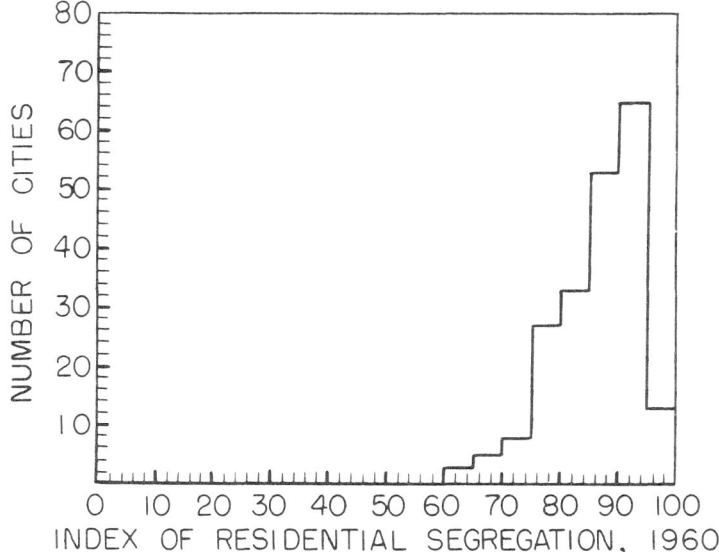

FIGURE 1.—*Histogram of Indexes of Residential Segregation for 207 Cities, 1960* (Source: *Table 1*)

tracts was much greater than variability in other socioeconomic characteristics of tracts.[5]

The high degree of residential segregation that exists between whites and non-whites in the cities of the United States can be illustrated less abstractly with some results of an analysis of data from the 1950 census concerning a group of 188 large cities.[6] In 47 of these cities, more than one-fourth of non-whites lived in city blocks that contained *no* white residents. In only two of the 188 cities were less than 50 per cent of whites living in all-white blocks.

No further analysis is necessary to reach some broad generalizations concerning racial segregation: In the urban United States, there is a very high degree of segregation of the residences of whites and Negroes. This is true for cities in all regions of the country and for all types of cities—large and small, industrial and commercial, metropolitan and suburban. It is true whether there are hundreds of thousands of Negro residents, or only a few thousand. Residential segre-

5. Leslie Kish, "Variance Components of the Distribution of Population Characteristics" (Abstract), *Population Index*, XXV, No. 3 (July, 1959), pp. 97–98.

6. Karl E. Taeuber, "Residential Segregation by Color in United States Cities" (unpublished Ph.D. dissertation, Harvard University, 1959), chap. IV.

gation prevails regardless of the relative economic status of the white and Negro residents. It occurs regardless of the character of local laws and policies, and regardless of the extent of other forms of segregation or discrimination.

These are broad general conclusions. There are variations among cities in the specific levels of index values, but these variations occur at the high end of the scale. In this chapter and the next, we will be concerned with describing further the intercity variation in residential segregation, and will try to relate it to variaton in other city characteristics.

It is possible to search through the index values for individual cities (Table 1) for evidence to add to the propaganda game sometimes played by civil-rights advocates that "city X is the most segregated in the country." Although the 207 cities can be ranked from low to high on this particular index, we wish to discourage such usage. Other methods would produce somewhat different rank orderings, and no such measure fully captures the rather vague ideas about the severity of discrimination in the housing market which are the concern of those speaking for civil rights. We can, however, provide some relevant information on variations in actual residential patterns between different regions of the country, and between cities with various numbers and percentages of Negro residents.

The average values of the segregation index for cities in each region of the country are shown in Table 2. For all 207 cities, the mean value is 86.2. The average value for cities outside the South is below this grand mean; the average for Southern cities is higher. There is, however, considerable variation among the parts of the North and West, with cities in the Northeast and West having lower average values than those in the North Central region. Let us caution that these figures refer to actual residential patterns, not the nature or severity of the discrimination and other forces producing these patterns. Further, the regional averages conceal a wide range of index values among the individual cities within each region.

Values of the segregation index vary more by region than by size of total population, size of non-white population, or percentage of non-whites in the city (Table 3). When cities are grouped according to total population, average index values display little variation between the groups. There is some tendency for average index values to increase as the size or percentage of non-white population increases. However, this finding is perhaps an alternate way of viewing the regional relationships, for the proportion of Southern cities also increases directly with size and percentage of non-white population. None of the categories of cities thus far considered has an average

TABLE 2

AVERAGE INDEXES OF RESIDENTIAL SEGREGATION FOR REGIONS
AND CENSUS DIVISIONS, 207 CITIES, 1960

Region and Division	Number of Cities	Mean Segregation Index
Total, All Regions	207	86.2
North and West, Total	122	83.0
Northeast	39	79.2
New England	10	76.2
Middle Atlantic	29	80.2
North Central	54	87.7
East North Central	44	87.5
West North Central	10	88.4
West	29	79.3
Mountain	6	81.6
Pacific	23	78.7
South, Total	85	90.9
South Atlantic	44	91.1
East South Central	15	90.5
West South Central	26	90.8

index value which is low in any absolute sense; it would be accurate
to say only that the averages for some groups of cities are relatively
higher or lower.

☐ CHANGES IN NEGRO RESIDENTIAL
SEGREGATION, 1940–1960

Segregation indexes have been computed for 1940, 1950, and 1960,
for all 109 cities for which the census included the required data
for city blocks, and which in 1940 contained more than 1,000 dwelling
units occupied by non-whites. With index values for these three
census years, we can obtain the changes in index values over the two
intercensal periods, 1940–50 and 1950–60. These data are presented
in Table 4.

In 83 of the 109 cities the segregation index for 1950 is higher
than that for 1940. The average change during this decade was 2.1
points. During the succeeding decade (1950–60), only 45 of the 109

TABLE 3

AVERAGE INDEXES OF RESIDENTIAL SEGREGATION FOR 207 CITIES
GROUPED ACCORDING TO SIZE OF TOTAL POPULATION, SIZE OF
NON-WHITE POPULATION, AND PERCENTAGE NON-WHITE, 1960 °

Variable and Quintile	Number of Cities	Mean Segregation Index
Size of total population:		
Smallest fifth	41	87.2
Second fifth	41	86.0
Middle fifth	42	87.0
Fourth fifth	41	84.5
Largest fifth	42	86.4
Size of non-white population:		
Smallest fifth	41	84.3
Second fifth	41	84.7
Middle fifth	42	86.2
Fourth fifth	41	87.2
Largest fifth	42	88.7
Percentage non-white:		
Smallest fifth	41	83.2
Second fifth	41	84.7
Middle fifth	42	85.0
Fourth fifth	41	87.8
Largest fifth	42	90.4

° The classifications by size and percentage non-white are based on occupied housing units rather than population.

cities had an increase, and there was an average decrease of 1.2 points. These averages, however, conceal considerable variation in the amount and direction of change experienced by individual cities. For each decade, the standard deviation of the changes in index values is greater than the magnitude of the average change.

Although on the average, residential segregation increased between 1940 and 1950 and decreased between 1950 and 1960, this did not occur in every city. Many cities had decreases in both decades, while other cities experienced increases in both decades. For all cities, the pattern of change is based on observations at only three points in time. Hence the changes are net changes, concealing whatever variation there may have been in the direction and rate of change during the period.

For example, the segregation index for Buffalo (N. Y.) was 1.4 points lower in 1960 than in 1940, but this net decrease was the result of an increase of 1.6 points in 1940–50, and a decrease of 3.0

TABLE 4

INDEXES OF RESIDENTIAL SEGREGATION FOR 109 CITIES,
1940, 1950, 1960 °

Region and City	1940	1950	1960	Change 1940–50	Change 1950–60
Northeast:					
Atlantic City, N.J.	94.6	94.0	89.2	− 0.6	− 4.8
Boston, Mass.	86.3	86.5	83.9	0.2	− 2.6
Bridgeport, Conn.	78.8	74.4	69.7	− 4.4	− 4.7
Buffalo, N.Y.	87.9	89.5	86.5	1.6	− 3.0
Cambridge, Mass.	74.3	75.6	65.5	1.3	− 10.1
Camden, N.J.	87.6	89.6	76.5	2.0	− 13.1
Chester, Pa.	85.1	88.1	87.4	3.0	− 0.7
East Orange, N.J.	85.3	83.7	71.2	− 1.6	− 12.5
Elizabeth, N.J.	75.9	76.1	75.2	0.2	− 0.9
Harrisburg, Pa.	87.2	89.8	85.7	2.6	− 4.1
Hartford, Conn.	84.8	84.4	82.1	− 0.4	− 2.3
Jersey City, N.J.	79.5	80.5	77.9	1.0	− 2.6
Mt. Vernon, N.Y.	78.9	78.0	73.2	− 0.9	− 4.8
Newark, N.J.	77.4	76.9	71.6	− 0.5	− 5.3
New Bedford, Mass.	83.4	86.8	81.6	3.4	− 5.2
New Haven, Conn.	80.1	79.9	70.9	− 0.2	− 9.0
New Rochelle, N.Y.	80.6	78.9	79.5	− 1.7	0.6
New York, N.Y.	86.8	87.3	79.3	0.5	− 8.0
Paterson, N.J.	79.8	80.0	75.9	0.2	− 4.1
Philadelphia, Pa.	88.0	89.0	87.1	1.0	− 1.9
Pittsburgh, Pa.	82.0	84.0	84.6	2.0	0.6
Providence, R.I.	85.8	85.5	77.0	− 0.3	− 8.5
Rochester, N.Y.	85.5	86.9	82.4	1.4	− 4.5
Trenton, N.J.	81.9	83.0	79.6	1.1	− 3.4
Yonkers, N.Y.	82.0	81.7	78.1	− 0.3	− 3.6
North Central:					
Akron, Ohio	82.2	87.6	88.1	5.4	0.5
Canton, Ohio	89.9	89.3	81.5	− 0.6	− 7.8
Chicago, Ill.	95.0	92.1	92.6	− 2.9	0.5
Cincinnati, Ohio	90.6	91.2	89.0	0.6	− 2.2
Cleveland, Ohio	92.0	91.5	91.3	− 0.5	− 0.2
Columbus, Ohio	87.1	88.9	85.3	1.8	− 3.6
Dayton, Ohio	91.5	93.3	91.3	1.8	− 2.0
Des Moines, Iowa	87.8	89.3	87.9	1.5	− 1.4
Detroit, Mich.	89.9	88.8	84.5	− 1.1	− 4.3
East Chicago, Ind.	74.5	79.6	82.8	5.1	3.2
East St. Louis, Ill.	93.8	94.2	92.0	0.4	− 2.2
Evanston, Ill.	91.5	92.1	87.2	0.6	− 4.9
Evansville, Ind.	86.2	92.4	91.2	6.2	− 1.2
Flint, Mich.	92.5	95.3	94.4	2.8	− 0.9
Gary, Ind.	88.3	93.8	92.8	5.5	− 1.0

TABLE 4

INDEXES OF RESIDENTIAL SEGREGATION FOR 109 CITIES,
1940, 1950, 1960° (CONT.)

Region and City	1940	1950	1960	Change 1940–50	Change 1950–60
Indianapolis, Ind.	90.4	91.4	91.6	1.0	0.2
Kansas City, Kan.	90.5	92.0	91.5	1.5	− 0.5
Kansas City, Mo.	88.0	91.3	90.8	3.3	− 0.5
Milwaukee, Wis.	92.9	91.6	88.1	− 1.3	− 3.5
Minneapolis, Minn.	88.0	86.0	79.3	− 2.0	− 6.7
Omaha, Neb.	89.5	92.4	92.0	2.9	− 0.4
St. Louis, Mo.	92.6	92.9	90.5	0.3	− 2.4
St. Paul, Minn.	88.6	90.0	87.3	1.4	− 2.7
Springfield, Ohio	80.9	81.6	84.7	0.7	3.1
Terre Haute, Ind.	86.6	89.8	90.1	3.2	0.3
Toledo, Ohio	91.0	91.5	91.8	0.5	0.3
Topeka, Kan.	80.8	80.7	83.5	− 0.1	2.8
Wichita, Kan.	92.0	93.3	91.9	1.3	− 1.4
Youngstown, Ohio	80.0	83.5	78.5	3.5	− 5.0
West:					
Berkeley, Calif.	81.2	80.3	69.4	− 0.9	−10.9
Denver, Colo.	87.9	88.9	85.5	1.0	− 3.4
Los Angeles, Calif.	84.2	84.6	81.8	0.4	− 2.8
Oakland, Calif.	78.4	81.2	73.1	2.8	− 8.1
Pasadena, Calif.	84.2	85.9	83.4	1.7	− 2.5
Portland, Ore.	83.8	84.3	76.7	0.5	− 7.6
Sacramento, Calif.	77.8	77.6	63.9	− 0.2	−13.7
San Diego, Calif.	84.4	83.6	81.3	− 0.8	− 2.3
San Francisco, Calif.	82.9	79.8	69.3	− 3.1	−10.5
Seattle, Wash.	82.2	83.3	79.7	1.1	− 3.6
South:					
Asheville, N.C.	88.6	89.2	92.3	0.6	3.1
Atlanta, Ga.	87.4	91.5	93.6	4.1	2.1
Augusta, Ga.	86.9	88.9	93.0	2.0	4.1
Austin, Tex.	84.8	92.0	93.1	7.2	1.1
Baltimore, Md.	90.1	91.3	89.6	1.2	− 1.7
Beaumont, Tex.	81.0	89.6	92.3	8.6	2.7
Birmingham, Ala.	86.4	88.7	92.8	2.3	4.1
Charleston, S.C.	60.1	68.4	79.5	8.3	11.1
Charleston, W. Va.	80.3	79.6	79.0	− 0.7	− 0.6
Charlotte, N.C.	90.1	92.8	94.3	2.7	1.5
Chattanooga, Tenn.	86.5	88.5	91.5	2.0	3.0
Columbia, S.C.	83.0	88.1	94.1	5.1	6.0
Covington, Ky.	80.6	85.0	87.8	4.4	2.8
Dallas, Tex.	80.2	88.4	94.6	8.2	6.2
Durham, N.C.	88.2	88.8	92.7	0.6	3.9
Fort Worth, Tex.	81.3	90.4	94.3	9.1	3.9

Region and City	1940	1950	1960	Change 1940–50	1950–60
Galveston, Tex.	72.2	78.3	82.9	6.1	4.6
Greensboro, N.C.	93.1	93.5	93.3	0.4	− 0.2
Houston, Tex.	84.5	91.5	93.7	7.0	2.2
Huntington, W. Va.	81.6	85.8	88.8	4.2	3.0
Jacksonville, Fla.	94.3	94.9	96.9	0.6	2.0
Knoxville, Tenn.	88.6	89.6	90.7	1.0	1.1
Little Rock, Ark.	78.2	84.5	89.4	6.3	4.9
Louisville, Ky.	81.7	86.0	89.2	4.3	3.2
Macon, Ga.	74.9	77.1	83.7	2.2	6.6
Memphis, Tenn.	79.9	86.4	92.0	6.5	5.6
Miami, Fla.	97.9	97.8	97.9	− 0.1	0.1
Mobile, Ala.	86.6	89.4	91.9	2.8	2.5
Montgomery, Ala.	86.8	90.5	94.7	3.7	4.2
Nashville, Tenn.	86.5	88.7	91.7	2.2	3.0
New Orleans, La.	81.0	84.9	86.3	3.9	1.4
Norfolk, Va.	96.0	95.0	94.6	− 1.0	− 0.4
Oklahoma City, Okla.	84.3	88.6	87.1	4.3	− 1.5
Port Arthur, Tex.	81.7	91.3	90.4	9.6	− 0.9
Richmond, Va.	92.7	92.2	94.8	− 0.5	2.6
Roanoke, Va.	94.8	96.0	93.9	1.2	− 2.1
San Antonio, Tex.	79.6	88.3	90.1	8.7	1.8
Savannah, Ga.	84.2	88.8	92.3	4.6	3.5
Shreveport, La.	90.3	93.2	95.9	2.9	2.7
Tampa, Fla.	90.2	92.5	94.5	2.3	2.0
Tulsa, Okla.	84.6	91.2	86.3	6.6	− 4.9
Waco, Tex.	80.1	87.0	90.7	6.9	3.7
Washington, D.C.	81.0	80.1	79.7	− 0.9	− 0.4
Wilmington, Del.	83.0	86.2	79.8	3.2	− 6.4
Winston-Salem, N.C.	92.9	93.8	95.0	0.9	1.2

° All cities are listed for which data by city blocks were published in the 1940, 1950, and 1960 censuses, and which in 1940 had 1,000 or more non-white-occupied dwelling units.

points in 1950–60. It is also possible that the increase of 1.6 points is similarly a compound of a larger increase between 1940 and 1946, and a small decrease between 1946 and 1950. However, no information is available to permit us to analyze change in segregation over periods shorter than a decade.

The contrast between the two decades in the changes occurring in residential segregation is portrayed in Fig. 2. Rather than plotting the changes directly, we have plotted the index values at the end of the decade against the values at the beginning of the decade. If there were no change in a city's segregation index, it would be plotted on the diagonal line. Points above the diagonal represent increases in segregation; points below the diagonal represent decreases in segregation.

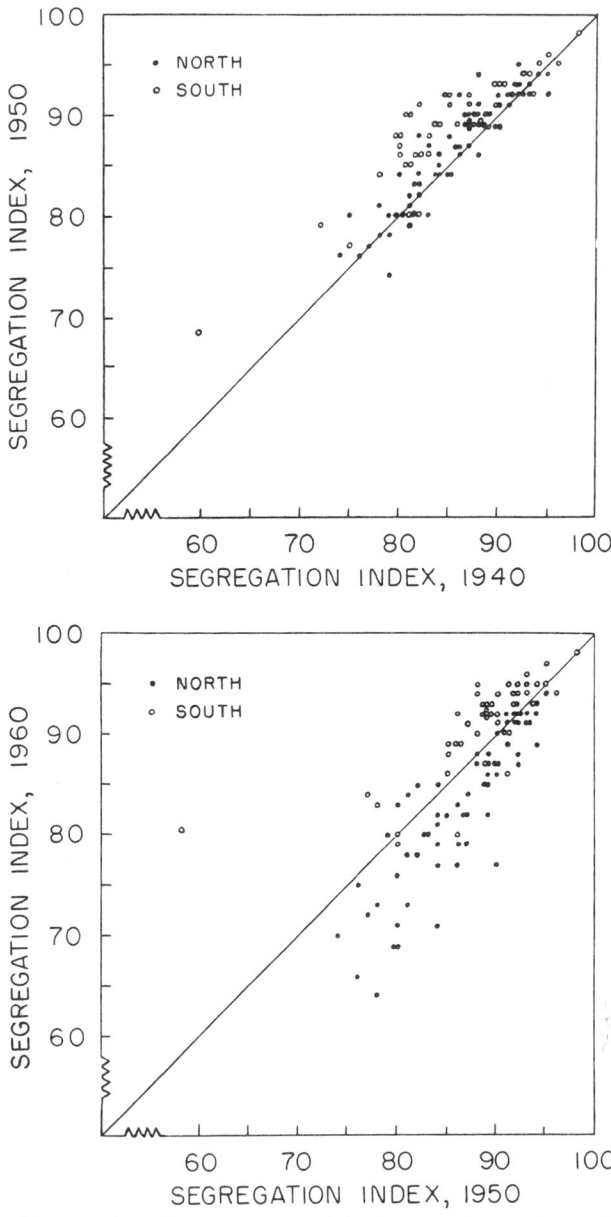

FIGURE 2. — *Scattergram of Indexes of Residential*
Segregation for 109 Cities, 1950
Against 1940, and 1960 Against 1950
(Source: Table 4)

In the first decade, the prevalent pattern was increasing segregation, with a slight tendency for larger increases in cities which initially had lower-than-average levels of segregation. An earlier examination of the changes for that decade led to the conclusion that all
cities seemed to be converging toward maximum levels of racial residential segregation.[7] The scattergram for the 1950–60 decade, however, gives quite a different impression. There are many cities below
the diagonal, with the greatest deviations from the diagonal accounted
for by large decreases in segregation occurring in cities with lower-
than-average levels of segregation. In contrast with the preceding
decade, there is a tendency for cities with high levels of segregation
to move still higher up the scale. Thus, in 1950–60, there was a pronounced divergence in levels of segregation. The standard deviation
of index values for the 109 cities was 5.8 in 1940 and 5.5 in 1950, but
jumped to 7.6 in 1960. The standard deviation of the changes increased from 2.8 in the first decade to 4.5 in the later period.

Presentation of data for the various regions and divisions (Table
5) brings out some interesting patterns in the changes in residential
segregation. Between 1940 and 1950, increases were slight in the
Northeast and in the West, moderate in the North Central, and larger
in the South. A number of cities in Texas experienced very large increases, contributing to the large average increase for the West South
Central cities. In no region or division was there an average decrease
in segregation. On the other hand, during the 1950–60 decade, cities
in every Northern and Western division experienced average decreases in segregation, whereas cities in all of the Southern divisions again experienced average increases in segregation.

The contrast between the two decades is brought out sharply in
Table 6, which is based on the behavior of individual cities rather
than group averages. In the 1940–50 decade, the great majority of
cities in both North and South experienced increases in segregation.
In the later decade, more than three-fourths of Southern cities again
experienced increases, as compared with 16 per cent of cities in the
North and West.

□ HISTORICAL TRENDS
IN RESIDENTIAL SEGREGATION

It is not possible to extend the set of indexes of residential segregation by city blocks to years prior to 1940, because earlier censuses
did not publish data for city blocks. For many cities, however, it is

7. *Ibid.*, chap. VII.

TABLE 5

AVERAGE VALUES AND STANDARD DEVIATIONS OF INDEXES OF
RESIDENTIAL SEGREGATION FOR REGIONS AND CENSUS DIVISIONS,
AND CHANGES IN INDEXES, 109 CITIES, 1940, 1950, 1960

Region and Division	Number of Cities	1940	1950	1960	Change 1940–50	Change 1950–60
Average Values of Segregation Indexes						
Total, All Regions	109	85.2	87.3	86.1	2.1	− 1.2
Northeast	25	83.2	83.6	78.9	0.4	− 4.7
New England	7	81.9	81.9	75.8	0.0	− 6.1
Middle Atlantic	18	83.7	84.3	80.0	0.6	− 4.3
North Central	29	88.4	89.9	88.4	1.5	− 1.5
East North Central	20	88.3	90.0	88.4	1.7	− 1.6
West North Central	9	88.6	89.8	88.3	1.2	− 1.5
West°	10	82.7	82.9	76.4	0.2	− 6.5
South	45	84.9	88.5	90.7	3.6	2.2
South Atlantic	22	86.9	88.7	90.6	1.8	1.9
East South Central	9	84.8	88.1	91.4	3.3	3.3
West South Central	14	81.7	88.5	90.5	6.8	2.0
Standard Deviations						
Total, All Regions	109	5.8	5.5	7.6	2.8	4.5
Northeast	25	4.5	5.1	6.1	1.6	3.6
New England	7	4.1	4.9	6.6	2.2	2.9
Middle Atlantic	18	4.6	5.1	5.5	1.3	3.7
North Central	29	4.7	4.0	4.2	2.2	2.6
East North Central	20	5.1	4.0	4.2	2.5	2.7
West North Central	9	3.2	3.6	4.1	1.5	2.4
West°	10	2.8	3.1	6.8	1.5	4.0
South	45	6.7	5.3	4.7	3.0	3.0
South Atlantic	22	8.2	6.9	5.9	2.3	3.4
East South Central	9	3.0	1.7	1.9	1.6	1.2
West South Central	14	4.0	3.8	3.7	1.9	2.8

Source: Table 4.

°Census divisions within the West are not shown separately because there is only one city (Denver) in the Mountain Division.

possible to put together a longer time series by making use of various data for other types of subareas, such as wards and census tracts. This procedure is, however, limited both by the availability of suitable data on the racial composition of the subareas, and by the fact that segregation indexes based on tracts or wards are not strictly comparable with each other or with indexes based on city blocks (see the

TABLE 6

DIRECTION OF CHANGE IN INDEX OF RESIDENTIAL SEGREGATION,
BY REGION, 109 CITIES, 1940–50 AND 1950–60

Intercensal Period	Region	Number of Cities With Change in Specified Direction		Percentage of Cities With an Increase
		Increase	No Change or Decrease	
1940-50	North and West	43	21	67.2
	South	40	5	88.9
1950-60	North and West	10	54	15.6
	South	35	10	77.8

Source: Table 4.

discussion in Appendix A). To illustrate the possibilities of this type of historical study and to provide the basis for some speculative hypotheses about long-term trends, we compiled various data for a longer time period for a few cities.

Charleston, South Carolina. — In 1940, at the beginning of the period for which we have systematic data, Charleston had the lowest index (60.1) of any of the 109 cities. During each succeeding decade, Charleston's index increased substantially, so that by 1960 it was no longer exceptionally lower than other cities. Was the 1940–60 trend for Charleston a continuation of a long-term trend, or was the level of residential segregation lower in 1940 than in earlier periods?

Charleston was one of the largest cities in the Colonies in the eighteenth century, and long remained a major urban center. It would be possible to trace at least some aspects of the development of residential patterns under slavery, but we begin our account with the situation in the early Civil War period. Distrusting the results of the 1860 federal census, the City Council of Charleston commissioned a census of the city in 1861.[8] The numbers of whites, slaves, and free colored persons residing in each of the eight wards, as reported by this census, are shown in Table 7. Negroes made up from 30 to 52 per cent of the population of each ward. Differences in the residential distributions of whites, slaves, and free colored can be measured with indexes of dissimilarity, based on data for eight wards rather than for hundreds of city blocks. (These indexes are based on the differences between the percentage distributions shown in the last three columns

8. Frederick A. Ford, *Census of the City of Charleston, South Carolina, for the Year 1861* (Charleston: Evans and Cogswell, 1861).

of Table 7.) Comparing the three groups in the population with each other, we obtain the following indexes of residential segregation:

Whites vs. Slaves...................... 11.4
Whites vs. Free Colored............. 23.2
Slaves vs. Free Colored............. 25.3

The magnitude of these indexes cannot be directly compared with the magnitude of indexes computed from blocks, but the three indexes can be compared with each other. The residential distributions of whites and slaves are very similar, and the free colored are clearly the most residentially segregated, both from whites and from slaves. All these indexes, however, are low compared with an index of the degree of residential segregation by socioeconomic status. This measure of status is indirect, based on an assumption that brick houses were more expensive and indicative of higher status than wooden houses. An index of dissimilarity for the distribution of brick and wooden houses among the eight wards is 51.0.

TABLE 7

DISTRIBUTION OF THE WHITE, SLAVE, AND FREE COLORED
POPULATIONS OF CHARLESTON, SOUTH CAROLINA,
BY WARDS, 1861

Ward	Population				Percentage of Total		Percentage Distribution by Wards		
	Total	White	Slave	Free Colored	Slave	Free Colored	White	Slave	Free Colored
Total	48,409	26,969	17,655	3,785	36.5	7.8	100.0	100.0	100.0
1	4,380	2,681	1,578	121	36.0	2.8	9.9	8.9	3.2
2	6,400	3,102	3,137	161	49.0	2.5	11.5	17.8	4.2
3	7,113	4,522	2,221	370	31.2	5.2	16.8	12.6	9.8
4	11,106	5,926	4,365	815	39.3	7.3	22.0	24.7	21.5
5	5,703	2,739	2,111	853	37.0	15.0	10.2	12.0	22.5
6	6,617	3,476	2,381	760	36.0	11.5	12.9	13.5	20.1
7	2,734	1,924	609	201	22.3	7.3	7.1	3.4	5.3
8	4,356	2,599	1,253	504	28.7	11.6	9.6	7.1	13.3

Source: Frederick A. Ford, *Census of the City of Charleston, South Carolina, for the Year 1861* (Charleston: Evans and Cogswell, 1861).

For the census years from 1910 to 1950, data are available on the racial composition of each of twelve wards in Charleston. (We were unable to determine the degree of correspondence between these twelve wards and the eight wards reported in the 1861 census.) The percentage of Negroes in the total population of each ward at each census is shown in Table 8. Wards 1–8 and ward 12 have relatively consistent patterns of decreasing percentages of Negroes over the entire 40-year period. In ward 9 the percentage of Negroes increases consistently, and in wards 10 and 11 it changes inconsistently. Indexes of over-all residential segregation between whites and Negroes, based on these data for 12 wards with constant boundaries, increased consistently from 1910 to 1950:

> 1910 ... 16.8 (white vs. Negro persons)
> 1920 ... 16.9 (white vs. Negro persons)
> 1930 ... 19.9 (white vs. Negro persons)
> 1940 ... 27.0 (white vs. Negro persons)
>   "   ... 26.6 (white vs. non-white households)
> 1950 ... 30.7 (white vs. non-white households)

Although the indexes based on eight wards for 1861 are not directly comparable with these based on twelve wards, the change in area units is probably not enough to account for the increase in value of the segregation index from 11.5 in 1861 (for white vs. Negro persons) to 16.8 in 1910. We may infer that the large increases in segregation evident from 1910 to 1960 represent the continuation of a trend already underway for half a century.

TABLE 8

PERCENTAGE NEGRO AMONG WARDS OF CHARLESTON, SOUTH CAROLINA, 1910 TO 1950

Ward	Percentage Negro (Population)				Percentage Non-white (Households)	
	1910	1920	1930	1940	1940	1950
Total	53	48	45	45	49	45
1	53	42	28	14	14	5
2	30	19	8	2	3	2
3	41	35	31	25	29	23
4	57	56	53	34	38	28
5	45	42	40	33	40	43
6	34	26	21	14	18	13
7	60	60	45	44	50	45
8	55	43	40	38	46	37
9	46	51	60	71	73	79
10	53	50	47	51	58	62
11	61	49	49	52	56	53
12	72	62	60	56	58	49

Source: U. S. Censuses of Population and Housing.

The distinctively low degree of residential segregation in Charleston has been noted by others, and attributed in part to the persistence of "the old southern pattern of housing Negro families in the backyards of the white families whom they serve."[9] A tourist guide to Charleston, published in 1939, suggested that this survival of past patterns was gradually disappearing:

> Here in Charleston there never has been a zoning ordinance to separate the living districts for the two races. But Charlestonians were always accustomed to having their domestic servants in residence back of the house; and after 1865 the custom continued, even though the blacks were emancipated and might work for any other master if they pleased. Nowadays, however, the Charleston negro is gradually moving into the sections of the city where his own people live. This is happening through natural conditions and desires rather than by law.[10]

A more detailed study of Charleston might be able to locate additional information on this pattern, and specify in what ways, if any, it differed from the location of Negro residences in alleys and back streets in cities such as Washington and Philadelphia, and why the pattern was more prevalent in Charleston than in other old Southern cities. In any case, it is clear that over a long period Negroes have been moving out of residences in many of the more expensive neighborhoods of the city. Wards 1 and 2, in particular, have come to be very desirable residential locations for whites. Although these wards contain predominantly older structures, some of their value derives from the associated "historical" character, and from the river-front location. Wards 3 and 4 include some high-income housing, as well as some of the piers and accompanying cheap lodgings catering to sailors. Certain undesirable locations, as near the site of old city dumps in wards 7 and 8 and around railroad yards in ward 9, have become Negro residential areas. The area around the Citadel, a men's college, has been occupied mainly by whites. The development of new housing in the northwestern part of the city and in rapidly growing suburbs has been mainly for middle-income whites.

Charleston is relatively small, and most of the city is accessible by foot or by short bus trips from any of the city's residential areas. Thus, for Charleston, it does not seem that Negro employment in domestic service has caused Negro residential areas to be located near the homes of upper-income whites, as has been suggested for

9. Donald O. Cowgill and Mary S. Cowgill, "An Index of Segregation Based on Block Statistics," *American Sociological Review*, XVI, No. 6 (December, 1951), p. 830. This pattern is mentioned by Charles S. Johnson, *Patterns of Negro Segregation* (New York: Harper and Brothers, 1943).

10. William Oliver Stevens, *Charleston* (New York: Dodd, Mead, and Co., 1939), pp. 62-63.

some larger cities.[11] If this were the case, it might be used in explanation of the increasing residential segregation, since there has been a great decline in the employment of domestic servants. The census in 1910 listed 6,166 female launderers and servants; in 1930, 5,313 Negro females in other domestic and personal service; in 1940, 4,055 non-white females in domestic service; in 1950, 2,628 non-white females in private household work; and in 1960, 2,300 non-white females in private household work. The declining Negro population in wards 1 and 2, and to a lesser extent in wards 3 and 4, might be related to the decline in domestic employment, but an alternative explanation seems more likely—that Negroes have been forced out of these wards by their inability to afford residence there. The renaissance of the old city—the increased value placed by wealthy whites on location in this area and the rebuilding and modernizing of old residences—may have involved increasing economic, and perhaps social, deterrents to continued Negro residence in the vicinity.

Public housing projects also may have contributed to the increasing residential segregation in recent decades. In 1959, the Housing Authority of the City of Charleston was operating ten projects, three built before 1940, five built 1940–50, and two built after 1950. Nine per cent of Charleston's housing was in these projects, which provided 1,000 units for white families and 850 units for Negro families. Families moving into public housing vacate other residences. Their places may or may not be taken by others. Thus the opening of public housing may inaugurate a considerable chain of residential relocation. Since the public housing is segregated, and since in 1940 in Charleston there was still, on a block basis, considerable racial intermixture, it is likely that the net effect has been to increase residential segregation as persons moved from older mixed neighborhoods to new segregated housing. The same argument applies to new private housing as well. Both within the city and in the suburbs there was much new private housing, mainly for whites and mainly in racially homogeneous areas.

Augusta, Georgia.—The general trend of residential segregation in Augusta since 1899 can be determined on the basis of data from a Work Projects Administration study.[12] Using city directories, the distribution of white and Negro families among 15 census tracts was reconstructed at five-year intervals from 1899 to 1939. With subsequent census data, this series may be extended to 1960. Computing

11. This was suggested for Philadelphia by W.E.B. DuBois, *The Philadelphia Negro* (Philadelphia: Publications of the University of Pennsylvania, 1899).

12. Federal Works Agency, Work Projects Administration of Georgia, *Population Mobility: A Study of Family Movements Affecting Augusta, Georgia, 1899–1939,* by Glenn Hutchinson and Maurice R. Brewster (Work Projects Administration, 1942).

segregation indexes from data on white and Negro families, 1899–1939, and on white and non-white households, 1940–1960, the following series is obtained:

1899 ... 49.9	1929 ... 70.6
1904 ... 56.1	1934 ... 72.4
1909 ... 58.8	1939 ... 72.2
1914 ... 63.2	1940 ... 73.1
1919 ... 66.4	1950 ... 74.6
1924 ... 68.7	1960 ... 79.7

The general trend in Augusta has been a continuing increase in residential segregation, with a slight exception between 1934 and 1939. Throughout the entire period, Augusta has apparently been considerably more racially segregated than Charleston.[13] Moreover, the distribution of whites and Negroes among the census tracts and the pattern of changes in the distribution differ from those observed for Charleston. Many of the tracts in Augusta have had fairly homogeneous populations, with percentages of Negroes above 80 or below 20 (Table 9). Only a few tracts show any consistent pattern of changes in the percentage of Negroes. Increasing segregation in Augusta has been mainly the result of increasing populations in tracts already predominantly white or Negro, rather than the Charleston pattern of changing racial balances within tracts. This has been especially true for tracts along the southern limits of the city, tracts 10, 11, and 12 being predominantly white, and tracts 9, 14, and 15, predominantly Negro.

For Augusta, it is possible to examine the changing residential distribution on a finer areal scale. For 1899, 1919, and 1939, racial composition was ascertained for "linear blocks"—not the ordinary city block, but the two facing sides of a block-long street segment.

> Taking into consideration the entire city of Augusta, there has been a large increase in the homogeneity of race by blocks. That is, a residential block is now more likely to be occupied entirely by white families or entirely by Negro families than was the case either in 1899 or in 1919. Thus, racial encroachment has tended toward complete racial succession on a block basis.
>
> In 1899 mixed blocks account for 42.3 percent of all occupied blocks in the city. This ratio declined to 24.6 percent in 1919 and to 14.1 percent in 1939. By individual census tracts, declines

13. Since five of Augusta's tracts had very small populations in the early years, the difference in number of subareas cannot account for the higher indexes for Augusta than for Charleston. In both cases, the use of the same set of areal units over time and the magnitude of the changes support the major conclusions, regardless of the general limitations to comparability of indexes based on small numbers of subareas.

TABLE 9

PERCENTAGE NEGRO AMONG CENSUS TRACTS OF AUGUSTA,
GEORGIA, 1899 TO 1960

Tract	Percentage Negro (By family units)									Percentage Non-white (Households)		
	1899	1904	1909	1914	1919	1924	1929	1934	1939	1940	1950	1960°
Total	46	47	46	44	45	44	45	45	45	44	39	42
1	− †	− †	− †	26	48	66	60	64	56	58	39	35
2	9	18	13	8	9	7	5	6	5	5	3	2
3	16	14	11	10	10	8	11	10	10	9	7	6
4	61	67	66	59	64	66	66	66	66	61	49	45
5	25	20	20	18	8	7	7	7	7	6	4	4
6	59	58	57	54	54	53	53	52	54	55	49	50
7	54	60	62	66	70	69	74	76	77	76	78	90
8	19	17	14	14	12	12	13	13	12	13	8	2
9	90	91	92	93	94	92	94	95	94	97	97	97
10	8	5	5	4	9	8	6	6	5	5	3	2
11	− †	− †	− †	1	4	7	4	4	4	5	3	3
12	− †	− †	− †	− †	1	1	1	1	0	1	0	0
13	− †	− †	− †	− †	− †	− †	− †	− †	40	57	49	38
14	− †	− †	− †	96	84	84	87	87	85	92	95	100
15	93	95	98	97	93	92	93	95	94	95	95	99

Source: Federal Works Agency, Work Projects Administration of Georgia, *Population Mobility: A Study of Family Movements Affecting Augusta, Georgia, 1899–1939* (Published by the Administration, 1942), Appendix Table 1, p. 69, and U. S. Censuses of Population and Housing.

° 1960 tracts adjusted to be comparable with 1950 tracts.

† Total population of tract less than 100.

occurred from 1899 to 1919 and from 1919 to 1939 in tracts 3, 4, 5, 6, 7, 8, 9, and 10.[14]

Local catastrophes, such as fires and floods, are noted as stimulating population redistribution. Particular features of a site are noted as making it generally desirable or undesirable as a place of residence, and thus being conducive to white or Negro occupancy. Once an area becomes predominantly white or Negro, this in turn becomes a major factor in determining subsequent racial composition.

Augusta has had a rapid growth of population outside the city limits. The main suburban developments have been relatively high-grade, representing in part simple extensions of high-grade neighborhoods within the city. The whites who move into these developments have not been living in cheap housing. Thus, any racial succession taking place as a result of such moves must occur indirectly through a series of residential changes. Residential developments for Negroes outside the city have tended to be expansions of low-rent peripheral Negro areas in the vicinity of heavy industry, commercial

14. Federal Works Agency, *op. cit.*, pp. 64–65.

structures, and swampland. At least until 1939, the growth of residential areas outside the central city and their racial composition seemed to depend to a great extent on particular features of the site and on historical accident, and to be only loosely connected with patterns of residential succession within the city. There is nothing in the data for Augusta to suggest any close correlations between racial patterns of suburban residential developments and the extent of racial residential segregation within the central city.

Jacksonville, Florida. — Jacksonville was among the most highly segregated cities according to the indexes based on block data for 1940, 1950, and 1960. Although some earlier data are available, they are much less satisfactory than for Charleston and Augusta, and our presentation is designed to indicate some of the difficulties with this type of historical study. Census data showing the racial composition of wards are available for 1910 to 1950, but the number of wards increased from year to year with the rapid increase of the population and land area of the city. Thus, only rough comparisons can be made between segregation at different time periods.

The indexes, based on data for Negro and white persons, 1910–1940, and for white and non-white households, 1940–1950, do not reveal so consistent a trend as in the other cities:

1910 . . . 39.4 (9 wards; city population, 58,000)
1920 . . . 46.6 (11 wards; city population, 92,000)
1930 . . . 44.8 (15 wards; city population, 130,000)
1940 . . . 44.7 (18 wards; city population, 173,000)

1940 . . . 47.1 (18 wards; city population, 173,000)
1950 . . . 47.5 (18 wards; city population, 205,000)

The increasing number of wards tends for methodological reasons to increase the observed level of the segregation index. It is also surprising that the absolute levels of the indexes are so low, in comparison, say, with those for Augusta, which were based on 15 subareas. On a block basis in 1940, the index for Augusta was 86.9 and for Jacksonville, 94.3. Inspection of a map showing racial occupancy on a block basis indicates that the wards in Jacksonville are poorly delineated with respect to representing the extent of residential segregation. Subareas with different boundaries could be drawn so that much higher index values would be obtained. Hence, we are not able to determine from the available data whether the high levels of residential segregation obtaining in Jacksonville in 1940 resulted from a long trend of increasing segregation, as in Charleston and Augusta, or from some other pattern of historical changes.

As a methodological note, it is apparent that historical data for a consistent set of area units are most likely to be available for a city such as Charleston, which has had stable boundaries and a relatively stable population size. These very circumstances, however, make the city very unusual. Special sources of data sometimes exist, as for Augusta, but the specific types of data are unlikely to be available for other cities, and the contribution of such special sources to comparative urban analysis may therefore be limited.

Selected Northern Cities. – For Northern cities, we present a 50-year series of segregation indexes for Cleveland and a 60-year series for Chicago, and then cite the findings concerning Negro segregation made in a study concerned mainly with residential segregation of European ethnic groups in American cities.

The census tract program of the Bureau of the Census was begun in 1910, with a few cities participating; from the beginning, the advantages of maintaining constant tract boundaries were often affirmed but seldom adhered to. Only for Cleveland is it possible to assemble a fully consistent series of segregation indexes for the entire 50-year period of the census tract program:

> 1910 ... 69.2
> 1920 ... 71.6
> 1930 ... 82.8
> 1940 ... 85.8
> 1950 ... 82.3
> 1960 ... 83.5

The principal feature of this series is the increase in the degree of residential segregation between 1910 and 1930. Since then there has been some fluctuation, but no sustained trend. For comparison, the indexes based on block data for 1940, 1950, and 1960 are, respectively, 92.0, 91.5, and 91.3.

The results for Chicago are rather similar. This series of indexes[15] is slightly different from the one we have been using regularly. The index is a Gini index, which is conceptually very similar to the index of dissimilarity. It was computed in an unusual fashion, from data for tracts and blocks, but the method was adequate for portraying the trend within Chicago:

> 1898 ... 91.8
> 1910 ... 92.4
> 1920 ... 94.0
> 1930 ... 98.4
> 1940 ... 98.9
> 1950 ... 98.7

15. David A. Wallace, "Residential Concentration of Negroes in Chicago" (unpublished Ph.D. dissertation, Harvard University, 1953).

The regular block indexes from Table 4 are 95.0 for 1940; 92.1 for 1950; and 92.6 for 1960. Again we have a series which clearly increases from the earliest observation to 1930, and then fluctuates with no obvious trend.

From Lieberson's study of ethnic assimilation in American cities,[16] we have reproduced (Table 10) segregation indexes between native whites and Negroes for ten cities for four census years. The indexes for 1910 and 1920 were computed from ward data, and for 1930 and 1950 from tract data. Hence comparability is not perfect, but the principal conclusion is so strongly supported as to be beyond dispute. Residential segregation between native whites and Negroes increased sharply in each of the ten cities between 1910 and 1930, and remained at a high level or increased further by 1950.

TABLE 10

INDEXES OF RESIDENTIAL SEGREGATION BETWEEN NEGROES AND NATIVE WHITES, 10 NORTHERN CITIES, 1910, 1920, 1930, AND 1950

	1910°	1920°	1930†	1950†
Boston	64.1	65.3	77.9	80.1
Buffalo	62.6	71.5	80.5	82.5
Chicago	66.8	75.7	85.2	79.7
Cincinnati	47.3	57.2	72.8	80.6
Cleveland	60.6	70.1	85.0	86.6
Columbus	31.6	43.8	62.8	70.3
Philadelphia	46.0	47.9	63.4	74.0
Pittsburgh	44.1	43.3	61.4	68.5
St. Louis	54.3	62.1	82.1	85.4
Syracuse	64.0	65.2	86.7	85.8

Source: Stanley Lieberson, *Ethnic Patterns in American Cities* (New York: The Free Press of Glencoe, 1963), Table 38, p. 122.

° Indexes computed from ward data.

† Indexes computed from census tract data, except community areas used for Chicago.

The most consistent finding in these historical investigations for various cities is a sharp increase in residential segregation between 1910 and 1930 in every city, both Northern and Southern, for which we have data. For most of the Northern cities, this was their first period of large-scale in-migration of Negroes, and it witnessed the initial development of large, racially homogeneous areas of Negro

16. Lieberson, *op. cit.*, Table 38, p. 122.

residence. Those cities in both North and South which already had sizable Negro populations in 1910 generally gained additional Negroes between 1910 and 1930, and housed them in an increasingly segregated pattern. We are not claiming that residential segregation originated during this period, or that other types of segregation and discrimination necessarily followed the same course. On a more speculative basis, we would argue that Negroes in cities have always been residentially segregated to some extent, and that from the Civil War to World War II there was probably a general tendency for residential segregation to increase with the growth of Negro population.

□ PATTERNS OF SEGREGATION IN METROPOLITAN AREAS

The description of levels of residential segregation and changes during the last two decades has been based on data for cities. Yet in contemporary society, population is not concentrated in a number of isolated, independent cities. Rather the nodal units in the residential organization of American society are large metropolitan areas, each of which embraces one or more large central cities along with a variety of other incorporated and unincorporated places. Residential segregation can be studied not only by taking the incorporated city as the unit of analysis, but also by taking the metropolitan area as the unit of analysis, and tracing the differing residential distribution of whites and Negroes among the component parts of the entire area. Much attention has been centered on the "new" patterns of segregation thus revealed:

> The white and non-white citizens of the U. S. are being sorted out in a new pattern of segregation. In each of the major urban centers the story is the same: the better-off white families are moving out of the central cities into the suburbs; the ranks of the poor who remain are being swelled by Negroes from the South. This trend threatens to transform the cities into slums, largely inhabited by Negroes, ringed about with predominantly white suburbs. The "racial problem" of the U. S., still festering in the rural South, will become equally, perhaps most acutely, a problem of the urban North.[17]

We cannot afford to overlook metropolitan areas entirely in our study of residential segregation, but the nature of available data forces us to ignore them during the course of most of our analysis. In

17. Morton Grodzins, "Metropolitan Segregation," *Scientific American*, CXCVII, No. 4 (October, 1957), p. 33.

this section, we will briefly describe metropolitan segregation patterns, and relate them to the analysis based on city data.

In census terminology, a Standard Metropolitan Statistical Area (SMSA) consists of a central city (or twin central cities) with 50,000 inhabitants or more, the county containing the central city, and contiguous counties which are socially and economically integrated with the central city.[18] A simple division of a metropolitan area may be made between the population inside and outside the central city. The balance of the metropolitan area outside the central city is often called the *ring,* or the suburban ring. Since the ring is defined in a residual fashion, it embraces a variety of types of residence — incorporated and unincorporated cities and villages, as well as rural farm and non-farm areas. Despite the many theoretical limitations of these simple definitions, the resulting tabulations of data provide a useful general picture of metropolitan patterns.

The racial composition of metropolitan areas in the United States from 1900 to 1960 is shown in summary fashion in Table 11. Of the white population in 1960, 63 per cent lived within the 212 SMSA's recognized in the census, as compared with 65 per cent of the Negro population. Of the metropolitan Negro population in 1960, 80 per cent lived in central cities, and 20 per cent lived in the rings. Metropolitan whites were more evenly distributed, with a slight majority living in the suburban rings. Thus, Negroes composed 17 per cent of the population in central cities, but less than 5 per cent of the population outside central cities.

The trends in these various percentages are in part explained by the northward movement of Negro population. In the North, there has never been any significant amount of rural and village settlement by Negroes, and they have been excluded from nearly all new housing developments in the suburbs. In the South, by contrast, Negroes have long resided in many rural and village places that have been brought into the metropolitan sphere as urban settlement expanded outward. Within both North and South, the rapid urbanization of Negro population has contributed disproportionately to the growth of Negro population inside rather than outside central cities. For whites, particularly in the older and larger metropolitan areas, the central city population has been growing slowly if at all, while there has been a large migration to the suburbs.

There are many ways to qualify and elaborate the data in Table 11, but they suffice to show the disparity between whites and Negroes

18. For a more complete definition, see U. S. Bureau of the Census, *U. S. Census of Population: 1960, Selected Area Reports, Standard Metropolitan Statistical Areas,* Final Report PC(3)-1D (Washington: U. S. Government Printing Office, 1963), Introduction.

TABLE 11

DISTRIBUTION OF POPULATION WITHIN METROPOLITAN AREAS °
BY RACE, 1900–1960

Year	Total	White	Negro
	Population in Metroplitan Areas (in 000's)		
1960	112,385	99,509	12,194
1940	72,576	66,487	5,840
1920	52,508	48,779	3,547
1900	31,836	29,399	2,352
	Percentage Living in Central Cities		
1960	51.4	47.8	79.6
1940	62.7	61.6	74.6
1920	66.0	65.9	67.2
1900	62.1	62.8	54.5
	Percentage by Race, Inside Central Cities		
1960	100.0	82.4	16.8
1940	100.0	90.1	9.6
1920	100.0	92.9	6.9
1900	100.0	93.3	6.5
	Percentage by Race, Outside Central Cities		
1960	100.0	95.0	4.6
1940	100.0	94.1	5.5
1920	100.0	93.0	6.5
1900	100.0	90.7	8.9

Source: U. S. Bureau of the Census, *U. S. Census of Population: 1960, Selected Area Reports, Standard Metropolitan Statistical Areas,* Final Report PC(3)-1D (Washington: U. S. Government Printing Office, 1963), Table 1.

° The historical data pertain to Standard Metropolitan Statistical Areas as defined in the 1960 census, with no adjustment for changing city boundaries.

in suburbanization. These data are aggregated over all SMSA's, however; a few figures based on data for individual SMSA's may indicate the consistency of the patterns. Of 211 SMSA's (excluding Honolulu), there are only 21 where more than half the Negro population resides outside the central city; 15 of these are in the South. Of 134 Northern and Western SMSA's, there are only 14 in which the percentage Negro of the total central city population did not increase between 1940 and 1960.

A simple index of metropolitan centralization may be used to assess the relation of residential segregation within the central city to the differential distribution of whites and Negroes between central cities and rings of metropolitan areas. This index is defined as the difference between the percentage of the SMSA's Negro population living in the central city and the corresponding percentage for whites. Thus, in Birmingham (Alabama) in 1960, 61.5 per cent of the Negroes and 49.5 per cent of the whites lived inside the central city. The index of metropolitan centralization for Birmingham is 12.0. For Montgomery (Alabama) the corresponding percentages are 73.2 for Negroes and 83.2 for whites, and the index is −10.0. The larger this index, the greater the disproportionate concentration of Negroes in the central city rather than in the ring.

Of the 207 cities for which we have presented segregation indexes for 1960, 154 are principal central cities of metropolitan areas. The median index of metropolitan centralization for these 154 SMSA's is 30.0, with only ten areas having negative values. The median is higher for the Northern areas, 38.5; and lower for the Southern areas, 15.0. The degree to which Negroes are disproportionately living in the central city shows little correlation with the degree of racial residential segregation within the central city for 154 SMSA's. A similar analysis for 1950, using data for whites and non-whites in 138 metropolitan areas, also revealed no association between the two measures. Apparently the broad pattern of distribution of population between city and ring is unrelated to the detailed pattern of residential segregation within the central city.

Of the 207 cities for which we have indexes of residential segregation for 1960, 168 are central cities of SMSA's, 30 are suburbs (located within SMSA's, but not central cities), and 9 are independent cities (not located in SMSA's). Computing mean index values for each group of cities, we obtain the following:

Central cities................ 86.8
Suburbs....................... 82.3
Independent cities......... 89.5

On an aggregate basis, suburbs tend to be less segregated, and independent cities more so, than central cities. These results, however, pertain to a very peculiar sample of suburbs and independent cities − those few for which block data were available and which had at least 1,000 non-white households in 1960.

Another way of examining the segregation indexes for the 30 suburbs is to compare each to the index for the corresponding central city (Table 12). This does not improve the representativeness of the sample of suburbs, but does provide a more appropriate set of comparisons. In 13 comparisons, the index for the suburb is lower than for the central city, while in 16 the suburb is higher. There is one tie. From these data, it is not possible to draw any firm conclusions. The most significant aspect of the data is perhaps the small number of suburbs having 1,000 or more non-white households, and this is merely another indication of the existence of racial segregation among the component parts of metropolitan areas.

TABLE 12

INDEXES OF RESIDENTIAL SEGREGATION FOR 30 SUBURBS AND
THEIR RESPECTIVE CENTRAL CITIES, 1960

Central City	Index	Index	Suburb
Baltimore, Md.	89.6	80.9	Annapolis
Birmingham, Ala.	92.8	87.9	Bessemer
Boston, Mass.	83.9	65.5	Cambridge
Buffalo, N.Y.	86.5	82.3	Niagara Falls
Chicago, Ill.	92.6	87.2	Evanston
		90.2	Joliet
Cincinnati, Ohio	89.0	87.8	Covington
Detroit, Mich.	84.5	77.4	Highland Park
		95.0	Inkster
		90.5	Pontiac
Los Angeles, Calif.	81.8	84.4	Compton
		83.4	Pasadena
		83.3	Santa Monica
Newark, N.J.	71.6	71.2	East Orange
		75.2	Elizabeth
		80.3	Montclair
New York, N.Y.	79.3	73.2	Mount Vernon
		79.5	New Rochelle
		79.3	White Plains
		78.1	Yonkers
Paterson, N.J.	75.9	87.9	Englewood
Philadelphia, Penn.	87.1	76.5	Camden
		87.4	Chester
St. Louis, Mo.	90.5	88.6	Centreville
		92.0	East St. Louis
San Francisco, Calif.	69.3	69.4	Berkeley
		77.3	Richmond
		87.6	San Mateo
		83.1	Vallejo
Washington, D.C.	79.7	87.8	Alexandria

Source: Table 1.

The metropolitan ring, as we have previously indicated, is a heterogeneous area, and is not composed solely of residential tract-developments. This is particularly necessary to keep in mind when assessing the suburbanization of Negro population in Northern metropolitan areas. In the Chicago SMSA, for instance, there were in 1960 about 77,500 Negroes living outside the central city. More than half of these Negroes lived in nine large industrial suburbs, most of which, like the central city itself, have older, predominantly Negro neighborhoods. More than 20 per cent of the Negroes outside the central city lived in what might be termed "Negro suburbs," communities or separate sections of communities which have been developed expressly to provide new housing for Negroes.[19] Suburbanization of Negroes has not been proceeding at a rapid pace, and much of what has occurred has had little effect on patterns of residential segregation.

Cowgill has recently presented a set of "Segregation Scores for Metropolitan Areas," arguing that

> To measure any part of the community separately, whether suburban or central city, is to reflect only part of the spectrum. If there is real segregation present, as there is in all American cities, the larger the portion of the total community which is included in the measurement, generally speaking, the higher will be the segregation index.[20]

In Appendix A, we express some reservations about the usefulness of Cowgill's index; however, we cite his work here because it is one of two previous efforts to deal with residential segregation on a metropolitan rather than a city basis. Cowgill, like ourselves, utilized block data for the computation of his index. His approach to developing aggregate scores for metropolitan areas as of 1950 was to compute an index based on the combined block data for all possible cities within a metropolitan area. He then presented a table, much like Table 12, but comparing the separate scores for each central city and suburb with the aggregate score. The limitation of this approach is that block data are generally available only for the largest cities of a metropolitan area, and thus the aggregate score is not for the entire metropolitan area.

The only direct approach to the computation of segregation indexes for metropolitan areas is to use data for census tracts. This was done, again for 1950, by Bell and Willis.[21] The Bell index also has weaknesses for this type of study (see Appendix A), and in 1950 only

19. This account of Negro suburbanization in Chicago draws on data presented in Karl E. Taeuber and Alma F. Taeuber, "The Negro Population in the United States," *The American Negro Reference Book* (New York: Prentice-Hall, 1965).

20. Donald O. Cowgill, "Segregation Scores for Metropolitan Areas," *American Sociological Review*, XXVII, No. 3 (June, 1962), p. 401.

a few metropolitan areas were fully tracted. Partly because of methodological features of the index, the scores for adjacent areas were in many cases quite different from the corresponding central city scores. In aggregate metropolitan scores, however, the situation in the central city tended to dominate so that the two were usually similar.

To gain some perspective on the effect of confining our analysis to data for cities, we have computed segregation indexes for a dozen metropolitan areas, using the same dissimiliarity index as with block data but computed from census tract data. The areas selected, with one exception, had all of the SMSA tracted in 1960, with tract data for 1950 also available for the same area or for most of it. For each city and metropolitan area, the number of tracts changed little during the decade. The metropolitan indexes were computed for a constant area — as much of the entire 1950 tracted area as could be matched with the 1960 tract data.

There are several ways to examine the data in Table 13. First, we may compare the city and metropolitan indexes for a given year. For these twelve cases, there is a high correlation between the two series. Only for Greensboro is there more than a few points difference between city and metropolitan indexes. On a tract basis, therefore, it would appear that an analysis of data for cities would produce

TABLE 13

INDEXES OF RESIDENTIAL SEGREGATION FOR 12 CITIES AND
METROPOLITAN AREAS, 1950–1960

Central City	City Index (Tract)			Metropolitan Index° (Tract)			Change in City Index (Block)
	1950	1960	Change	1950	1960	Change	
Chicago, Ill.	89.0	89.8	0.8	88.1	89.7	1.6	0.5
Cleveland, Ohio	85.3	84.8	−0.5	86.6	89.7	3.1	−0.2
Dayton, Ohio	86.9	88.0	1.1	86.4	90.0	3.6	−2.0
Detroit, Mich.	80.4	79.9	−0.5	83.3	86.7	3.4	−4.3
Greensboro, N.C.	77.7	83.4	5.7	58.7	66.5	7.8	−0.2
Houston, Tex.	73.4	78.7	5.3	70.7	79.2	8.5	2.2
Indianapolis, Ind.	75.2	76.2	1.0	77.2	79.9	2.7	0.2
Milwaukee, Wis.	85.8	85.0	−0.8	85.7	86.0	0.3	−3.5
Philadelphia, Pa.	73.3	78.5	5.2	71.1	76.4	5.3	−1.9
Pittsburgh, Pa.	68.6	74.3	5.7	68.7	75.2	6.5	0.6
San Diego, Calif.	65.8	68.9	3.1	64.9	69.2	4.3	−2.3
Tacoma, Wash.	65.0	61.2	−3.8	61.9	55.5	−6.4	−3.6

Source: City and metropolitan tract indexes computed from Census Tract Bulletins for 1950 and 1960. Change in city block indexes from Table 4, except value for Tacoma computed from Block Bulletins.

° Metropolitan indexes were computed for the entire 1950 tracted area that was also tracted in 1960, in each case covering most of the Standard Metropolitan Statistical Area.

21. Wendell Bell and Ernest M. Willis, "The Segregation of Negroes in American Cities," *Social and Economic Studies*, VI, No. 1 (March, 1957).

results very similar to an analysis of data for metropolitan areas.

Second, we may compare the changes in city indexes between 1950 and 1960 with the changes in metropolitan indexes. Because of the prevalence of rapid suburbanization for whites during the decade, we might expect to find some large differences between the two series. For three of the twelve cases, the direction of change in the value of the segregation index is different on a city basis than on a metropolitan one. In eleven of the twelve cases, there is a greater increase in segregation on a metropolitan than on a city basis. This finding reflects the tendency for suburban areas, even more than central city areas, to be predominantly white. Nevertheless, there is a high correlation between city and metropolitan changes.

A final comparison we can make is between changes in city and metropolitan tract indexes and changes in our original block indexes. For these twelve areas, the association is quite loose. In Appendix A we discuss the differences between segregation on a block and on a tract basis, and present cross-sectional data showing only a moderate correlation between them. Hence, we cannot intersperse the indexes computed from tract data with the block indexes used elsewhere in our analysis. From the results for tracts, however, we hypothesize that if block data were available for entire metropolitan areas, there would be a high correlation, both cross-sectionally and through time, between the series for cities and the series for metropolitan areas.

□ CENTRALIZATION OF NEGROES
WITHIN CITIES

According to the principal theory of urban growth, there are gradients in residential land use, with persons of lower socioeconomic status living closer to the central business district.[22] Just as metropolitan Negroes tend to live in the central city, so might it be anticipated that within the central city, Negro residential areas would tend to be centrally located. The problem of measuring the degree of centralization of Negroes relative to whites is much easier than the problem of measuring most other aspects of the location of Negro residential areas; some relevant data are already available.[23]

22. Ernest W. Burgess, "The Growth of the City: An Introduction to a Research Project," *The City*, ed. Robert E. Park, Ernest W. Burgess, and Roderick D. McKenzie (Chicago: University of Chicago Press, 1925). Extensive citations to additional literature are given in Richard W. Redick, "A Study of Differential Rates of Population Growth and Patterns of Population Distribution in Central Cities in the United States: 1940–1950" (unpublished Master's thesis, University of Chicago, 1954), chaps. I and II.

23. "Contributions to the Theory of Segregation Indexes," *Urban Analysis Report*, No. 14, Prepared Under Contract with the Human Resources Research Institute, Air University, Maxwell Air Force Base, Montgomery, Alabama (hectographed preliminary

For the centralization index, census tracts are grouped into concentric zones around the central business district, and the racial composition of each zone is determined. From these data an index is computed, somewhat like a segregation index, with a value of 100 representing a situation in which all non-whites live closer to the city center than all whites; a value of −100 the opposite situation; and a value of 0 a situation in which whites and non-whites are identically distributed by distance. Methodologically, the procedure is convenient for intercity studies, since the areal units for each city are concentric zones and there are no serious problems of comparability. But the index measures only the relative centralization of non-whites with respect to whites, and does not measure specific locational features of residential distributions. For instance, a high centralization index may occur because of a single major non-white residential area adjoining the central business district, or it might result from a renewed central zone of racially mixed housing surrounded by predominantly white residential areas in the rest of the city.

With data for 1940, positive centralization indexes were found for 50 of 51 cities, confirming the prevalence of the hypothesized pattern of non-white centralization.[24] For the 51 cities, the median value of the index was 40.0, with cities in the North and West having higher values (median, 50.0) than those in the South (median, 34.5). Centralization can be viewed as a component of segregation. Thus, the overall segregation between whites and non-whites can be regarded as composed of two parts: the uneven distribution of white and non-white households among the concentric zones, and the uneven distribution within each zone.

In Appendix A we mention that the Gini segregation index is very similar to the index of dissimilarity we have been using for a segregation index. The absolute magnitude of the centralization index can never be greater than the Gini segregation index, and the ratio of the one to the other is a measure of the extent to which over-all segregation is accounted for by the degree of centralization. For 25 of the 51 cities, this ratio is greater than one-half, indicating that more than half of the total unevenness in residential distribution is accounted for by the relative centralization of non-white population. Surprisingly, however, there is no significant correlation for these 51 cities between the Gini segregation index and the centralization index.

Redick has reported on changes between 1940 and 1950 in the

report, Chicago Community Inventory, University of Chicago, February, 1953), pp. 71–75. See also Redick, *op. cit.*, and "Population Growth and Distribution in Central Cities, 1940–1950," *American Sociological Review*, XXI, No. 1 (February, 1956).

24. "Contributions to the Theory...," *op. cit.*

centralization of whites and non-whites in 23 cities. Two of his findings are pertinent to this discussion:

> Nonwhite population was centralized with respect to the white population both at the beginning and the end of the decade. Nevertheless, by 1950 the distribution of nonwhite population in eleven cities was tending, however slightly, to approach that of the white population, whereas in the remaining cities the distributions of the two populations were tending toward a greater divergence.
>
> The extent and direction of this change in the distribution of nonwhites with respect to whites appeared to have been due, in large measure, to the magnitude of nonwhite population growth and redistribution during the decade rather than to that of the white population.[25]

In all 23 cities, the white population was less centralized in 1950 than in 1940. The same was true for the non-white population in 21 cities. But in about half the cities, non-whites were decentralizing faster than were whites, and were thus becoming less centralized with respect to whites. Redick found the changes in centralization to be inversely correlated (−.60) with the rate of growth of non-white population during the decade; the more rapid the non-white growth, the greater the decline in relative centralization of non-whites with respect to whites. Despite the fact that centralization is a major component of segregation, there is no correlation between changes in the centralization index and changes in an over-all measure of residential segregation.

□ RESIDENTIAL SEGREGATION OF OTHER RACIAL AND ETHNIC GROUPS

Most of our analyses are concerned with residential segregation between Negroes and whites. In this section, we broaden the focus to consider the situation of several other racial and ethnic groups. Our purpose is twofold. First, we wish to provide some perspective on the way in which the situation of Negroes compares with that of other minority groups. Second, since our measure of segregation is based on data for whites and non-whites, we wish to provide a rough indication of how this comparison is affected when minorities other than Negroes are numerous in a city.

In a recent study of trends in racial and ethnic segregation in Chicago, we compared the situation of Negroes with that of various immigrant groups.[26] In contrast with earlier patterns for European immigrant groups, Negro residential segregation has remained at a

25. Redick, "Population Growth...," op. cit., p. 43.
26. Karl E. Taeuber and Alma F. Taeuber, "The Negro as an Immigrant Group:

high level, despite considerable social and economic advancement. Negro residential segregation is high even in comparison to that of Puerto Ricans and Mexicans, groups that on economic measures are less well off than Negroes. In 1960, based on data for 75 community areas in Chicago, the segregation index comparing Negroes and whites was 83; that for persons of Mexican birth or parentage and native whites of native parentage was 54; and that for persons of Puerto Rican birth or parentage and native whites of native parentage was 67.

New York City has been the principal destination for hundreds of thousands of Puerto Ricans who have migrated to the U. S. mainland since World War II. In 1960, New York's total population of 7,782,000 included 1,088,000 Negroes and 613,000 Puerto Ricans. For the purpose of comparing the residential segregation between Puerto Ricans, other whites, and Negroes, we shall assume that all Puerto Ricans are white (in the U. S., 3.9 per cent were listed as non-white in the 1960 census), and we shall leave out of consideration the 53,000 persons of other non-white races. Using census tract data,[27] we obtain the following segregation indexes for 1950 and 1960:

	1950	1960
Puerto Ricans and other whites.........	72.2	73.0
Negroes and other whites	84.9	79.8
Negroes and Puerto Ricans	74.6	62.2

Looking first at 1960, we see that residential segregation between Negroes and other whites was the highest, and segregation between Negroes and Puerto Ricans, though pronounced, was the lowest. The Puerto Rican population increased rapidly between 1950 and 1960, and many Puerto Ricans moved to other boroughs than Manhattan. By 1960, there was a lower degree of dissimilarity between the residential distributions of Negroes and Puerto Ricans than there had been in 1950. Puerto Rican segregation from whites, however, remained unchanged.

The segregation indexes computed from city block data compare whites with non-whites. In New York City, virtually all of the non-whites are Negroes, but a sizable minority of the whites are Puerto Ricans. If Negroes are less segregated from Puerto Ricans than from other whites, then an increase in the percentage of Puerto Ricans

---

Recent Trends in Racial and Ethnic Segregation in Chicago," *American Journal of Sociology*, LXIX, No. 4 (January, 1964).

27. Census tract data for Puerto Ricans for 1950 were obtained from *Population of Puerto Rican Birth or Parentage, New York City: 1950, Data for Boroughs, Health Areas, and Census Tracts* (New York: Research Bureau, Welfare and Health Council of New York City, 1952).

should tend to reduce the over-all Negro-white segregation. On a block basis, white — non-white segregation in the city declined by 8 points between 1950 and 1960. On a tract basis, segregation between Negroes and whites (including Puerto Ricans) also declined by 8 points, from 83.4 to 75.2. From the set of separate indexes for Negroes, Puerto Ricans, and other whites, we see that the decline was less (5 points) between Negroes and other whites. The increasing Puerto Rican population and the declining residential segregation between Puerto Ricans and Negroes apparently can account for somewhat less than half of the drop in the over-all white-Negro segregation index.

In several cities of the West and Southwest, Mexican Americans are a large segment of the white population, but one of rather low socioeconomic status with some problems of discrimination and segregation. Using census tract data on the white population with Spanish surnames, we may identify this group and analyze its segregation patterns in the same way as for Puerto Ricans in New York City. For illustration, we use data for San Antonio (Tex.), a city with a very large Spanish surname population (244,000, or 45 per cent of all whites) and a smaller but still sizable Negro population (42,000). The results for 1960 follow:

Spanish surname and other whites......... 63.6
Negroes and other whites 84.5
Negroes and Spanish surname.............. 77.4

Again the residential segregation between Negroes and other whites is greater than between the other pairs. The Spanish surname population, however, is also residentially segregated to a moderately high degree both from other whites and from Negroes. On a tract basis, the segregation between Negroes and all whites in 1960 is 80.8, a smaller figure than is obtained when the whites of Spanish surname are removed from the comparison.

In Los Angeles, there are large Negro (335,000) and Spanish surname (260,000) populations, but there are also many persons of other non-white races (82,000). The latter group is composed mainly of Japanese (51,000) and Chinese (15,000), but the details of the residential distribution are not available for the separate groups. Dividing the total population of Los Angeles into four groups, we obtain the following six segregation indexes from tract data for 1960:

Spanish surname and other whites......... 57.4
Negroes and other whites 87.8
Other races and other whites................. 60.5
Spanish surname and Negroes.............. 75.5
Spanish surname and other races 50.3
Negroes and other races...................... 66.2

Each group is residentially segregated from the others, but the highest index obtains for Negroes and other whites. The second and third highest indexes are for the comparisons between Negroes and the other two groups. On a tract basis, the segregation between all whites and all non-whites is 77.0, in contrast to the value of 87.8 obtained for Negroes and other whites.

San Francisco has had a stable system of census tracts for several decades, and we have prepared a series of segregation indexes for 1940–60 for whites, Negroes, and other races. In 1940, San Francisco's population included 603,000 whites, 5,000 Negroes, and 27,000 persons of other races (18,000 Chinese, 5,000 Japanese, 3,000 Filipinos). By 1960, the distribution had changed: 604,000 whites, 74,000 Negroes, and 62,000 persons of other races (36,000 Chinese, 9,000 Japanese, 12,000 Filipinos). Accompanying the changes in population were changes in segregation:

	1940	1950	1960
Whites and non-whites	73.8	66.2	57.6
Whites and Negroes	71.3	70.8	70.2
Whites and other races	76.2	67.8	51.4
Negroes and other races	61.4	65.2	65.4

During this period, the other races were dispersing residentially, becoming less segregated from whites, and, in the process, more segregated from Negroes. Negroes remained at about the same level of segregation from whites in all three years. The index which lumps together Negroes and other races follows an intermediate course, declining much more rapidly than the index for whites and Negroes, and less rapidly than the index for whites and other races.

Census data on the Spanish surname population of census tracts are not available for the entire 1940–60 period, but more detail may be added to the description of the intergroup segregation patterns as of 1960. In that year, there were 52,000 white persons of Spanish surname in San Francisco, with the following segregation from other groups:

Spanish surname and other whites	37.3
Spanish surname and Negroes	65.7
Spanish surname and other races	59.7

Persons of Spanish surname and persons of other races are more residentially segregated from each other than either group is segregated from whites. The greatest segregation, as usual, obtains for Negroes.

In his study of ethnic residential segregation, Lieberson briefly compared the situation of various European immigrant groups to that of Negroes in ten Northern cities, using ward data for 1910 and 1920 and census tract data for 1930 and 1950:

> In summarizing the findings about Negro-European immigrant housing patterns, we may observe that although at one time certain specific immigrant groups in a city have been somewhat less segregated from Negroes than from native whites or more segregated than Negroes were from the native whites, the general summary figures indicate that Negroes and immigrant groups have moved in opposite directions, *i.e.*, declining segregation for immigrants and increasing segregation for Negroes. In terms of sheer magnitude, the Negroes are far more highly segregated than are the immigrant groups.[28]

This review of a variety of miscellaneous information on the residential segregation of other minorities in comparison to that of Negroes has revealed some remarkably consistent patterns. The data reveal each minority group to be residentially segregated, usually to a high degree, not only from whites but from each other minority. In nearly every comparison, however, segregation of a group from Negroes is greater than its segregation from any other minority. These findings suggest that the segregation indexes between whites and non-whites, reported in previous sections, are likely to be understatements of the degree of segregation obtaining between Negroes and whites. To the extent that the non-white population in a city includes many Chinese, Japanese, or members of other non-white races, the segregation index tends to be lower than it would be if the data referred only to Negroes. Similarly, if Negroes were compared not to the total white population, but to whites excluding persons of Spanish surname or of other ethnic identities, then the magnitude of the segregation index would generally be higher.

Taken together, these data provide strong and consistent support for the conclusion that Negroes are by far the most residentially segregated large minority group in recent American history.

28. Lieberson, *op. cit.*, p. 132.

4

□

SOCIAL AND ECONOMIC FACTORS IN RESIDENTIAL SEGREGATION

A variety of alternative approaches to the study of residential segregation were enumerated in Chapter 2. Taken together, the somewhat divergent approaches suffice to provide a relatively coherent picture of the status of the Negro in the United States, of the general character of urban residential segregation, and of the relationships between residential segregation and other facets of race relations. Because of the prevalent concern with elucidating general patterns, however, there has been little emphasis on the nature and causes of variation among cities.

Previous studies utilizing segregation indexes include a few discussions of intercity variation.[1] Little confidence can be placed in the empirical results of such studies because of serious methodological weaknesses in the measurement of segregation (see Appendix A). In these studies, intercity variation in segregation at one point in time has been related to the variations in other characteristics at the same time. Such a cross-sectional design presents both conceptual and methodological difficulties. Conceptually, it would be difficult to argue on the basis of 1960 data, say, that Charleston's low segregation index compared to Augusta's is due to its higher percentage of Negroes, or to the higher average educational or occupational levels of its Negro population, or to any other city characteristics as of 1960. The lesser degree of residential segregation in Charleston can be traced back at least fifty and probably a hundred years. Current differences among cities reflect past differences, modified by the differential patterns of change taking place over long periods of time. A cross-sectional analysis based on data for 1940 would yield somewhat different results from one based on 1960 data; neither one, by itself, could yield much information on the differential patterns of change.[2]

1. A review of the literature on measurement of residential segregation is included in Appendix A.

2. The appropriate use of cross-sectional data for longitudinal inferences is extremely difficult, and there are no examples in the segregation literature. For some

A longitudinal analysis does not face difficulties of the same sort. Consider, for example, the finding that in 1940 the average segregation index for Southern cities was below the average for cities outside the South, whereas in 1960 the situation was reversed. Few of the variables that might be included in a cross-sectional analysis — percentage of Negroes, size or socioeconomic status of Negro population, economic base of city, and so forth — display patterns of regional variation sufficiently different in 1960 than in 1940 to explain the changed pattern of intercity variation in segregation. It is, however, a tenable assumption that changes in residential patterns during a given time are affected by changes in other city characteristics during that time; a longitudinal analysis seems to be able to capture substantively meaningful relationships. In such an analysis, questions of the historical origins of low levels of segregation in Charleston and other cities can be bypassed, and the problem becomes one of relating Charleston's recent rapid increases in segregation to concurrent changes in other relevant city characteristics.

□ INTERCITY VARIATION IN
SEGREGATION CHANGES

The small number of cities for which longitudinal data are available permits consideration of only a few explanatory variables. Since the index of residential segregation is a measure of the areal distribution of the Negro population relative to the white population within a city, it is appropriate to focus on the types of change which might affect population redistribution within a city. The analyses of long-term changes in Charleston, Augusta, and other cities demonstrate the relevance of population change, both white and Negro; of the building-up of new residential areas, both within the city and in the suburbs; and of various local factors unique to each city. In the broad intercity analysis to be reported, it was feasible to include measures of population growth, residential construction, and suburbanization. In addition, a measure of the changing socioeconomic status of Negroes in the city is included because rapid up-grading in recent decades may have improved the competitive position of Negroes in the housing market.

methodological discussion of the problem, see Otis Dudley Duncan, Ray P. Cuzzort, and Beverly Duncan, *Statistical Geography: Problems in Analyzing Areal Data* (Glencoe, Ill.: The Free Press, 1961); for a successful example of this type of study, see Donnell M. Pappenfort, *Journey to Labor: A Study of Births in Hospitals and Technology* (Chicago: Population Research and Training Center, University of Chicago, 1964).

In the multivariate analysis of segregation changes utilized here, each of the two decades for which data are available is treated separately. Not only does this provide two sets of analyses of segregation changes, but it provides an opportunity to ascertain why changes in segregation 1940–50 differ from those 1950–60. To maximize comparability, the same five variables were used in the analysis for each decade:

1. *White population change.* The measure used was obtained by calculating the percentage of the 1950 white population of the city comprised by the 1940 white population, and similarly for 1950–60. The measure was computed inversely to avoid giving undue weight to the few cities with very rapid population growth. Hence, the larger the value of the population-change measure, the smaller the increase in population; figures over 100 represent decreases in population. (The amount of change was adjusted for annexations to the city by subtracting from the terminal population in each decade an estimate of the white population of annexed areas.[3])

2. *Non-white population change.* The measure used was computed in the same way as the measure of white population change. It must be kept in mind that this also is an inverse measure, with smaller figures representing greater increases in population.

3. *Suburbanization.* The percentages of the metropolitan area population which resided outside the city at the beginning and end of each decade were computed, after adjusting the terminal population for any population in annexed areas. The percentage-point change in this measure is an index of suburbanization, with positive figures indicating increasing suburbanization.[4]

4. *New construction.* The percentage of all housing units in the

3. Estimates of total annexed population for 1940–50 were taken from Donald J. Bogue, *Components of Population Change, 1940–50: Estimates of Net Migration and Natural Increase for Each Standard Metropolitan Area and State Economic Area* (Oxford, Ohio, and Chicago: Scripps Foundation and Population Research and Training Center, 1957), Table II, and for 1950–60 from U. S. Bureau of the Census, *U. S. Census of Population: 1960.* Vol. I, *Characteristics of the Population,* Part A, *Number of Inhabitants* (Washington: U. S. Government Printing Office, 1961), Table 9 for states. Estimates of annexed population by color were made utilizing city block data from the 1940, 1950, and 1960 Censuses of Housing, except for 1950–60 data for some cities taken from Ann Ratner Miller and Bension Varon, *Population in 1960 of Areas Annexed to Large Cities of the United States between 1950 and 1960 by Age, Sex, and Color* Technical Paper No. 1 (Philadelphia: Population Studies Center, University of Pennsylvania, 1961).

4. For a discussion of the merits of various measures of suburbanization, see Donald J. Bogue and Dorothy L. Harris, *Comparative Population and Urban Research Via Multiple Regression and Covariance Analysis* (Oxford, Ohio: Scripps Foundation, Miami University, 1954); and Beverly Duncan, Georges Sabagh, and Maurice D. Van Arsdol, Jr., "Patterns of City Growth," *American Journal of Sociology,* LXVII (January, 1962).

city in 1950 (or 1960) which were in structures built during 1940–50 (or 1950–60) is an index of new housing opportunities.

5. *Non-white occupational change.* This measure refers to non-white civilian employed males age fourteen years and over, who reported occupation in the decennial census. The percentage with white-collar or skilled jobs (professionals, managers, clerical workers, sales workers, and craftsmen) was calculated for each census date. The percentage-point change in this measure indicates the degree of occupational advance by non-whites during the decade, and is a general index of change in the socioeconomic status of non-whites.

Although data on changes in segregation during the 1940's and 1950's are available for 109 cities, only 69 cities were included in the analysis. The segregation indexes are based on data for whites and non-whites. Because patterns of residential segregation among non-whites other than Negroes differ from patterns for Negroes, those cities (all in the West) in which Negroes were less than 90 per cent of the total non-white population at any of the three census dates were omitted from the analysis. Thus, the regression results can be interpreted as referring to changing patterns of Negro segregation. Suburban cities also were omitted, because our reasoning about the effects of social and economic changes on residential segregation implicitly refers to central cities. The cases of twin central cities for a single metropolitan area posed a potential problem, but in most cases the two cities were sufficiently separate to be retained in the analysis. In one situation of adjoining central cities — Minneapolis and St. Paul — the data for the two cities were combined and treated as referring to a single city.

The successive decennial censuses are not fully comparable with one another either in questions asked or in the details of tabulation and publication; this led to a further attrition in the number of cities that could be included in the analysis. Social and economic characteristics of the non-white population were published in 1940 only for cities of 100,000 population or more; in 1950 only for Southern cities; and in 1960 for all cities with 1,000 or more non-white residents. The omission of data for Northern cities in 1950 is a serious gap, which can be partially rectified by tedious summation over census tracts of those cities with such data. Other cities, however, had to be excluded for lack of the basic data.

The omission of cities with large Oriental populations, of suburbs, and of cities for which not all measures could be computed, subtracted 39 Northern and Western cities and one Southern city from the original list of 109, leaving 25 Northern and Western cities and 44 Southern cities in the analysis. For comparability, the same 69 cities were included in the analysis for each decade.

Results, 1940–50. — Zero-order correlation coefficients permit a quick overview of the interrelationships among the variables used in the multiple-regression analysis. Intercorrelations among the independent variables, as well as the correlations of each independent variable with the dependent variable, are shown in the top panel of Table 14. Among the independent variables, the only large correlation (−.72) is that between white population change and new construction. Greater increases in segregation (or smaller decreases) are predicted for a city with the greater percentage of new construction, the greater white population increase, the greater suburbanization, and the less non-white population increase.

TABLE 14

INTERCORRELATIONS OF MEASURES USED IN ANALYSES OF
SEGREGATION CHANGE IN 69 CITIES, 1940–50 AND 1950–60

Decade and Independent Variable	*Dependent Variable*	*Independent Variables*			
	Segregation Change	*Population Change†*		*Suburbanization*	*New Construction*
		White	*Non-white*		
1940–50					
Population change—white†	−.27°				
Population change—non-white†	.30°	−.26°			
Suburbanization	.20	.05	.21		
New construction	.51°°	−.72°°	.29°	.28°	
Non-white occupational change	.06	−.20	.19	.14	.36°°
1950–60					
Population change—white†	−.19				
Population change—non-white†	.64°°	−.05			
Suburbanization	.01	.24°	−.11		
New construction	.28°	−.69°°	.18	.07	
Non-white occupational change	−.57°°	.16	−.48°°	.07	−.31°°

† The population-change measures are inverse (see text for definitions), so that, for example, the negative correlations between white population change and new construction mean that the greater the increase in white population, the greater the amount of new construction.

° Statistically significant at the .05 level.

°° Statistically significant at the .01 level.

The predictive power of the independent variables is better indicated by the data in Table 15, which show how much of the intercity variance in segregation change can be accounted for by various combinations of the independent variables. Together, the two population-change measures account for 13 per cent of the variance in segregation change, but once the intercorrelations with new construction and other independent variables are taken into account, the

power of the population-change measures is sharply diminished, to a
final net figure of 7.4 per cent.

TABLE 15

PERCENTAGE OF VARIANCE IN SEGREGATION CHANGE
EXPLAINED BY VARIOUS LINEAR COMBINATIONS OF INDEPENDENT
VARIABLES, FOR 69 CITIES, 1940–50 AND 1950–60 †

Independent Variables	Variables Held Constant	Percentage Explained of Variance in Segregation Change	
		1940–50	1950–60
Population changes – white and non-white	None	12.8°	42.8°°
Population changes – white and non-white	Non-white occupational change	12.6°	26.7°°
Population changes – white and non-white	All other independent variables	7.4	27.1°°
New construction	None	26.0°°	8.1°
New construction	All other independent variables	20.9°°	0.0
Non-white occupational change	None	0.4	32.6°°
Non-white occupational change	Population changes – white and non-white	0.1	13.6°°
Non-white occupational change	All other independent variables	3.6	13.5°°

† The per cent of variance explained is based on the square of the coefficient of multiple
partial correlation, defined in Frederick E. Croxton and Dudley J. Cowden, *Applied General
Statistics,* 2nd ed. (Englewood Cliffs, N. J.: Prentice-Hall, 1955), p. 551.
   ° Statistically significant at the .05 level.
   °° Statistically significant at the .01 level.

The measures of suburbanization and of new construction were
included as an index of the availability to city residents of alternative,
presumably highly segregated, housing. New construction is the most
powerful of the five independent variables. After all other independent
variables are controlled, this single measure accounts for more than
one-fifth of the intercity variance in segregation change 1940–50. The
suburbanization measure, however, has little explanatory power, and
hence is not shown separately in Table 15.

    A regression equation using linear combinations of all five in-
dependent variables can explain one-third of the variance in segrega-

tion change during the 1940's (Table 16). The net regression coefficients, expressed in standard form, indicate the weight given to each variable, with other variables controlled, in predicting segregation change. New construction clearly is the most important of the independent variables in predicting change in residential segregation. The position of a city on any of the other four independent variables has little effect on the predicted value of segregation change unless that measure is extremely high or low.

TABLE 16

MULTIPLE REGRESSION ANALYSIS OF SEGREGATION CHANGE AND FIVE INDEPENDENT VARIABLES, FOR 69 CITIES, 1940–50 AND 1950–60

Results of Multiple Regression Analysis	1940–50	1950–60
Percentage of Variance Explained	33.4°°	51.9°°
Net regression coefficients:		
Population change – white†	.077	−.039
Population change – non-white†	.038	.097°°
Suburbanization	−.016	.086
New construction...	.215°°	−.003
Non-white occupational change...........................	−.212	−.377°°
Net regression coefficients, in standard form:		
Population change – white†	.254	−.145
Population change – non-white†	.200	.486°°
Suburbanization	−.027	.119
New construction...	.702°°	−.010
Non-white occupational change...........................	−.172	−.324°°
Standard deviation of dependent variable...................	2.96	3.42
Standard error of regression estimate	2.51	2.47
Average values (means):		
Segregation change..	2.7	0.6
Population change – white†	91.1	108.9
Population change – non-white†	77.0	76.0
Suburbanization	7.5	11.9
New construction...	17.2	20.7
Non-white occupational change...........................	4.1	4.2

† The population-change measures are inverse (see text for definitions), so that the smaller the measure, the greater the increase in population.

°° Statistically significant at the .01 level.

Results, 1950-60. – The correlation and regression results for 1950–60 differ from those for 1940–50. Again there is a high zero-order correlation between white population change and new construction (Table 14). A moderate positive relationship exists between non-white occupational change and non-white population increase.

The main correlates of segregation change are non-white population change and non-white occupational change. The predictive power of these two measures is shared jointly, since each explains some of the variance in segregation change even after controlling for all other independent variables (Table 15). In striking contrast to the previous decade, there is a negligible association between new construction and segregation change, holding constant the other independent variables.

The regression analysis for 1950–60 explains more than one-half the variance in segregation change (Table 16). Non-white population change and non-white occupational change predominate in predicting a city's segregation change: the greater the increase in Negro population or occupational status, the greater the decrease (or the less the increase) in segregation. The amount of new construction in a city makes no difference in this decade, and there is only a slight association between increasing segregation and increasing white population or suburbanization.

Discussion. – The virtual hiatus in residential construction during World War II and the severe housing shortages during the immediate postwar years produced a very tight housing market in most cities throughout the 1940's. Furthermore, many central cities did not have large quantities of vacant land for extensive new residential developments. The percentage of dwelling units existing in 1950 which had been built during the decade ranged from 3.6 to 37.7 per cent among the 69 cities. Where this figure was high, increases in residential segregation were facilitated by the development of new housing, most of which was in racially homogeneous neighborhoods. Where this figure was low, there was usually little change in existing residential patterns, since, in a tight housing market, neither whites nor Negroes had enough residential alternatives to permit rapid change in housing patterns. In the context of such a restricted housing market, neither the pressures of a growing population nor the changing socioeconomic status of Negroes could have much impact on patterns of residential segregation.

In the 1950's, the supply of housing in most cities caught up with the demand. Not only was there a great expansion in suburban housing, but it became much easier for both whites and Negroes to locate housing within the city. With higher vacancy rates and a wider variety of housing alternatives than in the 1940's, housing patterns could change rapidly in response to changing socioeconomic circumstances. In this decade, Negro gains in occupational and income levels could be translated into improved housing, often in less segregated neighborhoods. Thus, the changing context of the housing market is the principal explanation for the differing trends in residential segregation in the two decades.

That non-white population change emerges as the strongest variable in predicting segregation change, 1950–60, is also a consequence of the greater looseness of the housing market in that decade, and the great expansion of Negro residential areas stands in contrast to the crowding and congestion of the preceding decade.[5] The direction of the association between Negro population growth and changes in segregation, however, is contrary to that usually assumed. In the 1950's, the greater the increase in Negro population, the greater the decrease in residential segregation. This association may depend more on short-run changes in residential distributions than on fundamental long-run changes. Consider the following discussion, based on an analysis of residential patterns in Chicago:

> This suggests that the "mixed" areas observed . . . are transitory, *i.e.*, that non-Negroes will continue to leave the areas and Negroes will continue to enter the areas and that, with time, the "mixed" areas will become almost exclusively Negro residential areas. A highly segregated population, expanding under pressure of sheer numbers, can appear "less segregated" during the expansion phase without any permanent change in residential patterns.[6]

The Chicago experience suggests that the immediate effect of an increase in Negro population may be to augment the number of racially mixed areas at the periphery of established Negro areas. This temporary mixture – temporary for any given area – may tend to lower the segregation index. But the continuing transition of mixed areas to solidly Negro areas would operate to raise the segregation index eventually. Hence, there is a limit to the magnitude of a decrease in segregation that can reasonably be attributed to the effect of "temporary mixture."

Thus far, the regression results have been discussed without reference to region. Region, as such, was not included among the explanatory variables because its meaning is vague. Any "regional effect" must be attributable to specific regional differences in appropriate independent variables. Comparisons of actual values of segregation change with those predicted from the regression equations show that Northern and Southern cities are about equally often underpredicted or overpredicted. Thus, there is no regional variation in changes in segregation indexes beyond that which can be explained by the five independent variables.

5. The contrast between the two decades is discussed in greater detail in Chapter 7.

6. Otis Dudley Duncan and Beverly Duncan, *The Negro Population of Chicago: A Study of Residential Succession* (Chicago: University of Chicago Press, 1957), pp. 98–99.

☐ RESIDENTIAL SEGREGATION BY RACE AND BY SOCIOECONOMIC STATUS

Although residential segregation between whites and Negroes is the central focus of this study, there are types of residential segregation other than that between racial groups. As familiar as the differentiation of a city into Negro and white neighborhoods is its differentiation into wealthy neighborhoods and slums. Expensive housing tends to be located in separate neighborhoods from inexpensive housing, and persons with high incomes and upper-level jobs tend to live apart from persons with low incomes and more menial jobs. Obviously, the residential segregation of racial groups is not completely independent of the residential segregation of socioeconomic groups. Negroes, on the average, score much lower on measures of socioeconomic status than do whites, and this fact alone would produce some degree of racial residential segregation, even in the absence of any racial prejudice or housing discrimination. Can it be inferred that racial segregation would virtually disappear if urban Negroes were to catch up to whites in measures of economic well-being? In this section, several models are presented which permit a careful assessment of the interrelations between racial and socioeconomic residential segregation. It is necessary to utilize data for census tracts rather than blocks, so caution is necessary in comparing segregation indexes reported in this section with those used previously (see Appendix A).

Macon, Georgia: An Illustrative Approach. — There are many status measures that might be used in studying these interrelations, and for a first approach we use a measure of quality of housing. Residential segregation of the population by socioeconomic status is accompanied by residential segregation of high-quality from low-quality housing. Several censuses provide tabulations of the structural condition and plumbing facilities of dwelling units, permitting a classification of all units into "standard" and "substandard" categories.[7]

Census tract data for Macon for 1940 include both the city and some adjoining built-up area. Segregation indexes (indexes of dissimilarity) may be computed to compare residential distributions of standard housing occupied by whites, standard housing occupied by non-whites, substandard housing occupied by whites, and substandard housing occupied by non-whites. There are six paired comparisons:

7. In 1940, "standard" includes all dwellings with private bath and not needing major repair, while all other dwellings are "substandard." Analogous definitions apply to 1950 and 1960.

White standard vs. non-white standard dwellings 49.8
White substandard vs. non-white standard dwellings 49.6
White standard vs. non-white substandard dwellings 47.7
White substandard vs. non-white substandard dwellings 35.2
Non-white standard vs. non-white substandard dwellings 30.7
White standard vs. white substandard dwellings 28.3

The four highest indexes each involve a white-non-white comparison. Taking quality of housing as an index of socioeconomic status, the high-status whites maintain a high degree of residential segregation from non-whites, whether of high or low status. Moreover, the high-status non-whites are more highly segregated from low-status whites than from low-status non-whites. In sum, interracial segregation is quite pronounced in comparison with the much weaker patterns of segregation by housing quality within each racial group.

A Model of Residential and Economic Segregation. — Arguments as to the relations between the residential segregation of whites and Negroes and that of persons of differing economic status are seldom stated in completely deterministic fashion. If carried to the extreme, however, an hypothesis of the following sort would be reached: Residential segregation between whites and Negroes is no greater than that to be expected on the basis of (1) the lower economic status of Negroes, and (2) the existing residential segregation by economic status.

In practice, residential segregation by race and by economic status exist simultaneously, and it is something of a chicken-and-egg problem to assign priority to one or the other. Assuming for analytical purposes the priority of residential segregation by economic status, the above hypothesis may be phrased as a simple model:

$$
\underbrace{\left\{\begin{array}{c}\text{Segregation}\\\text{of whites}\\\text{and}\\\text{Negroes}\\\text{by}\\\text{area}\end{array}\right\}}_{A}=\underbrace{\left\{\begin{array}{c}\text{Segregation}\\\text{of whites}\\\text{and}\\\text{Negroes}\\\text{by}\\\text{economic}\\\text{status}\end{array}\right\}}_{B}\times\underbrace{\left\{\begin{array}{c}\text{Segregation}\\\text{of}\\\text{economic}\\\text{status}\\\text{groups}\\\text{by}\\\text{area}\end{array}\right\}}_{C}+\left\{\begin{array}{c}\text{R}\\\text{Residual}\end{array}\right\}
$$

The hypothesis suggests that the residual term in the equation will be zero.

Although such a model may perhaps clarify the analytical problem, it generally cannot be applied literally in evaluating these relationships empirically. There is a special case in which the arithmetic operations of the equation do make sense. If economic status is measured by a dichotomy (high or low), and segregation is in each instance measured with the index of dissimilarity, then the direct algebraic application of the model is meaningful, and is equivalent to an indirect standardization technique that will be discussed later.

In applying the model, the over-all racial residential segregation, A, is to be explained by the product, BC. The residual, R, indicates how much of A remains unexplained. Hence, we are interested in obtaining two ratios — BC/A, representing the proportion of the racial segregation explained by the model; and R/A, representing the proportion of racial segregation left unexplained by the model.

For illustrative purposes, we have applied the model to census tract data for 1940 and 1950 for Macon (Ga.) and Charleston (S.C.). Economic status is indexed by quality of dwelling units, with standard units representing high status and substandard units representing low status. Owing to changes in census procedures, the quality classifications for the two years are not strictly comparable, but that does not seriously affect this illustrative analysis.

The components specified by the model are defined operationally as follows:

A = Index of dissimilarity between the distribution of whites and non-whites over census tracts.

B = Index of dissimilarity between the distribution of whites and non-whites over standard and substandard dwelling units.[8]

C = Index of dissimilarity between the distribution of standard and substandard dwelling units over census tracts.

The values of the components for the two cities are given in Table 17.

In the data for 1940, the magnitudes of the components for the two cities are quite different. For Charleston, component C is small, indicating that standard and substandard dwellings are not very segregated from each other, and thus that residential segregation by economic status (quality of dwelling unit) is not very great. In 1940 in Charleston, 91 per cent of dwelling units occupied by non-whites were substandard, as compared to 29 per cent for units occupied by whites. Hence, component B, the color differential in economic status, is quite large (91.2 − 28.5 = 62.7). Taken together, components B and C can account for only a moderate degree of racial segregation; but since in 1940 Charleston had a rather low segregation index, the

8. This index is similar to the index of metropolitan centralization used in Chapter 3, and is equal to the absolute value of the difference between the percentage of standard units among dwelling units occupied by whites and the percentage of standard units among dwelling units occupied by non-whites.

product BC is 65 per cent of A. Thus only 35 per cent of the racial residential segregation is unaccounted for by this simple model of the influence of residential segregation by economic status.

For Macon, the situation is different. Compared with Charleston, Macon in 1940 had a greater degree of residential segregation by economic status (component C) and a smaller color differential in status (component B). The color segregation expected from economic factors (BC) is higher for Macon than for Charleston, but so is actual segregation by color. The per cent explained is therefore lower—42 per cent—leaving 58 per cent of racial residential segregation unaccounted for by the model.

Between 1940 and 1950, racial residential segregation increased in both Charleston and Macon. Color differentials in quality of dwelling units decreased in both cities, but segregation between standard and substandard units increased. The component BC was greater in 1950 than in 1940, but not sufficiently so to account for all the increase in racial segregation, so that the percentage explained by the model diminished in both cities.

Before leaving this illustrative model, we may note that it inherently tends to exaggerate the impact of economic factors. Residential segregation between standard and substandard dwelling units is treated as if it were a measure of only economic segregation, but it is obviously affected by the degree of racial segregation. If most Negroes live in substandard housing and most whites live in standard housing, and there is a high degree of segregation, the two factors of racial segregation and segregation by economic status cannot be measured separately. Using a different measure of economic status might produce somewhat different results in the model, but it would not get around this inherent confounding of the two types of residential segregation. Although the more elaborate technique described in the next section cannot solve this confounding, it does permit the use of more refined measures of economic status.

Techniques Utilizing Indirect Standardization. — The technique may be illustrated with hypothetical data, using once again the quality of dwelling units as an indicator of economic status. For a city, we have the following racial breakdown by economic status:

	Total	Non-white	Proportion Non-white
Total occupied dwelling units	100	50	.50
Standard units	50	10	.20
Substandard units	50	40	.80

For each census tract, the distribution of occupied dwelling units by quality is known. Assume there are two tracts in the city, as follows:

	Tract 1	Tract 2
Total occupied dwelling units	50	50
Standard units...............................	30	20
Substandard units	20	30

For this hypothetical city, .20 of the standard units and .80 of the substandard are occupied by non-whites. If these proportions are applied in each tract, there would be 6 non-whites residing in standard units in Tract 1 (.20 times 30), and 4 non-whites in standard units in Tract 2 (.20 times 20). Similarly, there would be 16 non-whites in substandard units in Tract 1 (.80 times 20), and 24 non-whites in substandard units in Tract 2 (.80 times 30). Altogether, then, on the basis of housing quality, there should be 6 plus 16, or 22 non-whites in Tract 1, and 4 plus 24, or 28 non-whites in Tract 2, as shown:

	Tract 1	Tract 2
Standard units...............................	6	4
Substandard units	16	24
Expected units occupied by non-whites	22	28

The *actual* number of units occupied by non-whites in each tract is also known — 10 in Tract 1 and 40 in Tract 2. The actual and expected numbers of non-whites may be compared.

One simple approach is to compute two segregation indexes, one for the actual distribution of whites and non-whites, and a second for the expected distribution of whites and non-whites. For the example, the segregation index based on the actual distribution is 60, while the segregation index based on the expected distribution is 12. Thus the expected index is one-fifth the actual index. In this example, then, economic status can account for only 20 per cent of the actual racial residential segregation.[9]

This technique has been carried out for Macon and Charleston, and relevant data are presented in Table 18. When economic status is measured in only two categories, the percentage explained that is obtained from the previously described simple model is identical with the percentage explained that is obtained by the indirect stand-

9. The approach used here is adapted from one devised by Otis Dudley Duncan and Beverly Duncan and reported in "Contributions to the Theory of Segregation Indexes," Urban Analysis Report, No. 14, Prepared under Contract with the Human Resources Research Institute, Air University, Maxwell Air Force Base, Montgomery, Alabama (hectographed preliminary report, Chicago Community Inventory, University of Chicago, February, 1953).

ardization technique. Hence, the figures in the bottom row of Table 18 are identical with those in the next to last row of Table 17. The findings for Macon and Charleston are presented primarily to illustrate techniques, but they suggest that racial residential segregation is becoming less dependent on either economic differentials or residential segregation by economic status, primarily because economic differentials between whites and non-whites are decreasing.

TABLE 17

EVALUATION OF A SIMPLE MODEL RELATING RESIDENTIAL SEGREGATION BY COLOR TO RESIDENTIAL SEGREGATION BY ECONOMIC STATUS, MACON (GA.) AND CHARLESTON (S.C.), 1940 AND 1950

Components of the Model	Macon		Charleston	
	1940	1950	1940	1950
A = Residential segregation by color	47.8	52.0	26.6	30.7
B = Color differentials in economic status	54.0	52.2	62.7	61.1
C = Residential segregation by economic status	37.5	39.2	27.7	31.6
Product, BC	20.2	20.4	17.2	19.3
Residual, R = A − BC	27.6	31.6	9.4	11.4
Per cent explained = 100(BC/A)	42	39	65	63
Per cent unexplained = 100(R/A)	58	61	35	37

Source: Census Tract Bulletins.

TABLE 18

EVALUATION OF AN INDIRECT STANDARDIZATION TECHNIQUE FOR RELATING RESIDENTIAL SEGREGATION BY COLOR TO RESIDENTIAL SEGREGATION BY ECONOMIC STATUS, MACON (GA.) AND CHARLESTON (S.C.), 1940 AND 1950

Summary Measure	Macon		Charleston	
	1940	1950	1940	1950
Per cent non-white of occupied dwelling units:				
Total	47	40	49	45
Standard	9	15	10	17
Substandard	68	65	75	79
Per cent substandard of occupied dwelling units:				
Whites	40	29	29	15
Non-whites	94	81	91	76
Segregation index:				
Actual	47.8	52.0	26.6	30.7
Expected	20.3	20.5	17.4	19.3
Per cent expected of actual	42	39	65	63

Source: Census Tract Bulletins.

Additional data on intercity variation in the percentage of racial segregation accounted for by economic segregation, and on trends in that percentage, are needed in order to determine whether the findings for Macon and Charleston are general. For a preliminary assessment, we have experimented with three different measures of economic status. For quality of housing and for labor force and occupational status, data were assembled for eleven Southern cities for 1940 and 1950. For a classification of dwelling units by value of owner-occupied homes and by rent of renter-occupied homes, data were assembled for fifteen cities, including four in the North, for 1940, 1950, and 1960. The expected segregation indexes, actual segregation indexes, and per cent expected of actual are presented in Tables 19 and 20.

These data confirm the earlier finding that patterns of economic residential segregation do not account for the observed levels of

TABLE 19

EXPECTED INDEXES OF RACIAL RESIDENTIAL SEGREGATION BASED
ON INDIRECT STANDARDIZATIONS FOR QUALITY OF DWELLING
UNIT AND LABOR-FORCE AND OCCUPATIONAL STATUS OF
PERSONS, AND PER CENT EXPECTED INDEX IS OF ACTUAL INDEX,
11 SOUTHERN CITIES, 1940 AND 1950

City	Expected Index°				Per Cent Expected of Actual†			
	Based on Quality		Based on Occupation		Based on Quality		Based on Occupation	
	1940	1950	1940	1950	1940	1950	1940	1950
Atlanta, Ga.	26.3	19.1	17.6	17.1	32.8	23.0	21.9	20.6
Baltimore, Md.	19.2	15.3	13.4	11.5	23.0	18.9	16.0	14.2
Birmingham, Ala.	30.7	24.1	12.9	12.2	44.9	36.3	18.9	18.4
Dallas, Tex.	20.1	11.2	15.7	14.9	30.8	14.8	24.0	19.7
Houston, Tex.	12.1	11.3	14.3	13.0	17.5	15.2	20.6	17.5
Louisville, Ky.	21.9	14.9	9.6	9.7	31.9	20.4	14.0	13.3
Memphis, Tenn.	28.5	23.1	12.9	12.1	49.4	35.4	22.4	18.6
Nashville, Tenn.	26.9	15.8	11.9	11.5	40.0	21.8	17.7	15.9
New Orleans, La.	25.8	21.8	9.3	9.2	41.5	34.3	15.0	14.5
Richmond, Va.	25.6	22.8	15.4	14.4	36.8	31.2	22.1	19.7
Washington, D.C.	12.1	9.7	13.5	11.3	19.7	15.7	22.0	18.3

° Expected indexes were computed from the distribution of whites and non-whites expected on the basis of the indirect standardizations. Each standardization was made using as detailed a classification by economic status as the census tract data for each year permit.

† Actual segregation indexes were computed from the distribution of occupied dwelling units, by color of household head, among census tracts. The actual indexes are listed in Table 20.

TABLE 20

EXPECTED INDEXES OF RACIAL RESIDENTIAL SEGREGATION BASED
ON INDIRECT STANDARDIZATION FOR TENURE, VALUE, AND RENT
OF OCCUPIED DWELLING UNITS, ACTUAL SEGREGATION INDEXES,
AND PER CENT EXPECTED INDEX IS OF ACTUAL INDEX,
15 CITIES, 1940, 1950, AND 1960

City	Expected Index°			Actual Index†			*Per Cent Expected of Actual*		
	1940	*1950*	*1960*	*1940*	*1950*	*1960*	*1940*	*1950*	*1960*
Atlanta, Ga.	37.2	36.3	26.1	80.3	83.1	85.6	46.3	43.7	30.5
Baltimore, Md.	24.5	24.0	25.3	83.6	81.1	82.8	29.3	29.6	30.6
Birmingham, Ala.	40.9	37.4	25.2	68.3	66.4	70.1	59.9	56.3	35.9
Dallas, Tex.	29.7	25.6	27.4	65.3	75.5	87.1	45.5	33.9	31.5
Houston, Tex.	29.6	18.8	23.7	69.3	74.1	79.3	42.7	25.4	29.9
Louisville, Ky.	32.1	25.8	21.6	68.6	73.0	78.1	46.8	35.3	27.7
Memphis, Tenn.	38.8	37.8	30.4	57.7	65.2	77.7	67.2	58.0	39.1
Nashville, Tenn.	30.8	24.1	13.6	67.3	72.4	72.8	45.8	33.3	18.7
New Orleans, La.	29.0	21.5	19.8	62.1	63.5	67.2	46.7	33.9	29.5
Richmond, Va.	43.7	39.9	28.9	69.6	73.0	81.7	62.8	54.7	35.4
Washington, D.C.	25.4	15.4	12.1	61.4	61.6	67.8	41.4	25.0	17.8
Cleveland, Ohio	22.3	10.5	8.5	86.4	85.7	84.1	25.8	12.3	10.1
Detroit, Mich.	20.2	17.2	17.5	82.7	80.6	79.0	24.4	21.3	22.2
Philadelphia, Pa.	21.9	23.3	18.9	69.9	75.0	78.5	31.3	31.1	24.1
St. Louis, Mo.	28.6	20.7	12.4	84.6	86.0	84.9	33.8	24.1	14.6

° Expected indexes were computed from the distribution of whites and non-whites expected on the basis of the indirect standardizations. Each standardization was made using as detailed a classification by tenure, value, and rent as the census tract data for each year permit.

† Actual segregation indexes were computed from the distribution of occupied dwelling units, by color of household head, among census tracts.

racial residential segregation. In only six of 89 comparisons is the per cent expected of actual greater than 50 per cent, and in the majority of cases the figure is less than 30 per cent. Furthermore, intercity variation in racial residential segregation is unrelated to variation in economic residential segregation, for there is no significant correlation between actual and expected indexes.

The importance of economic status in explaining racial residential segregation declined for Southern cities between 1940 and 1950, for each of the three measures of economic status. Comparing the per cent expected of actual in 1940 with 1950, 32 of 33 comparisons are in the anticipated direction. A decline in the percentage explained by economic status is also evident between 1940 and 1950 from the tenure, value, and rent standardization for four Northern cities (Table

20). For this latter measure, declines also prevailed during 1950–60, with but three exceptions among the 15 cities.

Examining the magnitudes of the expected indexes, the most common pattern among the eleven Southern cities in both 1940 and 1950 is for the index based on tenure, value, and rent to be largest, that based on quality of unit to be second, and that based on labor force and occupational status to be smallest. There are large differentials between Negroes and whites in rates of home-ownership, as well as in the distribution of owned units by value and of rented units by rent. It is this standardization that seems to capture most directly the economic functioning of the real estate market as a factor in racial residential segregation. The standardization by quality of housing is less satisfactory, since the classification is made on the basis of the condition of the unit and of plumbing facilities available, factors which are rather peripheral measures of economic status. The standardization by labor force status and occupation is weak as an explanation because of the unavoidable inclusion of the categories "under 14 years old" and "not in the labor force." Racial differences in these categories are slight, and little related to residential segregation.

The magnitude of the expected indexes for tenure, value, and rent tends to be lower for Northern than for Southern cities, and the percentages expected of actual are correspondingly lower. Where racial economic differentials are less, the ability of economic factors to explain residential segregation is less. These data, thus, are consistent with the findings and interpretations for Charleston and Macon. Racial residential segregation appears to be largely independent of economic residential segregation.

Components of Variance Analysis of Standardized Percentages. — The procedure described in the preceding section for relating an expected segregation index to an actual one is useful for demonstrating the low degree of expected segregation, but statistically it is not a very satisfying method. An alternative approach, based on the data yielded by the indirect standardization, has been developed within the conventional statistical framework of regression and analysis of variance.[10]

The indirect standardization proceeds in the same manner, applying the proportions non-white in each economic-status category for the city to the economic-status distribution for each tract. The result is the expected number of non-whites in each tract. Instead of

10. This approach is described in Duncan, Cuzzort, and Duncan, *op. cit.*, pp. 121–128.

proceeding to computation of an expected segregation index, the regression approach requires computation of the actual and expected percentages of non-whites in each tract. Where there is no racial residential segregation, the actual percentage non-white in each tract will be equal to the city percentage non-white. Where there is segregation, the actual percentages non-white will vary from tract to tract. The variance of these actual percentages is computed, and it is this variance which we may try to explain statistically by consideration of the percentages non-white expected on the basis of economic status.

The expected percentages non-white will also vary from tract to tract, and their variance may be computed. If this variance is large, it means that there is considerable variation among tracts in composition by economic status, which is sufficient by itself to produce considerable racial segregation. If this variance is small, it means that variation among tracts in composition by economic status is not such as to produce much racial residential segregation by itself. Consider as an example Nashville (Tennessee), and the distribution of standard and substandard dwellings among census tracts in 1950. The variance in actual percentages non-white among the city's 40 census tracts is 1184.9; the variance in expected percentages is 55.2. Thus, tract variations in the distribution of housing of differing quality is not great enough to account for much tract variation in percentages non-white. Only 4.7 per cent of the variance in actual percentages is accounted for by the variance in expected percentages.

The ratio of the two variances may be termed the "net effect of composition." To what is the rest of the variance in actual percentages attributable? A decomposition of the actual variance may be made, beginning with a consideration of the regression of actual on expected percentages. This regression is shown for Nashville in Fig. 3. If the economic-status composition of tracts were the only factor involved, then we might expect the actual percentages to equal the expected percentages, and all points in the scattergram would lie on the diagonal (solid line) which would also be the regression line. In the case of Nashville, the regression line is much steeper (slope = 2.9) than the diagonal. A steep regression line is characteristic of other analyses of this type applied to problems of racial and ethnic segregation.[11] Apparently, where tract composition by economic status is such that the expected percentage non-white is a bit lower than the city average, the actual percentage is usually near zero. Where the tract composi-

---

11. Otis Dudley Duncan, "Residential Segregation and Social Differentiation," in *International Population Conference, Vienna, 1959* (Vienna: International Union for the Scientific Study of Population, 1959), pp. 571–577.

tion by economic status is such that a higher percentage non-white is expected, the actual percentage is much greater.

Although the actual and expected percentages non-white are not equal, knowledge of the expected percentages can clearly be helpful

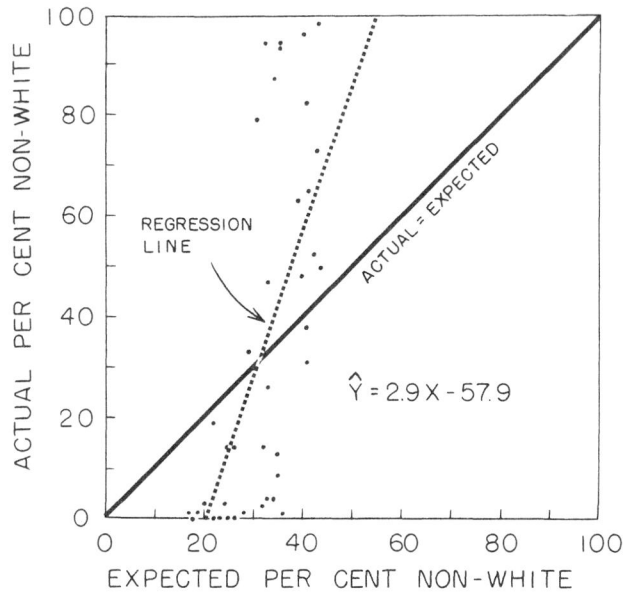

FIGURE 3. —*Nashville: Scattergram and Regression Line Showing Relationship of Actual Percentages Non-white to Expected Percentages Non-white (by Indirect Standardization for Quality of Dwelling Units) for Census Tracts, 1950*

in predicting (or statistically explaining) the actual percentages. The correlation of actual and expected percentages for the Nashville example is .64. The square of this coefficient, .41, indicates that 41 per cent of the variance in actual percentages can be explained by the regression of actual on expected percentages. Five per cent of the variance has previously been attributed to the net (direct) effect of composition, and this is clearly one component of the total 41 per cent explained by the regression. The difference of 36 per cent can be divided into two components, one an interaction term and the other representing the effect of variation among tracts in the racial composition of economic-status categories. In the Nashville example, 18 per cent of the variance is attributable to each of these two components. Unexplained by the regression is 59 per cent of the variance, and this represents the share of racial residential segregation which may be regarded as due to factors having no association with the particular measure of economic-status composition or with color differentials in economic status.

To summarize this decomposition of variance, let us note that tracts vary in "composition" (relative numbers of units or people in each economic-status category) and in "rates" (proportions non-white among economic-status categories). For convenience, we may assign letters to symbolize each component of the total variance in actual percentages non-white:

N = net effect of composition
J = joint effect of composition and associated variables; the interaction term
R = effect of rate variation associated with composition
U = variance unexplained by the regression; effect of rate variation not associated with composition.

Methodologically, the specific percentages of total variance accounted for by each component will depend to some extent on the particular economic-status variable, and hence there is no unique solution to the question of the relation between economic and racial segregation. Furthermore, the presence of the interaction term, J, precludes a neat separation of the total variance into one component due to composition and one due to rates. There is no satisfactory way to allocate the J component to either the N component or the R + U component. For the Nashville example, the percentage allocation of variance may be summarized as follows:

Total variance 100
N 5
J 18
R 18
U 59

Five per cent of the variance is attributable to the net effect of composition, and 77 per cent (*i.e.*, 18 + 59) to the net effect of rates. The other 18 per cent (*i.e.*, 100 −5 −77) is attributable to the interaction of composition and rates. If some portion of the interaction effect were added to the net effect of composition, the gross effect of composition could range upwards from 5 per cent to as much as 23 per cent. Adding some portion of the interaction effect to the rate effect could produce a gross effect of rates ranging from 77 to 95 per cent. Because of the interaction term, we can only specify a range for the gross effect of composition or rates.

For the same set of cities, census dates, and economic-status variables for which actual and expected segregation indexes were previously presented, estimates were prepared of the components of variance according to the scheme just outlined. The results are shown in Tables 21, 22, and 23.

TABLE 21

COMPONENTS OF VARIANCE IN ACTUAL PERCENTAGES NON-WHITE, BASED ON INDIRECT STANDARDIZATIONS FOR QUALITY OF DWELLING UNITS, 11 CITIES, 1940 AND 1950 [°]

City and Year	Total Variance	Component of Variance			
		N	J	R	U
1940					
Atlanta, Ga.	100.0	12.2	25.4	13.1	49.3
Baltimore, Md.	100.0	5.5	19.6	17.3	57.6
Birmingham, Ala.	100.0	19.3	41.9	22.7	16.1
Dallas, Tex.	100.0	14.3	16.4	4.7	64.6
Houston, Tex.	100.0	3.8	10.9	7.9	77.4
Louisville, Ky.	100.0	8.3	21.2	13.5	57.0
Memphis, Tenn.	100.0	25.3	39.6	15.4	19.7
Nashville, Tenn.	100.0	15.9	28.4	12.6	43.1
New Orleans, La.	100.0	16.6	22.6	7.7	53.1
Richmond, Va.	100.0	11.7	33.4	23.8	31.1
Washington, D. C.	100.0	3.5	15.8	17.9	62.8
1950					
Atlanta, Ga.	100.0	5.9	18.8	14.8	60.5
Baltimore, Md.	100.0	3.5	14.1	14.1	68.3
Birmingham, Ala.	100.0	13.7	35.6	23.0	27.7
Dallas, Tex.	100.0	2.5	6.1	3.7	87.7
Houston, Tex.	100.0	3.5	10.5	7.9	78.1
Louisville, Ky.	100.0	3.2	14.0	15.1	67.7
Memphis, Tenn.	100.0	14.1	30.1	16.1	39.7
Nashville, Tenn.	100.0	4.7	18.3	18.0	59.0
New Orleans, La.	100.0	11.7	27.0	15.5	45.8
Richmond, Va.	100.0	8.9	29.2	24.1	37.8
Washington, D. C.	100.0	2.8	13.8	17.3	66.1

[°] Standardizations were made using as detailed a classification by quality of units as the census tract data for each year permit. See text for definitions of components.

TABLE 22

COMPONENTS OF VARIANCE IN ACTUAL PERCENTAGES
NON-WHITE, BASED ON INDIRECT STANDARDIZATIONS FOR
LABOR-FORCE AND OCCUPATIONAL STATUS OF PERSONS,
11 CITIES, 1940 AND 1950

City and Year	Total Variance	Component of Variance			
		N	J	R	U
1940					
Atlanta, Ga.	100.0	5.2	31.8	48.5	14.5
Baltimore, Md.	100.0	3.0	25.7	54.9	16.4
Birmingham, Ala.	100.0	3.6	28.8	58.3	9.3
Dallas, Tex.	100.0	4.2	27.7	45.4	22.7
Houston, Tex.	100.0	3.6	28.8	56.8	10.8
Louisville, Ky.	100.0	1.8	20.8	61.7	15.7
Memphis, Tenn.	100.0	4.6	31.9	55.5	8.0
Nashville, Tenn.	100.0	3.4	27.2	54.8	14.6
New Orleans, La.	100.0	2.9	24.1	49.9	23.1
Richmond, Va.	100.0	5.3	32.2	49.1	13.4
Washington, D. C.	100.0	4.6	30.5	50.0	14.9
1950					
Atlanta, Ga.	100.0	4.6	30.1	49.5	15.8
Baltimore, Md.	100.0	1.9	22.7	66.9	8.5
Birmingham, Ala.	100.0	3.4	28.0	56.8	11.8
Dallas, Tex.	100.0	3.9	28.7	52.9	14.5
Houston, Tex.	100.0	3.8	25.4	42.7	28.1
Louisville, Ky.	100.0	1.6	20.1	63.2	15.1
Memphis, Tenn.	100.0	3.1	26.6	56.0	14.3
Nashville, Tenn.	100.0	2.8	25.4	58.9	12.9
New Orleans, La.	100.0	3.0	22.4	42.4	32.2
Richmond, Va.	100.0	4.2	29.7	52.4	13.7
Washington, D. C.	100.0	3.5	27.7	54.1	14.7

° Standardizations were made using as detailed a classification by labor-force and occupational status as the census tract data for each year permit. See text for definitions of components.

In discussing the results of this procedure, component N will be emphasized, since it represents the net effect of economic segregation in explaining racial segregation. Two comparisons may be made with the results presented in the preceding section based on comparisons of expected and actual segregation indexes. First, the cities are ranked in pretty much the same order by percentage of residential segregation attributable to economic factors. Rank correlations comparing the two different approaches are above .80 for each economic-status measure at each date. Second, the magnitude of component N

TABLE 23

COMPONENTS OF VARIANCE IN ACTUAL PERCENTAGES
NON-WHITE, BASED ON INDIRECT STANDARDIZATIONS FOR
TENURE, VALUE, AND RENT OF OCCUPIED DWELLING UNITS,
15 CITIES, 1940, 1950 AND 1960 °

City and Year	Total Variance	Component of Variance			
		N	J	R	U
1940					
Atlanta, Ga.	100.0	23.0	18.7	3.8	54.5
Baltimore, Md.	100.0	8.4	22.3	15.0	54.3
Birmingham, Ala.	100.0	31.5	37.6	11.3	19.6
Dallas, Tex.	100.0	18.3	16.0	3.5	62.2
Houston, Tex.	100.0	12.8	19.7	7.5	60.0
Louisville, Ky.	100.0	16.0	21.3	7.1	55.6
Memphis, Tenn.	100.0	41.7	31.7	6.0	20.6
Nashville, Tenn.	100.0	22.2	22.0	5.5	50.3
New Orleans, La.	100.0	24.7	21.5	4.7	49.1
Richmond, Va.	100.0	30.5	29.4	7.1	33.0
Washington, D. C.	100.0	16.5	24.7	9.2	49.6
Cleveland, Ohio	100.0	4.2	12.2	8.9	74.7
Detroit, Mich.	100.0	3.4	11.3	9.5	75.9
Philadelphia, Pa.	100.0	11.0	13.5	4.1	71.3
St. Louis, Mo.	100.0	9.3	13.3	4.7	72.7
1950					
Atlanta, Ga.	100.0	20.0	31.4	12.3	36.3
Baltimore, Md.	100.0	7.4	20.9	14.7	57.0
Birmingham, Ala.	100.0	29.1	37.3	12.0	21.6
Dallas, Tex.	100.0	10.3	14.4	5.0	70.3
Houston, Tex.	100.0	6.4	14.3	8.0	71.3
Louisville, Ky.	100.0	9.1	20.5	11.5	58.9
Memphis, Tenn.	100.0	31.1	32.2	8.3	28.4
Nashville, Tenn.	100.0	11.6	26.5	15.0	46.9
New Orleans, La.	100.0	14.3	27.3	13.0	45.4
Richmond, Va.	100.0	24.6	34.7	12.2	28.5
Washington, D. C.	100.0	6.8	24.4	22.1	46.7
Cleveland, Ohio	100.0	1.6	6.9	7.8	83.7
Detroit, Mich.	100.0	2.4	10.3	11.0	76.2
Philadelphia, Pa.	100.0	12.4	21.2	9.0	57.4
St. Louis, Mo.	100.0	5.8	12.5	6.7	75.0
1960					
Atlanta, Ga.	100.0	14.4	14.3	3.6	67.8
Baltimore, Md.	100.0	3.6	13.9	13.4	69.1
Birmingham, Ala.	100.0	15.9	30.2	14.4	39.6
Dallas, Tex.	100.0	10.5	12.8	3.9	72.9
Houston, Tex.	100.0	9.8	9.5	2.3	78.4
Louisville, Ky.	100.0	7.1	13.4	6.3	73.2
Memphis, Tenn.	100.0	18.1	28.8	11.5	41.6

City and Year	Total Variance	Component of Variance			
		N	J	R	U
Nashville, Tenn.	100.0	4.3	15.1	13.2	67.4
New Orleans, La.	100.0	11.6	18.4	7.3	62.7
Richmond, Va.	100.0	14.5	23.2	9.3	53.0
Washington, D. C.	100.0	5.0	16.9	14.4	63.8
Cleveland, Ohio	100.0	1.2	7.9	13.1	77.8
Detroit, Mich.	100.0	4.7	13.1	9.2	73.0
Philadelphia, Pa.	100.0	9.7	15.9	6.6	67.8
St. Louis, Mo.	100.0	3.2	8.7	5.9	82.2

° Standardizations were made using as detailed a classification by tenure, value, and rent as the census tract data for each year permit. See text for definitions of components.

is always much lower than the corresponding "per cent expected of actual" shown in Tables 19 and 20. Apparently, the more refined the statistical technique, the less the percentage of residential segregation attributable directly to economic status.

Since the results from the two procedures are so highly correlated, the pattern of intercity variation and change over time is roughly the same. The net effect of economic factors diminished over time, according to both techniques and all measures. The components of variance based on labor-force standardization highlight the usefulness of the refined statistical techniques (Table 22). The magnitude of the U component is usually rather small, indicating high correlations between actual and expected percentages non-white, which suggests at first glance that racial segregation is dependent on economic segregation. Yet the net effect of composition (component N) is very small.

Although knowledge of the labor force and occupational composition of a tract can lead to a good prediction of the tract's racial composition, this is apparently because certain aspects of occupational composition are an effective clue to racial composition. For instance, any tract whose residents include more than a trivial percentage of domestic servants in the labor force is likely to be a tract with a very high percentage of Negroes. The variation in actual percentages of Negroes, however, is far greater than the variation in expected percentages of Negroes. The composition of a tract's population by labor-force and occupational status serves as a clue to, but not an explanation of, the racial composition of the tract. In a tract with many domestic servants, most of the professional workers, sales workers, operatives, laborers, and others are Negroes. In a tract with few domestic servants, most of the professional workers, sales workers, operatives, laborers, and others are whites. Hence, it makes more sense to argue that the degree of residential segregation of economic-

status groups is affected by the degree of racial segregation than that
the former accounts for the latter.[12] Are Negro domestic servants
residentially segregated because they are servants or because they
are Negroes? How about Negro lawyers, or Negro stenographers?
Similarly, it is implausible to attribute the high degree of residential
segregation of Negroes from whites to differences in the rents they
pay and the value of the homes they own. Can such differences explain the virtually complete absence of Negro residents from most
"white" high-rent areas, or the existence of high-rent areas within
the "Negro" areas of many large cities? An area with low average
rents, for example, may be predominantly Negro, but how much of the
racial segregation can be assigned to economic causes when even the
few high-rent dwellings in this area are Negro-occupied, while low-
rent dwellings in another neighborhood are entirely white-occupied?

The models were constructed by attributing to economic status as
much as possible of the racial segregation. The relative weight given
to economic factors is an upper limit of their explanatory power. To
the extent that it makes sense to attribute some of the economic
residential segregation to racial residential segregation, the models
overstate the causal importance of economic factors in explaining
racial segregation. If a more elaborate theory and methodology were
developed for assessing the direct causal importance of economic
factors, their explanatory power would be shown to be even less
than indicated here.

According to the models, the net effect of economic factors in
explaining residential segregation is slight. Their power in explaining
racial residential segregation diminishes as differentials between the
races in the quality of the housing they occupy, in the occupations
they hold, and in the rents they pay also diminish. Economic differentials diminish, but residential segregation persists. These results
complement the previously reported finding from the regression
analysis of segregation change that only in the context of a permissive
housing market situation was there a significant tendency for improvement in Negro occupational status to be accompanied by declines in a
city's segregation index. Extrapolating the regression relationships
for 1950–60 ten decades into the future, segregation indexes could be

12. One study of residential segregation of occupational groups found the percentage non-white to be an important explanatory variable. See Arthur H. Wilkins,
"The Residential Distribution of Occupation Groups in Eight Middle-sized Cities of
the United States in 1950" (unpublished Ph. D. dissertation, University of Chicago,
1956). For Chicago for 1950, it has been shown that holding constant occupation makes
very little difference in the segregation index. See Otis Dudley Duncan and Beverly
Duncan, Chicago Community Inventory, *Chicago's Negro Population: Characteristics
and Trends* (Chicago: Office of the Housing and Redevelopment Coordinator and the
Chicago Plan Commission, 1956).

expected to decline an average of only 15 points, if non-white occupational status continued to improve during each decade as much as it did 1950–60, and if changes in other explanatory factors are ignored. Clearly, residential segregation is a more tenacious social problem than economic discrimination. Improving the economic status of Negroes is unlikely by itself to alter prevailing patterns of racial residential segregation.

Part Two

THE PROCESS OF NEIGHBORHOOD
CHANGE

5

□

THE PREVALENCE OF
RESIDENTIAL SUCCESSION

Changes in the distribution of population within a city underlie changes in the level of residential segregation. Segregation indexes, however, are summary measures, and provide no clues to the nature of neighborhood changes in racial composition. In the race relations literature, attention has been given primarily to one specific type of change, the replacement of white by Negro population in city neighborhoods. Generalizations concerning such racial residential succession have been based mainly upon observations of processes occurring in a few large Northern cities. The only systematic empirical analysis of Negro residential succession is based on the experience of Chicago in the 1940's. From an analysis of census tract data, three main conclusions emerged:

1. Negro residential succession in Chicago was an irreversible process, and any area which gained more than a few Negro residents tended to become all Negro.

> Areas inhabited by substantial proportions of Negroes tended to increase their Negro proportions...whereas a decrease seldom occurred, once an area had reached a proportion of, say, ten per cent Negroes.[1]

Any given census tract with Negro occupants could, therefore, be classified by "stage" of succession.

2. "Piling up" of population was a concomitant of each stage of succession during the 1940–50 decade. Failure of the housing supply to keep pace with the rapid population increase resulted in increasing population density and room-crowding in Negro residential areas.

3. The Negro population entering a neighborhood resembled the displaced white population in relative status on several social and economic measures. Thus, there was a high degree of stability

1. Otis Dudley Duncan and Beverly Duncan, *The Negro Population of Chicago: A Study of Residential Succession* (Chicago: University of Chicago Press, 1957), p. 11.

of various characteristics of an area despite partial or complete racial turnover.

Systematic statistical study of residential patterns in Chicago can provide verification and elaboration of earlier observations, but cannot provide a firm basis for generalizations about other cities. Processes of succession by which a high degree of residential segregation is maintained in Chicago may or may not typify patterns and processes in other cities. In this chapter, we attempt a systematic comparison of processes of racial residential succession in other large cities. The approach developed by Duncan and Duncan for their study of Chicago pointed the way to the application of available census data to this problem, and their work has been taken as a point of departure for the present analysis. In this chapter, the findings of the Chicago study are examined in a comparative framework in order to determine the conditions leading to varying patterns of racial residential succession, and to specify the limits under which the patterns observed for Chicago (1940–50) will prevail.

□ PROCEDURES

In most discussions of racial residential succession, the irreversibility or inevitability of the process is emphasized. While recognizing that it was logically possible for the process to be halted or even reversed, Duncan and Duncan acknowledged that unless this was unlikely, their use of a scheme of "stages of succession" would be hard to justify.[2] Irreversibility is implicit in the widely accepted concept of a "tip point," defined as the percentage Negro in an area which "exceeds the limits of the neighborhood's tolerance for inter-racial living."[3] Once the percentage Negro passes the tip point, it is assumed that whites will leave the area at an accelerated rate and be replaced by Negroes until the neighborhood has become entirely Negro. In addition to this notion of irreversibility, the concept of racial residential succession usually refers implicitly to the replacement of white families by Negro families in existing dwellings. Logically, however, a change in racial composition toward all-Negro occupancy could be accomplished in other ways: by a rapid exodus of whites from the area, and a less rapid exodus of Negroes; or by development of formerly vacant land for residential use, with Negroes occupying a disproportionate share of the new dwellings.

It is also logically possible for the racial composition of an area

2. *Ibid.*, p. 12.

3. Morton Grodzins, *The Metropolitan Area as a Racial Problem* (Pittsburgh: University of Pittsburgh Press, 1958).

to change toward lower Negro proportions, or to remain relatively stable over time. In fact, Burgess in 1928 argued that the situation in the South was quite different from that in the North. Only in the North where the Negro population was growing rapidly did Negro residential patterns resemble the succession patterns of an immigrant group.[4] Unfortunately, the literature contains few studies of the relationship between racial composition and residential differentiation in Southern cities or in Northern cities other than those experiencing large-scale Negro in-migration.[5]

Most discussions of racial residential succession, therefore, have taken for granted two empirical assumptions: (1) that the process occurs in an irreversible sequence of stages; and (2) that it occurs as the replacement of white families by Negro families in existing dwellings. It is important to separate these two assumptions from the basic definition of succession, in order that they may be subjected to empirical test. In our comparative investigation, we question whether racial residential succession as ordinarily conceived is a universal phenomenon among American cities. It is therefore necessary to determine the specific types of racial change which do occur in urban neighborhoods, and to account for differences among cities in this respect.

The choice of cities and approach was dictated in part by the nature of available data. Although our interest is in Negro residential succession, most of the small-area data which appear in decennial census publications refers to non-whites. The study is therefore restricted to cities in which Negroes comprise more than 95 per cent of the non-white population, and Puerto Ricans and Mexican Americans are not a significant element in the white population. Moreover, since analysis of neighborhood changes within a city must be based on census tract data, it was necessary to have roughly comparable census tract grids for the 1940, 1950, and 1960 censuses. To ensure

4. Ernest W. Burgess, "Residential Segregation in American Cities," *Annals of the American Academy of Political and Social Science,* Publication No. 2180 (November, 1928).

5. Burgess cites a study of New Orleans that found a correlation between Negro population movement and number of feet of depression of various areas below the level of the Mississippi River. Later findings are reported in Harlan Gilmore, "The Old New Orleans and the New: A Case for Ecology," *American Sociological Review,* IX, No. 4 (August, 1944). There have been some studies of cities with small Negro populations: William K. Brussat, "Incidental Findings on Urban Invasion," *American Sociological Review,* XVI, No. 1 (February, 1951); Bulkeley Smith, Jr., "The Reshuffling Phenomenon: A Pattern of Residence of Unsegregated Negroes," *American Sociological Review,* XXIV, No. 1 (February, 1959); and Arnold M. Rose, Frank J. Atelsek, and Lawrence R. McDonald, "Neighborhood Reactions to Isolated Negro Residents: An Alternative to Invasion and Succession," *American Sociological Review,* XVIII, No. 5 (October, 1953).

enough census tracts for the analysis, only cities with a non-white population in 1950 of 100,000 or more were considered. Ten cities met these specifications: Detroit, Cleveland, Philadelphia, St. Louis, Washington, Baltimore, New Orleans, Atlanta, Birmingham, and Memphis. In terms of region as defined by the census, the first four cities are in the North and the last six in the South. Washington and Baltimore, however, will generally be identified as "border cities," and distinguished from the other four Southern cities.

Delineation of patterns of racial residential change among census tracts in the ten cities will be explained first for the 1940–50 decade. Census tracts in which the population was predominantly white in both years are omitted from the classification. The available census data provide a reasonable, albeit arbitrary, definition of "predominantly white," since census tract data for non-whites for 1940 and 1950 are published only for tracts with 250 or more non-white residents. Within each city, the group of census tracts upon which the classification is based includes all tracts in the 1940 tract grid which by 1950 contained 250 or more non-whites. In each city, more than 95 per cent of the non-white population resided in these tracts.

Census tracts in areas annexed by these cities since 1940 are excluded by this procedure. Three of the Southern cities annexed populated territory during this decade. Estimates of the 1950 population of areas annexed during the 1940's for these three cities are: Atlanta, 3,002 (2,452 whites and 550 non-whites); Birmingham, 28,482 (17,832 whites and 10,650 non-whites); Memphis, 37,042 (29,346 whites and 7,696 non-whites).[6] Population in annexed areas constituted 0.9 per cent of the total 1950 population in Atlanta, 8.7 per cent in Birmingham, and 9.4 per cent in Memphis. The only other tracts omitted from the analysis were those few in which most of the non-white population was institutional rather than residential.

☐ THE CLASSIFICATION SYSTEM

In Chicago during the 1940–1950 decade, virtually all tracts in which Negro population increased experienced a decrease in white population that resulted in an increase in percentage Negro. Preliminary examination of data for other cities showed that the Chicago pattern did not recur in all of them. Figure 4 presents scattergrams

6. Estimates of total population of annexed area are taken from Donald J. Bogue, *Components of Population Change, 1940–50: Estimates of Net Migration and Natural Increase for Each Standard Metropolitan Area and State Economic Area* (Oxford, Ohio, and Chicago: Scripps Foundation and Population Research and Training Center, 1957), Table II. Estimates by color of population in annexed area were made utilizing city block data from the 1940 and 1950 Censuses of Housing.

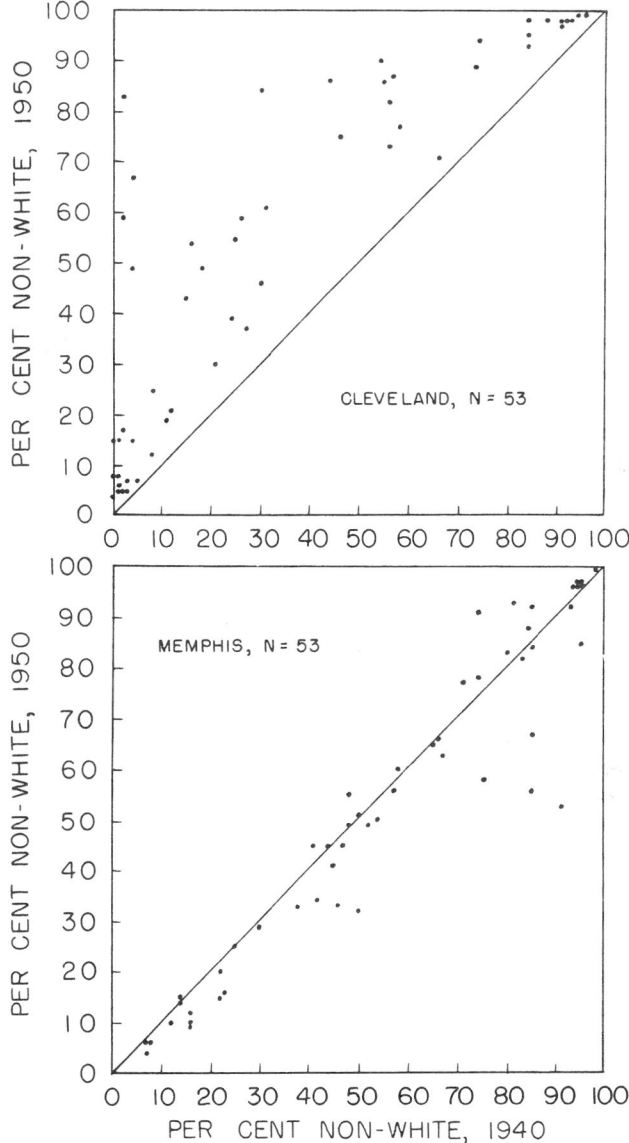

FIGURE 4. — *Cleveland and Memphis: Scattergrams
of Percentages Non-white, 1940 and
1950, for Census Tracts with 250 or
More Non-whites in 1950*

in which the percentages non-white in 1940 for each tract are plotted
against those for 1950, illustrating the difference between two cities,
Cleveland and Memphis. Tracts falling above the diagonal increased
in percentage non-white during the decade, while those falling below the diagonal decreased. The picture for Cleveland resembles that
for Chicago, with the overwhelming majority of tracts experiencing
large increases in percentage non-white. Memphis, however, deviates
markedly from this pattern, showing a predominance of declines in
percentage non-white. Replacement of white by non-white population was the prevalent pattern in Cleveland, while in Memphis new
residential construction permitted increases in both white and non-
white population.

As a consequence of such intercity differences, the scheme of
stages of succession developed for the Chicago study could not be
applied directly. A more general classification of census tracts by
type of racial change was developed, based on two criteria: (1)
change in percentage non-white between 1940 and 1950, and (2) net
change in numbers of whites and non-whites during the decade. An
increase in the percentage non-white within a census tract indicates
a movement toward all-Negro occupancy, while a decline in this
percentage indicates a movement toward all-white occupancy. Consideration of the net change in numbers of whites and non-whites
provides a basis for classifying tracts according to how change in
the percentage non-white occurred.[7]

Classification of census tracts with 250 or more non-whites in
1950 proceeded in the following sequence:

1. All tracts in which non-whites made up over 90 per cent of
the total population in both 1940 and 1950 were termed *Established
Negro Areas*. These areas were occupied almost exclusively by Negroes during the observation period. They may have become all-
Negro as a process of succession from an earlier stage of being all-
white, or they may have been settled initially by Negroes. The latter
alternative is more likely in Southern than in Northern cities.

2. Tracts in which both the white and non-white populations
were stable during the decade were designated *Stable Interracial
Areas*. For each color group, "stability" was defined as a change of
fewer than 100 persons *and* less than 10 per cent. This definition
of stability is quite stringent since it requires that an area remain
virtually stable in absolute numbers of whites and non-whites as well
as in proportion non-white. The definition permits emphasizing the
changes occurring within a tract. (Larger numbers of stable tracts

7. An increase of 100 or more persons *or* more than 10 per cent was termed an increase in population, and a loss of 100 or more persons *or* more than 10 per cent was
termed a decrease in population.

might have been delineated under broader alternative definitions.)

3. All remaining tracts in which the percentage non-white increased were termed *Consolidation.* Since Consolidation could be accomplished in a number of ways, these tracts were subdivided into four broad groups according to the nature of the net changes in white and non-white populations.

In *Succession* tracts, the non-white population numbered 250 or more in 1940, and increased between 1940 and 1950, while the white population decreased. In *Invasion* tracts, the white population again decreased, while the non-white population increased from fewer than 250 in 1940 to more than 250 in 1950. In *Growing* tracts, the non-white population increased more rapidly than the white population; the white population was, however, stable or growing over the decade. In *Declining* tracts, the non-white population, although stable or declining in numbers, decreased less rapidly than the white population. In each type of Consolidation tract, the proportion non-white rose over the decade. Only in Succession or Invasion tracts, however, did this increase in proportion non-white come about through an increase in non-whites and a concomitant decrease in whites, the type of racial change commonly recognized as racial residential succession.

4. Tracts in which the percentage non-white decreased over the decade were termed *Displacement.* This group of tracts was also split, into a "pure" type in which an increase in the white population was accompanied by a decrease in the non-white population, and into Growing and Declining tracts categorized like those under Consolidation.

The classification scheme is summarized in Table 24.

□ TYPES OF RACIAL CHANGE

Results, 1940–50. — The distribution of census tracts by the type of racial change that occurred during the 1940–50 decade differs substantially among the ten cities (Table 25). In Detroit and Cleveland, as in Chicago, virtually all tracts are classified as Established Negro Areas, Succession, or Invasion. In Philadelphia, St. Louis, Washington, and Baltimore, about two-thirds of the tracts are classified as Established Negro Areas, Succession, or Invasion. In the four Southern cities (New Orleans, Atlanta, Birmingham, and Memphis), only one-fifth to one-half the tracts are classified as Established Negro Areas or Succession, and no Invasion tracts are found. In the Southern cities, Consolidation occurred more frequently as a result of an increase in whites accompanied by more rapid growth of Negro population (Growing tracts) or of a decrease in both groups with a

TABLE 24

CRITERIA FOR CLASSIFYING CENSUS TRACTS ACCORDING TO
TYPE OF RACIAL CHANGE °

Type of Racial Change	Definition
Established Negro Areas	Over 90 per cent non-white in initial and terminal years of decade.
Consolidation: Succession	Increase in percentage non-white: non-white population increase accompanied by white population decrease; 250 or more non-whites in initial and terminal years of decade.
Invasion.........	Increase in percentage non-white: non-white population increase accompanied by white population decrease; less than 250 non-whites in initial year and over 250 in terminal year of decade.
Growing	Increase in percentage non-white: non-white population increases and white population increases or remains stable; non-white population increases at faster rate than white population.
Declining	Increase in percentage non-white: non-white population decreases or remains stable and white population decreases; non-white population decreases at slower rate than white population.
Stable Interracial Areas	Both white and non-white population change by less than 100 persons and less than 10 per cent.
Displacement: "Pure"	Decrease in percentage non-white: white population increase accompanied by non-white population decrease.
Growing	Decrease in percentage non-white: white population increases and non-white population increases or remains stable; white population increases at faster rate than non-white population.
Declining	Decrease in percentage non-white: white population decreases or remains stable and non-white population decreases; white population decreases at slower rate than non-white population.

° This scheme is applied to all census tracts in a city which had a non-white population of 250 or more in the terminal year of a decade, except for tracts annexed during a decade and a few tracts in which most of the non-white population is institutional. See text for definitions of "increase," "decrease," and "stable."

lesser rate of decline for Negroes (Declining tracts) than as a result of Succession. Displacement tracts appear with relatively high frequency in these cities. Displacement was less likely to occur in the "pure" form, however, than in the Growing or Declining classifications.

If racial succession were inevitable and irreversible, Stable Interracial Areas would appear infrequently, and, in fact, such areas are uncommon in the ten cities. However, the definition of stability is very stringent. Under a less restrictive definition, *e.g.*, a change of less than five percentage points in the tract percentage Negro, a

TABLE 25

PERCENTAGE DISTRIBUTION OF CENSUS TRACTS BY TYPE OF RACIAL CHANGE: 10 CITIES, 1940–50

Type of Racial Change	Detroit	Cleveland	Philadelphia	St. Louis	Washington	Baltimore	New Orleans	Atlanta°	Birmingham°	Memphis°
Tracts with 250 or more non-whites, 1950†	131	53	118	32	68	64	86	40	41	53
Established Negro Areas...	6.9	11.3	1.7	18.8	10.3	10.9	4.7	22.5	14.6	13.2
Consolidation	92.3	88.7	90.7	71.8	72.1	68.8	62.8	52.5	63.5	26.4
Succession	40.5	51.0	60.2	28.0	47.1	35.9	24.4	30.0	14.6	7.5
Invasion	43.4	24.5	5.1	15.6	7.4	17.2	...	...	...	...
Growing	6.1	13.2	17.8	21.9	8.8	9.4	10.5	12.5	39.1	11.4
Declining	2.3	...	7.6	6.3	8.8	6.3	27.9	10.0	9.8	7.5
Stable Interracial Areas ...	...	...	0.8	...	...	3.1	5.8	7.5	2.4	11.3
Displacement	0.8	...	6.8	9.4	17.6	17.2	26.7	17.5	19.5	49.1
"Pure"	...	...	1.7	3.1	7.4	3.1	2.3	7.5	7.3	9.4
Growing	0.8	...	3.4	6.3	8.7	11.0	15.1	7.5	12.2	26.5
Declining	...	...	1.7	...	1.5	3.1	9.3	2.5	...	13.2
Total	100.0	100.0	100.0	100.0	100.0	100.0	100.0	100.0	100.0	100.0

° Census tracts annexed during the decade are omitted.

† Excludes census tracts omitted from classification because the non-white population was primarily institutional. The number of such tracts is one for Cleveland, New Orleans, Atlanta, and Memphis; two for St. Louis and Washington; three for Baltimore; and six for Philadelphia.

majority of tracts in the four Southern cities would be classed as stable.

Results, Other Decades. — Patterns of racial residential change in some cities during the 1940–50 decade diverged markedly from the Chicago pattern. We turn now to the temporal generality of these findings — whether they are unique to circumstances prevailing during the 1940–50 decade. To examine this question, an analysis identical to that for 1940–50 was carried out for these same cities for each decade for which census tract data by color were available. Analysis was possible for all ten cities for 1950–60; for Detroit, Cleveland, Philadelphia, St. Louis, and Washington for 1930–40; and for Cleveland for 1910–20 and 1920–30.

Census tracts were classified by the same procedure as was used for the 1940–50 decade: the group of relevant tracts for a given decade is composed of all those that contained 250 or more non-whites in the terminal year of the decade. As before, tracts in areas annexed during a decade were, of necessity, excluded from the analysis, as were a few tracts with primarily institutional population. During the 1950–60 decade, the following cities annexed population: Atlanta, 171,467 (of whom 39,659 were non-white); Birmingham, 12,714 (180 non-white); and Memphis, 69,095 (1,994 non-white).[8] Cleveland annexed an estimated 52,000 persons, virtually all white, during the 1910–20 decade.

Using the two criteria of (1) direction of the change in the percentage non-white, and (2) net change in numbers of whites and non-whites, tracts were sorted into the various racial-change categories. Distributions of tracts among the categories are presented in Table 26 for the 1950–60 decade, and in Table 27 for the other decades analyzed.

In 1950–60, as in 1940–50, most tracts in the six Northern and border cities are classed as Established Negro Areas, Succession, or Invasion. Invasion is of somewhat greater importance than during 1940–50. Among the four Southern cities, however, the proportion of tracts classed in these three categories is much greater than in the previous decade, primarily because of an increase in Succession tracts. In most cities, in contrast to the previous decade, Declining tracts outnumber Growing tracts in both Consolidation and Displacement categories.

The patterns for the four Northern cities during the 1930's re-

---

8. Ann Ratner Miller and Bension Varon, *Population in 1960 of Areas Annexed to Large Cities of the United States between 1950 and 1960 by Age, Sex, and Color,* Technical Paper No. 1 (Philadelphia: Population Studies Center, University of Pennsylvania, 1961).

TABLE 26

PERCENTAGE DISTRIBUTION OF CENSUS TRACTS BY TYPE OF RACIAL CHANGE: 10 CITIES, 1950–60

Type of Racial Change	Detroit	Cleveland	Phila-delphia	St. Louis	Washing-ton	Baltimore	New Orleans	Atlanta°	Birming-ham°	Memphis°
Tracts with 250 or more non-whites, 1960†	192	72	116	41	77	85	82	38	41	54
Established Negro Areas...	12.0	18.1	2.6	9.8	9.1	14.1	8.5	28.9	14.6	20.4
Consolidation	85.9	76.3	94.8	78.0	83.1	77.7	79.3	60.6	56.1	64.8
Succession	32.8	30.5	43.9	31.7	45.4	29.5	51.2	42.2	29.2	37.0
Invasion	36.4	29.1	18.1	34.1	15.6	27.1	3.7	5.3	...	...
Growing	...	1.4	5.2	...	2.6	3.5	8.5	2.6	9.8	5.6
Declining	16.7	15.3	27.6	12.2	19.5	17.6	15.9	10.5	17.1	22.2
Stable Interracial Areas ...	...	...	...	...	...	...	3.7	...	...	...
Displacement	2.1	5.6	2.6	12.2	7.8	8.2	8.5	10.5	29.3	14.8
"Pure"	...	1.4	...	...	2.6	...	1.2	...	4.9	1.9
Growing	...	1.4	0.9	...	...	1.2	4.9	2.6	12.2	5.6
Declining	2.1	2.8	1.7	12.2	5.2	7.0	2.4	7.9	12.2	7.3
Total...	100.0	100.0	100.0	100.0	100.0	100.0	100.0	100.0	100.0	100.0

° Census tracts annexed during the decade are omitted.

† Excludes census tracts omitted from classification because the non-white population was primarily institutional. The number of such tracts is one for Cleveland, Washington, Baltimore, and Atlanta; two for St. Louis; three for Detroit; and five for Philadelphia.

TABLE 27

PERCENTAGE DISTRIBUTION OF CENSUS TRACTS BY TYPE OF RACIAL CHANGE: 5 CITIES, 1930–40; AND CLEVELAND, 1920–30 AND 1910–20

Type of Racial Change	1930–40 Decade					Cleveland	
	Detroit	Cleveland	Philadelphia	St. Louis	Washington	1920–30 Decade	1910–20 Decade°
Tracts with 250 or more non-whites, terminal year†	69	37	105	25	62	36	25
Established Negro Areas	7.2	2.7	…	4.0	6.5	…	…
Consolidation	79.8	78.4	66.7	76.0	66.1	97.2	100.0
Succession	42.1	51.4	42.0	44.0	14.5	47.2	16.0
Invasion	8.7	5.4	1.9	…	…	11.1	28.0
Growing	5.8	5.4	11.4	8.0	51.6	16.7	56.0
Declining	23.2	16.2	11.4	24.0	…	22.2	…
Stable Interracial Areas	…	…	5.7	…	…	2.8	…
Displacement	13.0	18.9	27.6	20.0	27.4	…	…
"Pure"	…	2.7	1.9	…	3.2	…	…
Growing	1.4	…	2.9	…	22.6	…	…
Declining	11.6	16.2	22.8	20.0	1.6	…	…
Total	100.0	100.0	100.0	100.0	100.0	100.0	100.0

° Census tracts annexed during the decade are omitted.

† Excludes census tracts omitted from classification because the non-white population was primarily institutional. The number of such tracts is one for St. Louis and Washington; and six for Philadelphia.

semble the patterns for these same cities during the 1940's and 1950's in the predominance of Succession over other types of racial change. These four cities during 1930–40 had relatively few Invasion tracts as contrasted with the other decades, while Displacement tracts were somewhat more common. The experience of Cleveland in 1920–30 is similar to its experience during the later decades.

Washington, 1930–40, presents a striking contrast to the other four cities. Growing tracts accounted for over three-fourths of all Consolidation tracts, while Succession was negligible, and there were no Invasion tracts.[9] In more than one-fourth of the tracts with 250 or more non-whites in 1940, the percentage non-white had declined during the 1930's. In virtually all of these, both white and Negro population had increased, with whites growing at a faster rate than Negroes. Cleveland's experience during the 1910–20 decade bears some similarity to Washington in the 1930's. Though in 1910–20, all tracts increased in percentage non-white, over one-half were Growing tracts, and only about one-sixth were Succession tracts. The chief contrast with Washington (1930–40) is the prevalence in Cleveland of Invasion tracts and the absence of Displacement tracts.[10] As will be seen subsequently, this appears to be a result of Cleveland's relatively small and rapidly growing Negro population in 1910–20, as compared to Washington's very large Negro population in 1930–40.

The Nature of Displacement. — In all cities, declines in percentage non-white were most likely to result from both races in an area increasing or decreasing, but with whites having the higher rate of increase or lower rate of decrease. The infrequency of "pure" Displacement suggests that the transfer of dwellings from Negro to white occupancy is similarly infrequent. The data presented thus far, however, refer to aggregate population changes within census tracts; the inference about patterns of racial change on a *household* basis can be examined directly with another set of data.

For dwelling units in the housing inventory in both 1950 and 1959, and for which 1950 records were available, tabulations of the color of the 1950 occupant by color of the occupant in 1959 appear in the 1960 Census of Housing. Thus we can determine the share of all white-occupied units in 1950 which by 1959 were occupied by

9. Five of Washington's 32 Growing tracts had fewer than 250 non-whites in 1930 and might be thought of as Invasion tracts.

10. Eleven of Cleveland's 14 Growing tracts in the 1910–20 decade had fewer than 250 non-whites in 1910 and might also be thought of as Invasion tracts. There were only seven tracts in Cleveland in 1910 which had more than 250 non-whites. Appendix B indicates, for all cities and decades, the number of tracts in each racial-change type which had fewer than 250 non-whites in the initial year of a decade.

non-whites, and the share of all non-white-occupied units in 1950 which by 1959 were occupied by whites. These figures are presented for the total metropolitan population of each census region in Table 28. The transfer of white-occupied dwellings to non-white occupancy is fairly common in all regions, but the reverse is much less frequent. Similar data are available for the metropolitan areas of seven of our ten cities (Table 29). There is much variation among these areas in the percentage of white-occupied units turned over to non-white occupancy by 1959, but the percentage of units transferred from non-white to white occupancy was generally small.

TABLE 28

TRANSFERS OF DWELLING UNITS° BY COLOR: SMSA'S BY REGION,
1959 BY 1950

Region	Non-white to White Succession		White to Non-white Succession	
	Non-white Occupied in 1950	White Occupied in 1959	White Occupied in 1950	Non-white Occupied in 1959
United States	1,346,341	95,320	19,167,545	978,598
Northeast	331,269	24,640	7,088,246	283,034
North Central	276,878	26,864	5,687,844	371,331
West.......................................	198,333	39,445	3,117,305	158,668
South.......................................	539,861	4,371	3,274,150	165,565

Source: U. S. Bureau of the Census, *U. S. Census of Housing: 1960,* Vol. IV, *Components of Inventory Change,* Final Report HC(4), Part 1A, No. 1 (Washington: U. S. Government Printing Office, 1962), Table 4.

° Data refer to dwelling units in the housing inventory in both 1950 and 1959, for which 1950 records were available.

These data for households are consistent with the data for tracts. The small numbers of units shifting from non-white to white occupancy, as compared with the much larger numbers of units shifting from white to non-white, are direct evidence of the virtual irreversibility of succession on a dwelling unit basis. Declines in percentage non-white in census tracts are seldom the result of a transfer of dwellings from non-white to white occupancy. Rather they result from racial selectivities in the occupancy of demolished houses and new construction. Individual examination of the few "pure" Displacement tracts indicated that they were no exception, for this type of racial

TABLE 29

PERCENTAGE DISTRIBUTION OF COLOR OF OCCUPANTS, FOR SAME
UNITS WITH 1950 RECORDS AVAILABLE: SELECTED SMSA'S,
1959 BY 1950

SMSA and 1950 Occupancy	Total Dwelling Units (in 000's)	1959 Occupancy				Percentage Displacement Tracts, 1950-60°
		Total	White	Non-white	Vacant	
Detroit:						
White	655.5	100.0	83.6	11.0	5.4	2.4
Non-white	47.9	100.0	3.5	85.6	10.9	
Cleveland:						
White	355.6	100.0	85.9	10.0	4.1	6.8
Non-white	30.8	100.0	7.5	85.1	7.1	
Philadelphia:						
White	729.7	100.0	88.4	6.8	4.8	2.7
Non-white	84.0	100.0	2.5	89.9	7.6	
St. Louis:						
White	377.5	100.0	90.0	6.3	3.7	13.5
Non-white	27.4	100.0	2.2	92.3	5.5	
Washington:						
White	266.2	100.0	84.8	13.0	2.2	8.6
Non-white	47.6	100.0	2.5	92.0	5.5	
Baltimore:						
White	241.7	100.0	84.4	12.1	3.5	9.6
Non-white	39.5	100.0	3.8	88.6	7.6	
Atlanta:						
White	109.8	100.0	90.1	4.9	5.0	14.8
Non-white	23.9	100.0	2.9	95.0	2.1	

Source: U. S. Bureau of the Census, *U. S. Census of Housing: 1960*, Vol. IV, *Components of Inventory Change*, Final Report HC(4), Part 1A (Washington: U. S. Government Printing Office, 1962), Table 4.

° Established Negro Areas omitted from the base in computing these percentages to facilitate comparisons among cities.

change usually resulted from the construction of housing projects for whites.

The role of new construction in displacing Negro population has been mentioned by Heberle in a discussion of the effect of recent industrialization in the South on the structure of Southern cities.[11] In Southern cities prior to industrialization, the wealthier, socially prominent families tended to live near the central business district,

11. Rudolf Heberle, "Social Consequences of the Industrialization of Southern Cities," *Cities and Society*, ed. Paul K. Hatt and Albert J. Reiss, Jr. (Glencoe, Illinois: The Free Press, 1957).

while the poorer classes, especially the Negroes, tended to live at the edge of town. (This type of residential pattern is consistent with other data on the locations of high- and low-status groups in cities of underdeveloped and non-industrialized nations.[12]) As Southern cities grew under the impact of industrialization, wealthy people moving toward the periphery of the city displaced the resident Negro population, and residential patterns became more similar to the gradient patterns typical of contemporary industrialized cities.

As these "pockets" of Negro residence on the undeveloped periphery of many Southern cities disappear with the expansion of cities, and as vacant land suitable for residential development becomes scarce, displacement caused by increases in both white and Negro population seems likely to become as infrequent in the South as it is in the North. Displacement, if it is to occur, would then have to come about through selective demolition, or through the direct transfer of existing dwellings from Negro to white occupancy. Although this latter process has been infrequent, it is likely to recur in the future in situations where whites of high socioeconomic status reclaim historical residences in the older sections of a city.

One example of this is the Georgetown section of Washington, once well along in the process of succession, which in recent decades has steadily declined in Negro population and risen in socioeconomic status. The following data are illustrative:

	Georgetown (Census tracts 1, 2)		Washington (City Total)	
	1940	1960	1940	1960
Percentage non-white	21.8	4.4	28.5	54.8
Median gross rent	$43	$129	$45	$81
Median value of owner units	$9,342	$25,000+	$7,568	$15,400

Similar changes have been observed in old sections of other cities, including Philadelphia and Charleston. In recent years, another type of displacement of Negroes by whites has sometimes occurred in the course of slum clearance and redevelopment on the part of governmental agencies. Thus, it seems likely that Displacement tracts will continue to be observed, but it is unlikely that their numbers in any single decade will be great.

12. Leo F. Schnore, "On the Spatial Structure of Cities in the Two Americas: Some Problems in Comparative Urban Research," in The Study of Urbanization, ed. Philip M. Hauser and Leo F. Schnore (New York: John Wiley & Sons, 1965).

☐ POPULATION GROWTH AND
TYPES OF RACIAL CHANGE

During the 1940–50 decade, Chicago experienced a high rate of Negro in-migration, along with a small net out-migration of white population. This demographic imbalance, according to Duncan and Duncan, probably contributed to the instability of "mixed" neighborhoods. The empirical applicability of a scheme of stages of succession was thought to be most appropriate during periods of rapidly increasing Negro population. New population has to be housed, and under conditions of rigid residential segregation, this will be accomplished through the consolidation of existing Negro neighborhoods and the invasion and subsequent consolidation of surrounding white residential areas. The likelihood of this pattern appearing is increased if new housing is not generally available to Negroes, and if established Negro areas can absorb only part of the increase in population. The Chicago study, focusing on one city during one decade, could not provide empirical evaluation of this line of reasoning, but a few studies suggest that Northern cities not experiencing large-scale Negro in-migration do not display a high prevalence of racial residential succession:

> Studies in Connecticut, in Kalamazoo, in Minneapolis, suggest that succession does not occur when Negroes constitute only a small percentage of the population. Nor do white residents flee, abandoning their homes behind them. The findings suggest that residents of Kalamazoo are neither less prejudiced nor less prone to "panic" than those of Detroit, but rather that they may know from observation and experience that the entrance of one or two Negro families into a middle-class neighborhood has had, in the past, a different outcome in Kalamazoo than it has had in Detroit. In the absence of imposed controls, biracial stability seems to occur as a result of the operation of demographic and market factors.[13]

For a wider empirical assessment of these arguments, the data showing types of racial change occurring in ten cities during several decades can be related to demographic patterns. Intuitively, it seems that the fortunes of residential neighborhoods will be quite different in a city where a high rate of Negro in-migration is accompanied by a high rate of white population growth than in a city where it is accompanied by stability or loss of white population. For this reason, we use as an index of demographic patterns the relationship between

---

13. Eleanor P. Wolf, "Some Factors Affecting Residential Decisions in a Racially Changing Neighborhood," paper delivered at the annual Institute of the Society for Social Research, University of Chicago, May, 1960. The paper was published in shorter form in *Journal of Intergroup Relations*, I, No. 3 (Summer, 1960).

white and Negro population growth rates rather than their specific levels. Our measure of the imbalance between white and non-white growth rates is the "growth differential," computed by subtracting the percentage change in white population from the percentage change in non-white population. The percentage changes in white and non-white population and the growth differentials for all cities and decades included in our study are shown in the first three columns of Table 30.

It was also necessary to choose a single index of the patterns of racial change occurring in a city's non-white neighborhoods. For this purpose, we use the percentage of census tracts in a city which increased in percentage Negro during a decade (among those tracts with at least 250 Negroes at the end of the decade). Although the detailed classification of tracts by type of racial change takes account of different patterns of population change by which a tract can experience an increase in percentage Negro, these variations will be overlooked for the moment. The single index chosen is shown in column 4 of Table 30.

Comparison of columns 3 and 4 of Table 30 indicates that the growth differential varies in much the same fashion as the percentage of census tracts increasing in percentage non-white. The zero-order correlation coefficient between the two measures is .83, and the regression equation $\hat{Y} = 70.1 + .342\,X$, where Y is the measure of racial change among tracts and X is the growth differential.[14] If the analysis is carried out using as independent variables the two growth rates separately, rather than combined into the growth differential, the multiple correlation is .83. The beta coefficients in standard form are .59 for the non-white growth rate, holding constant the white growth rate; and $-.47$ for the white growth rate, holding constant the non-white rate. Each of the growth measures exerts an effect independently of the other. This result supports our use of the growth differential rather than the non-white growth rate by itself.

From the zero-order regression equation we note that even when the growth differential is zero, an estimated 70 per cent of a city's

14. This correlation, and those presented subsequently, were computed omitting Cleveland, 1910–20 and 1920–30. In both decades, the percentage change in non-white population is not an accurate reflection of the net change in numbers of whites and non-whites in the city, owing to the small non-white population in Cleveland in the initial year of each decade. There were only 8,448 Negroes in Cleveland in 1910, and 34,451 in 1920. During the 1910–20 decade, a greater number of whites (159,000) was added to the city's population than Negroes (26,000), despite the fact that the percentage change in population is much higher for non-whites than for whites. Between 1920 and 1930, a net increase of 17,000 whites accompanied a net gain of 37,000 non-whites. Because of the small base population for non-whites, the percentage change in non-white population is enormous. Because the study was restricted to cities having large non-white populations in 1950, these difficulties are not present for later decades.

TABLE 30

RELATIONSHIP BETWEEN POPULATION GROWTH AND TYPES AND RATE OF RACIAL CHANGE: 10 CITIES, SELECTED DECADES

City and Decade	Percentage Change in Population			Percentage of Tracts		Average Increase in Percentage Non-white, Succession Tracts (6)
	Non-white (1)	White (2)	Differential (3)	Increasing in Percentage Non-white° (4)	Succession or Invasion† (5)	
1950-60						
Detroit	60.5	−23.5	84.0	97.4	78.7	42.2
Cleveland	69.6	−18.6	88.2	94.4	72.9	46.7
Philadelphia	40.7	−13.3	54.0	97.4	63.7	28.0
St. Louis	39.9	−24.0	63.9	85.4	73.0	34.8
Washington	46.6	−33.3	79.9	90.9	67.1	34.7
Baltimore	44.6	−15.6	60.2	90.6	65.8	33.5
New Orleans	28.6	1.2	27.4	91.5	60.0	11.3
Atlanta‡	21.2	−19.6	40.8	81.6	66.7	30.9
Birmingham‡	3.8	− 1.4	5.2	70.7	34.3	8.1
Memphis‡	24.1	− 1.2	25.3	85.2	46.5	20.7
1940-50						
Detroit	101.5	5.0	96.5	99.2	90.2	31.1
Cleveland	75.0	− 3.5	78.5	100.0	85.1	24.5
Philadelphia	49.9	0.8	49.1	93.2	66.4	14.6
St. Louis	41.4	− 0.6	42.0	90.6	53.8	21.4
Washington	49.9	9.2	40.7	80.9	60.7	19.3
Baltimore	35.7	4.5	31.2	79.7	59.6	17.4
New Orleans	22.0	12.5	9.5	70.9	25.6	5.5
Atlanta‡	15.5	4.9	10.6	72.5	38.7	12.9
Birmingham‡	9.6	12.3	− 2.7	75.6	17.1	9.1
Memphis‡	14.8	28.0	−13.2	43.4	8.7	10.7
1930-40						
Detroit	24.2	1.8	22.4	87.0	54.7	20.4
Cleveland	17.5	− 4.2	21.7	81.1	58.3	12.4
Philadelphia	14.2	− 2.9	17.1	69.5	43.8	9.4
St. Louis	16.2	− 2.9	19.1	80.0	45.8	13.6
Washington	41.8	34.0	7.8	72.6	15.5	11.0
1920-30						
Cleveland	108.7	8.6	100.1	100.0	58.3	47.5
1910-20						
Cleveland‡	307.8	28.7	279.1	100.0	44.0	18.4

° Percentages based on all tracts with 250 or more non-whites in the terminal year, except for a few tracts omitted from classification.

† Percentages based on all tracts as defined in the préceding note, except those classified as Established Negro Areas.

‡ Adjusted for annexations during decade.

tracts containing non-whites will increase in per cent non-white. Further, the slope is fairly low, indicating that sizable increments in the growth differential make only a slight difference in the share that such tracts form of all tracts. This is not surprising. Urban Negro populations grow by natural increase as well as by migration. Even in the absence of white or Negro migration to a city, many of these tracts would in all likelihood increase their percentage non-white because new households formed by Negroes would be restricted to existing Negro areas, whereas new white households would have a wide variety of choice in residential location and could avoid Negro areas.

Increases in percentage non-white among census tracts may occur through various combinations of white and Negro population change, of which Succession and Invasion are only two. Can the prevalence of these two specific types of racial change be predicted from the growth differential? Column 5 of Table 30 presents the percentage of all tracts (except Established Negro Areas) containing non-whites in the terminal year of a decade which experienced Succession or Invasion during that decade. Established Negro Areas were omitted from the base of this percentage because their number reflects the size of the Negro population of a city rather than patterns of racial change. The prevalence of Succession and Invasion tracts is highly related to the growth differential, as indicated by a zero-order correlation of .91. The regression equation is $Y = 29.8 + .634 X$, where Y is the percentage of Succession or Invasion tracts, and X is the growth differential. The degree of imbalance between white and Negro population growth rates is an important determinant of the amount of Succession and Invasion. Separate examination of Succession and Invasion reveals that Invasion is common only under extreme situations of Negro population increase and white population stability or decrease.

Finally, the evidence indicates that the *rate* at which succession proceeds is also a function of the growth differential. Column 6 of Table 30 presents the average percentage-point change in percentage non-white for Succession tracts in each city and each decade. Though this is a crude measure of the rate of racial transition, it is, nonetheless, adequate to reflect major differences among cities in this respect. The zero-order correlation between the growth differential and the average increase in percentage non-white in Succession tracts is .87, and the regression equation is $\hat{Y} = 8.5 + .326 X$, where Y is the average increase and X is the growth differential. If Negro and white population growth rates are in relative balance and the growth differential is zero, then in each Succession tract an average increase of 8.5 points in percentage non-white would be predicted on the basis of the observed relationship. Ordinarily, a smaller rate of racial change would be expected among types of racial change other than Succession, since a greater movement of population would be required to achieve an equivalent increase in percentage non-white in tracts, for example, where both populations are growing or declining than where Negroes are replacing whites.

The preceding discussion has been in terms of rates of population growth. Variation among cities in these rates is the result of intercity variation in migration experience. A population in a given area can increase either through natural increase (the excess of births over deaths) or net migration (the excess of in-migrants over out-migrants). Natural increase varies little from city to city, so that it is variation in migration experience that accounts for the large observed differences among cities in rates of growth. This is verified by data showing the components of population growth for our ten cities during the 1940–50 decade (Table 31). The extremely high growth differentials for the Northern and border cities are the result of a high rate of net in-migration of Negroes combined with a net out-migration of whites,

TABLE 31

ESTIMATED COMPONENTS OF POPULATION GROWTH, BY RACE: 10 CITIES, 1940–50

| City | Percentage Change in Population | | | | | |
| | White | | | Non-white | | |
	Total	Natural Increase	Net Migration	Total	Natural Increase	Net Migration
Detroit	5.0	14.5	− 9.5	101.5	22.0	79.5
Cleveland	− 3.5	13.3	−16.8	75.0	12.6	62.4
Philadelphia	0.8	9.4	− 8.6	49.9	15.9	34.0
St. Louis	− 0.6	9.6	−10.2	41.4	14.6	26.8
Washington	9.2	14.6	− 5.4	49.9	19.1	30.8
Baltimore	4.5	11.9	− 7.4	35.7	17.7	18.0
New Orleans	12.5	13.9	− 1.4	22.0	18.5	3.5
Atlanta°	4.9	19.1	−14.2	15.5	14.5	1.0
Birmingham°	12.3	15.6	− 3.3	9.6	15.8	− 6.2
Memphis°	28.0	14.1	13.9	14.8	10.4	4.5

Source: Donald J. Bogue, *Components of Population Change, 1940–50: Estimates of Net Migration and Natural Increase for Each Standard Metropolitan Area and State Economic Area* (Oxford, Ohio: Scripps Foundation, 1957), Part II, Table III.

°Adjusted for annexations during the decade.

TABLE 32

CLASSIFICATION OF CITIES BY PATTERN OF GROWTH AND PREVALENT TYPES OF RACIAL CHANGE

Negro Growth	White Growth	Prevalent Types of Racial Change	Growth Differential	City and Decade
High	Low	Predominance of Succession and Invasion No Stable Interracial Areas Few Displacement tracts	54.0 to 96.5	*1940–50* Detroit Cleveland *1950–60* Detroit Cleveland Philadelphia St. Louis Washington Baltimore
Moderate	Low	Predominance of Succession, little Invasion Few Stable Interracial Areas Some Displacement tracts	17.1 to 49.1	*1940–50* Philadelphia St. Louis Washington Baltimore *1920–30* Cleveland *1950–60* New Orleans Atlanta Memphis *1930–40* Detroit Cleveland Philadelphia St. Louis

Low	Low	Growing and Declining more important than Succession, no Invasion Some Stable Interracial Areas Displacement fairly common	− 2.7 to 10.6	*1940–50* New Orleans Atlanta Birmingham	*1950–60* Birmingham
High	High	Growing tracts predominant, Succession uncommon, little Invasion° No Stable Interracial Areas Displacement fairly common	7.8†	*1930–40* Washington	*1910–20* Cleveland
Low	High	Displacement predominant and accounted for by Growing tracts Succession negligible, no Invasion Some Stable Interracial Areas	− 13.2		*1940–50* Memphis

° Though Cleveland was deviant in this respect, we have taken the results for Washington as typical, for the study was initially restricted to cities with large Negro populations.

† The differential is presented only for Washington, since Cleveland's value is distorted because of its small Negro population in 1910. See text for full explanation.

whereas the growth of population in Southern cities is primarily the result of natural increase. Only in Memphis, which is unique in its distribution of tracts by type of racial change, did net in-migration play an important part in the growth of white population. Thus, demonstrating that variation among cities in the types of racial change is largely attributable to patterns of population growth also demonstrates that this variation is attributable to the migration experience of a city. In subsequent discussions, data on population growth are used to avoid the extra computation necessary to obtain estimates of net migration.

A relationship has been demonstrated between the growth differential and types and rates of racial change. This relationship and much of the previous discussion can be summarized by distinguishing four patterns of migration (growth) experience, each with a distinctive distribution of census tracts by type of racial change. This classification is presented schematically in Table 32 along with a list of the cities and decades exemplifying each pattern.

1. *High Negro Growth–Low White Growth.* – Cities in which extremely high rates of Negro population growth were combined with low levels of white population growth are characterized by a predominance of Succession and Invasion tracts. The prevalence of Invasion tracts under these circumstances suggests that under extreme pressure for Negro housing, the capacity of existing Negro areas to absorb incoming Negro population is limited. Stable Interracial Areas and Displacement tracts are rare under these circumstances. This pattern corresponds to the experience of Chicago, 1940–50.

A less extreme form of this pattern may be designated as a situation of *Moderate Negro Growth–Low White Growth.* It is characterized by a predominance of Succession tracts, but few Invasion tracts, indicating that the moderate increases in Negro population could be accommodated in existing Negro areas. There are no Stable Interracial Areas, but some Displacement tracts do appear.

2. *Low Negro Growth–Low White Growth.* – Under these growth conditions, the majority of tracts containing Negro population increases in percentage non-white, but this is unlikely to be caused by Succession. Rather, Growing and Declining tracts account for most of the tracts that increase in percentage non-white, and there are no Invasion tracts. Occasional Stable Interracial Areas are apparent, and Displacement is an important type of racial change.

3. *High Negro Growth–High White Growth.* – The combination of high levels of both white and Negro population growth is exemplified by two cities, Cleveland between 1910 and 1920, and Washington in the depression decade (1930–40). Consolidation prevails,

but Growing tracts account for over one-half of all tracts. Succession is of minor importance. There are no Stable Interracial Areas. The two cities, however, differ in one respect. One-fourth of Washington's tracts are classified as Displacement tracts and there are no Invasion tracts, while the reverse is true in Cleveland. This difference can be traced to the small size of the Negro population of Cleveland in 1910 (8,448) compared to Washington's Negro population of 132,068 in 1930. The increase of the Negro population of Cleveland from 8,448 in 1910 to 34,451 in 1920 required substantial expansion of Negro residential areas, but since whites also increased in these areas they are classified as Growing tracts. Since most of Cleveland's Growing tracts had fewer than 250 non-whites in 1910, they represent, like Invasion tracts, new areas of Negro residence. In Washington, on the other hand, the increase in Negro population was absorbed into areas already containing Negroes, with very little expansion into new areas. Displacement tracts in Washington were the result of increases in both white and Negro population with whites increasing at the faster rate.

 4. Low Negro Growth–High White Growth. —The final pattern, exemplified only by Memphis in the 1940–50 decade, combines a moderately high level of white in-migration with a low level of Negro net in-migration. Migration was of negligible importance in the growth of the Negro population of Memphis during this decade, while it accounted for about one-half the increase in the white population. As a consequence of this unusual pattern of growth, Displacement tracts (those tracts in which the percentage non-white declined) accounted for nearly one-half the tracts containing Negroes. Displacement occurred typically as the result of simultaneous increases in the populations of both races, with the whites increasing at a faster rate. Among the minority of tracts which increased in percentage non-white, Succession was uncommon and there were no Invasion tracts. Stable Interracial Areas, though infrequent, were more common than in any other city or decade.

 Established Negro Areas have been overlooked in the above summary of the relations between patterns of population change and types of racial change within cities. All these cities are characterized by a high degree of racial residential segregation. Under these conditions the prevalence of Established Negro Areas is a function not of growth patterns but of the city percentage Negro and the absolute number of Negroes in the city. Obviously, the number of census tracts which Negroes can completely fill is limited by the size of the Negro population. Given residential segregation, a city with 500,000 Negroes will have more all-Negro tracts than a city in which there are only 10,000 Negroes.

A city's rate of population growth is to some extent a function of the amount of land within the city limits still suitable for residential development. Population growth stimulates filling-in of available land, and as cities become increasingly built-up, additional increments of population tend to be housed outside the city limits in suburban areas. Certainly, the metropolitan areas of which our ten cities are a part have continued to grow, but this growth is less likely to be accommodated within the city than was once the case.

In the Southern cities, the Negro demand for housing has been met with new residential construction to a much greater extent than in Northern cities (Table 33). In some of these cities informal political

TABLE 33

PERCENTAGE OF HOUSING UNITS BUILT 1940–60,
BY COLOR, 1960

City	Percentage Built 1940–60	
	White	Non-white
Detroit	30.4	8.9
Cleveland	14.7	8.9
Philadelphia	21.6	5.0
St. Louis	11.7	9.1
Washington	39.4	32.3
Baltimore	31.4	16.4
New Orleans	32.4	33.7
Atlanta	47.3	40.8
Birmingham	42.3	29.3
Memphis	59.3	38.1

Source: Census Tract Bulletins for 1960.

agreements permitting "zoning" of portions of the city for white or Negro occupancy may have played a part in making available the requisite vacant land for building. Negroes in Southern cities may also have greater access to "suburbs" than do Negroes in Northern cities, because of old established peripheral Negro settlements. Southern cities have not yet experienced the marked net losses of white population typical of Northern cities, apparently because land suitable for residential development has so far been available within the city.

In the large Northern cities, white population growth, on net balance, tends to be absorbed in the suburbs, while increases in Negro population are absorbed in or adjacent to existing Negro areas in the central city. A high rate of Negro in-migration in a situation in which segregation is maintained through restrictions on available housing outside existing Negro areas will necessarily result in the replacement of white population by Negro population if, as is true of most Northern cities, these areas are already built-up to a point where new construction is unlikely. Although Negroes are confined mainly to Negro residential areas in both Northern and Southern cities, in the South such areas have had considerable land available for new construction. Due to the lesser volume of Negro migration and the alternative offered by new residential building, the pressure for Negroes to occupy dwellings formerly occupied by whites is less in Southern than in Northern and border cities. Despite these North-South differences in neighborhood patterns of racial change, however, additional population in every city has been housed in such a manner as to maintain a high degree of residential segregation.

Much of the sociologist's knowledge of the nature of racial change in urban neighborhoods has come from the study of Northern cities during decades of extremely high Negro in-migration coupled with net losses in white population. Terms such as "block-busting," "invasion," "resistance," and "encroachment" are products of Northern experience under this particular combination of circumstances. The data presented in this chapter demonstrate that the fortunes of residential neighborhoods in a city are to a large extent tied to broader changes occurring in the metropolitan area and the economy as a whole. An important implication of the findings here is that as the source of Negro population growth in cities shifts from a predominance of migration to a predominance of natural increase, and as the urban growth context is altered, modifications of the patterns of racial change in residential neighborhoods may be expected.

6

□

THE CHANGING CHARACTER OF NEGRO MIGRATION

The types of racial change experienced in urban neighborhoods and the rate at which racial change proceeds have been shown (in Chapter 5) to depend on the relationship between the volume of white and Negro migration to and from a city. Migration, therefore, is a major stimulus to alterations in the racial structure of cities. In this chapter we assess the character of Negro migration, attempting to answer two main questions: (1) What are the characteristics of Negro migrants to a given city, and what is their impact on the socioeconomic status of the resident Negro population? (2) How does the Negro migrant population distribute itself among the various subareas of a city?

□ CHARACTERISTICS OF NEGRO MIGRANTS

Contradictory expectations confronted us prior to our analysis of the characteristics of Negro migrants. On one hand, an extensive literature portrays a situation in which whites are abandoning cities to a Negro population that increases daily through the addition of low-status migrants who produce increasing burdens upon schools, welfare agencies, the police, and other public agencies. On the other hand, general demographic research on migration has usually shown that the higher status segments of a population are the most residentially mobile.

Much of what we know about the early period of large-scale Negro migration to cities is based upon fragmentary sources. Most of this literature agrees that Negro in-migrants to cities were of lower social and economic status than the resident Negro population. Increased racial tensions were blamed upon this heavy influx of Negroes of low socioeconomic status, and old Negro residents apparently shared in the resentment toward the new in-migrants:

Inevitably many of them were inclined to hold the migrants responsible for these increasing social restrictions and tended to resent the influx of other blacks, many of whom were inferior in education and culture to the northern Negroes and many of whom were unaccustomed to northern standards of living and modes of conduct.[1]

Contemporary evidence also exists that although the newcomers were lower in status than the urban resident, they were drawn from the higher status segment of the population of origin. Woodson, for example, lists Negro politicians and educated persons as being more likely to leave the South than certain business classes and poorer people, though "the largest number of Negroes who have gone North during this period . . . belong to the intelligent laboring class."[2]

Analyzing the characteristics of migrants is a complicated task. Migrants have both a place of origin and a place of destination, and their characteristics may be compared with non-migrants at either place. Furthermore, migrations are not all in one direction, but flow in complex and interlocking channels. Both in-migration and out-migration have an impact upon the socioeconomic status of the resident Negro population. The net effect upon the resident population is a function both of the socioeconomic composition of each migration stream and the relative volumes of in- and out-migration. Unfortunately, lack of data has usually prohibited precise determination of the differing character and relative importance of various migration streams, and much of the literature is empirically untrustworthy.

Recent Evidence: Migration, 1955–60.—The best available migration data for the United States refer to the 1955–60 period. From these data, it is possible to examine selected characteristics of non-white in-migrants to selected metropolitan areas (SMSA's) according to their place of residence in 1955—whether another SMSA or non-metropolitan area. Similar characteristics are also available for out-migrants from these SMSA's. Although most of the data we utilize pertain to metropolitan areas rather than cities, the overwhelming majority of the Negro population in each of our ten SMSA's resides in the central city rather than the suburban "ring."

The data are based upon a comparison between place of residence reported for April 1, 1955, and place of residence at the time of the census in April, 1960. A difference between the two places of residence indicates at least one move was made during the five years,

1. Louise V. Kennedy, *The Negro Peasant Turns Cityward* (New York: Columbia University Press, 1930), p. 222.

2. Carter G. Woodson, *A Century of Negro Migration* (Washington: The Association for the Study of Negro Life and History, 1918), p. 163.

though a person may well have made several moves during that period. The migration tabulations necessarily exclude children under five years of age, and those persons who moved between 1955 and 1960 but died before enumeration. The usual census problem of completeness of coverage appears to be especially critical in these data, since it is young, mobile adults who are most likely to be missed in an enumeration.

The origins and destinations of non-white in- and out-migrants for our ten SMSA's have been discussed elsewhere, and the findings may be briefly described here.[3] The general picture which emerges is one of a sizable intermetropolitan flow of population, both from Southern metropolitan areas to Northern metropolitan areas, and between Northern metropolitan areas. A significant local exchange of non-white population characterizes the four Southern metropolitan areas – the majority of their in-migrants are from non-metropolitan areas in the same state or those nearby, while a moderate share of their out-migrants return to such areas. Finally, there is a substantial movement of non-whites from Southern non-metropolitan areas to metropolitan areas in the Northern and border states, though such migrants are a minority of all in-migrants to these SMSA's. Also of smaller magnitude are movements from North to South (to both metropolitan and non-metropolitan areas) and movements between metropolitan areas within the South. Less than one-third of non-whites who left the four Southern SMSA's for other metropolitan areas remained in the South.

The number of in-migrants and out-migrants for each SMSA is presented in Table 34. Though Negro in-migrants are most numerous in the Northern and border areas and least numerous in the Southern areas, in each SMSA they account for less than 10 per cent of the total 1960 Negro population over five years of age. Substantial differences exist among SMSA's with regard to the predominant source of in-migrants. In the Northern and border SMSA's, in-migrants from other metropolitan areas are of greater significance than in the Southern SMSA's. Variation among SMSA's in the relative importance of in-migrants of non-metropolitan origin probably reflects not only the character of the immediate hinterland of the SMSA, but the extent to which the SMSA participates in a national intermetropolitan stream of migration.

The characteristics of the in-migrant group as a whole reflect differences in the origins of the migrants. To the extent that in-migrants from non-metropolitan places are of lower socioeconomic status than those from metropolitan areas, for example, the status of

    3. Karl E. Taeuber and Alma F. Taeuber, "The Changing Character of Negro Migration," *American Journal of Sociology*, LXX, No. 4 (January, 1965).

TABLE 34

NON-WHITE POPULATION BY MIGRATION STATUS, 1955–60 (IN 000'S)

SMSA	Total Population Age 5 and Over	Total In-Migrants	In-Migrants from —			Total Out-Migrants	Moved, 1955 Residence Not Reported
			Other SMSA	Non-Met. Area	Abroad		
Detroit	486.6	25.5	13.6	10.4	1.4	30.1	16.3
Cleveland	222.8	19.9	10.7	8.3	0.8	12.0	7.1
Philadelphia	589.9	37.4	18.3	15.8	3.4	22.6	18.5
St. Louis	252.7	14.1	5.5	7.9	0.6	14.7	10.9
Washington	429.5	44.5	18.4	20.6	5.5	22.2	21.6
Baltimore	328.3	21.6	8.8	11.3	1.5	13.2	12.8
New Orleans	228.1	11.2	3.0	7.6	0.6	14.3	5.2
Atlanta	199.1	10.8	3.1	7.4	0.4	11.5	4.5
Birmingham	190.1	8.9	3.0	5.7	0.3	15.3	1.8
Memphis	193.2	12.7	2.4	10.1	0.2	15.8	3.0

Source: U. S. Bureau of the Census, *U. S. Census of Population: 1960, Subject Reports, Mobility for Metropolitan Areas*, Final Report PC(2)-2C (Washington: U. S. Government Printing Office, 1963), Tables 1 and 5.

the total in-migrant group will be lower where they make up a larger share of the group than do the intermetropolitan migrants. The impact of migration upon the status of the resident Negro population is offset to a varying extent by out-migration. To the extent that Negro out-migrants are of high status relative to the resident population, this flow operates to reduce the socioeconomic status of the resident Negro population.

The volume of out-migration is fairly large relative to the volume of in-migration among the ten metropolitan areas. The difference between the numbers of in- and out-migrants is the number of net migrants. If out-migrants outnumber in-migrants, a net loss of population has occurred through migration; while an excess of in-migrants over out-migrants indicates a net gain in population from migration. From a comparison of the numbers and characteristics of Negro in-migrants and out-migrants, we may gain some insight into the net effect of migration, 1955–60, upon the socioeconomic status of the resident Negro population in 1960. Before proceeding, however, we note that the levels of net migration for the ten SMSA's are quite low. This is particularly surprising for the Northern areas, which experienced a large net in-migration of Negroes during the 1950–60 decade. In two SMSA's, Detroit and St. Louis, the data actually indicate a net loss of Negroes during the 1955–60 period. These results raise questions concerning the accuracy of the data. Estimates of net migration are invariably subject to many errors. In the present case, in addition to the obvious possibility that the course of migration during the last half of the decade may actually have differed from that prevailing during the first five years, possible sources of discrepancies are the restriction of the data to the population age five and over, misstatements of place of residence in 1955, the omission of out-migrants who moved abroad beyond coverage of the 1960 census, and general underenumeration of the Negro population.[4]

Probably the most serious defect of the 1955–60 data is the presence of a large group of persons who moved during the period but for whom place of residence in 1955 was not reported. Characteristics for this group were not published separately but were combined with those for migrants from abroad. Since the number of non-white migrants from abroad is small (see Table 34), we may treat this residual combined group as virtually synonymous with the "not reported" group. Selected characteristics of this group, presented in Table 35, indicate an overrepresentation of males, and of residents of institutions and other group quarters. Their degree of concentration

4. For a more complete discussion of census procedures and possible sources of error, see U.S. Bureau of the Census, *U. S. Census of Population: 1960, Subject Reports, Mobility for Metropolitan Areas*, Final Report PC(2)-2C (Washington: U. S. Government Printing Office, 1963), Introduction.

TABLE 35

SELECTED CHARACTERISTICS OF "MOVERS," 1955 RESIDENCE NOT REPORTED" AND "MOVERS," 1955 RESIDENCE ABROAD" COMBINED, FOR NON-WHITES

SMSA	Total (in 000's)	Sex Ratio	Percentage				
			Age 15–24 of Persons 15 and Over	In Armed Forces°	In Institutions	In Other Group Quarters	With 1+ Years High School
Detroit	17.7	123.7	18.7	2.3	12.1	5.9	55.8
Cleveland	8.0	126.5	18.5	1.0	8.2	11.0	56.2
Philadelphia	21.8	124.5	20.6	11.7	11.9	9.0	55.1
St. Louis	11.5	104.1	17.7	2.0	5.0	4.7	46.6
Washington	27.0	139.0	18.3	12.4	21.6	10.0	56.0
Baltimore	14.3	161.7	21.4	11.1	21.9	7.7	41.9
New Orleans	5.7	111.2	23.1	2.4	2.6	9.6	38.6
Atlanta	4.9	153.0	24.8	2.0	18.4	7.6	40.8
Birmingham	2.1	118.9	19.5	......	1.9	3.3	47.3
Memphis	3.1	129.3	24.0	3.4	8.4	4.0	31.3

Source: U. S. Bureau of the Census, U. S. Census of Population: 1960, Mobility for Metropolitan Areas, op. cit., Table 4.
° Base of percentage is male labor force.

in the young adult ages is similar to that among the non-migrant population, which is considerably less than prevails among in-migrants (compare with Table 37). Of the population in households, there is a surplus of primary individuals and non-relatives of household heads, and a corresponding deficiency of wives and children of household heads. There is an extremely high incidence of "not reporting" on all items for which such a category is tabulated. For educational attainment, however, non-responses were eliminated by a census editing procedure which utilized available information for the individual and information reported for a similar person in the same neighborhood. The resulting level of educational attainment, shown in Table 35, is somewhat higher than that of the total non-white population. Probably most of these persons would be classified as "local movers" if their migration status were known, but no precise determination can be made. In the absence of additional information, this group is omitted from further consideration. To the extent that some of these persons should be counted in one or another of the migration streams and that their characteristics differ from other migrants, our results will be biased by their exclusion. The numerically small group of in-migrants from abroad, comprised largely of immigrants and returning soldiers, is also disregarded.

An additional limitation of the data arises from the fact that the migration question was not restricted to the population in households. As a result, the volume of migration into or out of a particular SMSA may be distorted by the presence of a large institution, college, or military installation. The census tabulations group together these "special purpose" migrants with other migrants. The effect of this procedure upon the count of Negro in-migrants to our SMSA's is indicated in the following tabulation showing (for those SMSA's for which it is important) the percentage who were residents of group quarters in 1960. (Group quarters include institutions, barracks, dormitories, lodging houses, and the like.)

		Percentage in Group Quarters Among In-migrants from:		
SMSA	Total	Other SMSA	Non-metropolitan Areas	Major Type of Group Quarters
Philadelphia	10	14	6	Military
Washington	11	15	7	Howard U., military
Baltimore	15	24	7	Morgan State College, military
New Orleans	8	15	5	Dillard U., Xavier U., military
Atlanta	17	33	10	Federal Prison, Atlanta U.

Men in military service obviously make up a greater share of certain subgroups of in-migrants, such as all adult in-migrants or all in-migrants in the male labor force, than of all in-migrants. Mobility accompanying service in the armed forces also accounts for a substantial share of out-migration from metropolitan areas, and its impact is felt by all SMSA's, not just those containing military bases (Table 36). The effect of the military on mobility is probably underestimated since many migrants who moved in connection with military service were no longer in the service at the time of the census. Moves of dependents of military personnel, which may be numerous, cannot be identified from the available data. Table 36 also indicates that many out-migrants were residents of institutions at the time of the census in 1960.

TABLE 36

PERCENTAGE IN ARMED FORCES, INSTITUTIONAL GROUP
QUARTERS, AND OTHER GROUP QUARTERS,
FOR NON-WHITE OUT-MIGRANTS, 1955–60

SMSA	Percentage of Male Labor Force in Armed Forces	Percentage in Institutional Group Quarters	Percentage in Other Group Quarters
Detroit	26.0	10.6	11.8
Cleveland	20.1	11.7	9.9
Philadelphia	37.0	8.9	13.9
St. Louis	27.8	6.2	10.1
Washington	32.2	8.3	11.9
Baltimore	31.3	8.8	13.2
New Orleans	21.7	7.9	8.6
Atlanta	20.6	12.8	8.6
Birmingham	17.9	5.8	10.6
Memphis	16.1	1.6	8.1

Source: U. S. Bureau of the Census, *U. S. Census of Population: 1960, Mobility for Metropolitan Areas, op. cit.,* Table 6.

"Special purpose" migrants make up a substantial share of out-migrants from each SMSA, but are a large share of in-migrants only in those SMSA's that contain a large college, military base, prison, or other institution. The presence of inmates of institutions, members of the armed forces, and students is reflected in varying degrees in our measures of the characteristics of in- and out-migrants. The measure of educational attainment is based upon the total population over 25 years of age, while the measure of occupational status is based upon employed males age 14 and over in the civilian labor force. Probably most students and members of the armed forces (and many migrants as well) are too young to appear in the education statistics. Many college students are not in the labor force, while military personnel are not part of the civilian labor force. The institutional population appears in the education data, but not usually in the occupation statistics. Age and sex data, since they are classifications of the total population, are affected by all types of migrants.

The validity of the following discussion of the characteristics of Negro migrants rests upon the degree of confidence which can be placed in the 1955–60 statistics. The preceding discussion suggests that considerable caution should be exercised. Keeping in mind the deficiencies of the data, we now turn to an investigation of the characteristics of the various migration streams.

As compared to non-migrants, the in-migrants are younger, better educated, and more likely to be employed in white-collar occupations; and the ratio of males to females is similar (Tables 37 to 40). Two subgroups of Negro in-migrants may be distinguished: those moving from other metropolitan areas, and those of non-metropolitan origin. In-migrants of non-metropolitan origin are generally much younger than non-migrants or in-migrants from other SMSA's. In educational and occupational status, they are much lower than migrants from other metropolitan areas but rather similar to non-migrants. In-migrants from other SMSA's, on the other hand, are particularly

TABLE 37

PERCENTAGE AGE 15–24 OF ALL PERSONS AGE 15 AND OVER,
BY MIGRATION STATUS, 1955–60, FOR NON-WHITES

SMSA	Non-Migrants	Total In-Migrants°	In-Migrants from —		Total Out-Migrants°
			Other SMSA	Non-metropolitan Area	
Detroit	17.9	34.0	27.5	42.8	32.3
Cleveland	17.1	34.3	27.0	43.9	27.8
Philadelphia.........	19.1	36.6	30.5	43.7	33.9
St. Louis..............	19.3	34.0	26.0	40.0	35.1
Washington..........	18.4	41.0	36.5	45.2	31.9
Baltimore.............	20.7	38.9	35.2	41.7	36.5
New Orleans........	21.1	42.8	33.0	47.0	35.6
Atlanta.................	21.8	44.5	34.5	49.0	32.2
Birmingham	21.3	34.2	24.6	39.4	43.9
Memphis	20.4	36.8	28.0	39.1	38.8

Source: U. S. Bureau of the Census, U. S. Census of Population: 1960, Mobility for Metropolitan Areas, op. cit., Tables 4 and 5.

° Total in-migrants exclude persons who were abroad in 1955, and out-migrants exclude persons who were abroad in 1960. Both groups exclude those "not reported" who may have been migrants.

TABLE 38

SEX RATIO BY MIGRATION STATUS, 1955–60, FOR NON-WHITES

SMSA	Non-Migrants	Total In-Migrants°	In-Migrants from –		Total Out-Migrants°
			Other SMSA	Non-metropolitan Area	
Detroit	92.7	76.1	77.0	74.9	139.0
Cleveland	91.7	88.2	87.5	89.1	127.1
Philadelphia.........	89.1	94.1	97.6	90.1	127.9
St. Louis..............	85.3	87.2	92.0	83.9	106.7
Washington..........	89.6	97.6	104.6	91.7	118.4
Baltimore.............	92.1	101.3	111.4	94.0	126.9
New Orleans........	86.6	91.4	96.5	89.4	108.4
Atlanta.................	83.6	94.1	116.8	86.0	115.5
Birmingham.........	86.3	83.4	94.0	78.3	92.9
Memphis	87.3	89.3	99.2	87.1	93.2

Source: U. S. Bureau of the Census, *U. S. Census of Population: 1960, Mobility for Metropolitan Areas, op. cit.*, Tables 4 and 5.

° Total in-migrants exclude persons who were abroad in 1955, and out-migrants exclude persons who were abroad in 1960. Both groups exclude those "not reported" who may have been migrants.

TABLE 39

PERCENTAGE COMPLETING ONE OR MORE YEARS OF HIGH SCHOOL, BY MIGRATION STATUS, 1955–60, FOR NON-WHITES

SMSA	Non-Migrants	Total In-Migrants°	In-Migrants from –		Total Out-Migrants°
			Other SMSA	Non-metropolitan Area	
Detroit	51.4	59.8	65.5	50.0	59.9
Cleveland	54.2	63.5	66.6	58.2	62.3
Philadelphia.........	48.5	59.9	66.0	51.2	64.3
St. Louis..............	42.1	50.2	63.2	38.4	59.7
Washington..........	53.6	66.5	75.1	57.3	66.4
Baltimore.............	39.6	53.9	61.2	47.6	58.5
New Orleans........	30.5	39.6	56.0	30.6	50.4
Atlanta	37.2	43.2	56.1	35.8	51.1
Birmingham.........	34.4	40.0	55.8	29.5	54.5
Memphis	30.7	31.5	52.9	24.9	46.2

Source: U. S. Bureau of the Census, *U. S. Census of Population: 1960, Mobility for Metropolitan Areas, op. cit.*, Tables 4 and 5.

° Total in-migrants exclude persons who were abroad in 1955, and out-migrants exclude persons who were abroad in 1960. Both groups exclude those "not reported" who may have been migrants.

distinctive, being of substantially higher educational and occupational status than either in-migrants of non-metropolitan origin or non-migrants. Thus, the relatively high status of the total in-migrant

TABLE 40

PERCENTAGE OF EMPLOYED MALES IN WHITE-COLLAR
OCCUPATIONS, BY MIGRATION STATUS, 1955–60, FOR NON-WHITES

SMSA	Non-Migrants	Total In-Migrants°	In-Migrants from— Other SMSA	In-Migrants from— Non-metropolitan Area	Total Out-Migrants°
Detroit	14.3	24.7	31.3	15.1	18.4
Cleveland	15.9	17.9	22.0	13.2	24.2
Philadelphia	18.1	21.3	28.6	14.0	26.6
St. Louis	16.7	21.0	28.4	14.7	25.8
Washington	27.4	29.3	40.0	21.1	37.6
Baltimore	15.8	22.7	36.1	13.9	21.5
New Orleans	12.8	10.9	20.7†	7.1	24.9
Atlanta	12.1	14.7	25.1†	11.1	25.7
Birmingham	8.5	9.7	14.1†	7.4	17.6
Memphis	11.1	14.0	24.3†	11.6	18.0

Source: U. S. Bureau of the Census, U. S. Census of Population: 1960, Mobility for Metropolitan Areas, op. cit., Tables 4 and 6.

° Total in-migrants exclude persons who were abroad in 1955, and out-migrants exclude persons who were abroad in 1960. Both groups exclude those "not reported" who may have been migrants.

† Based on fewer than 1,000 persons.

group is due to the combination of the high-status intermetropolitan stream with the lower status (partially rural-to-urban) stream of non-metropolitan origin.

Compared to in-migrants, out-migrants have a similar concentration in the young adult ages and an excess of males (owing to the presence of members of the armed forces), but they tend to be of higher educational and occupational status. In fact, in this respect out-migrants resemble in-migrants from other metropolitan areas. This is not surprising since out-migrants from SMSA's generally become in-migrants to other SMSA's. Once Negroes become metropolitan residents, the tendency is to remain in metropolitan areas and participate in national streams of intermetropolitan migration.

On the basis of these data on the volume and characteristics of in- and out-migration, it is possible to make some inferences concerning the net effect of migration upon the socioeconomic status of the resident Negro population. Since net migration is small both absolutely and relative to the gross movement (see Table 34), the impact of migration, whether favorable or unfavorable, is slight.

The situation of the four Southern metropolitan areas is clear—migration has had a deleterious effect upon the educational and occupational advancement of the resident Negro population. This has happened because the depressing effect of an out-migration of a high-status group is not counteracted by in-migration because (1) there are fewer in-migrants than out-migrants; and (2) the status of the in-migrants is lower, being only slightly better than non-migrants, owing to the predominance of in-migrants of non-metropolitan origin.

The situation is more ambiguous in the Northern and border SMSA's. Although each area is characterized by out-migration of higher status Negroes, the countering effect of in-migration varies both in volume and status. Hence, the net impact of migration on the socioeconomic status of the resident Negro population is sometimes favorable and sometimes unfavorable.

In view of the differences in age composition of the various migration streams, we may inquire whether these differences account for differences in educational and occupational status observed among streams. Since young people have generally higher average levels of educational attainment, it is possible that the younger average age of the in-migrants is responsible for their higher educational level relative to non-migrants. Measures of educational attainment controlled for age, presented in Table 41, are very similar for the total in-migrant group and non-migrants, indicating that the favored position of in-migrants is largely accounted for by their favorable age composition. The age-standardized measures, however, still reveal a large difference in educational level between migrants from metropolitan areas and those from non-metropolitan areas. In-migrants from

TABLE 41

AGE-STANDARDIZED PERCENTAGE COMPLETING ONE OR MORE YEARS OF HIGH SCHOOL, BY MIGRATION STATUS, 1955–60, FOR NON-WHITES

SMSA	Non-Migrants	Total In-Migrants	In-Migrants from —	
			Other SMSA	Non-metropolitan Area
Detroit	51.9	51.9	55.9	44.7
Cleveland	55.0	55.3	58.4	50.3
Philadelphia	49.3	49.5	54.9	42.0
St. Louis	42.7	41.3	49.8	32.9
Washington	54.6	56.8	64.0	49.2
Baltimore	40.2	45.2	51.5	39.7
New Orleans	31.0	31.7	42.4	25.2
Atlanta	37.8	35.8	45.8	29.9
Birmingham	32.9	32.4	42.8	24.8
Memphis	31.1	26.9	40.9	21.9

° Standardized by the indirect method, using the age-sex-specific percentages for the non-white population of each SMSA as the standard set of rates.

other SMSA's are of uniformly higher status than those of non-metropolitan origin or the non-migrants, while migrants from non-metropolitan areas are of lower status than non-migrants. In sum, in-migrants of metropolitan origin are clearly of higher educational status than any non-migrants, even those of the same age. Migrants of non-metropolitan origin, though similar in educational status to all non-migrants, are of lower status than non-migrants of the same ages.

We have considered the socioeconomic status of in-migrant non-whites relative to the non-white population of SMSA's, but have not yet indicated their status relative to the resident white population. The percentages of high school graduates among the white populations of the ten cities are presented in Table 42, where they can be compared with the percentages among non-white in-migrants. (Because we are concerned only with in-migrants, data for cities rather than SMSA's can be used.) In their levels of educational attainment, non-white in-migrants to Northern and border cities resemble the resident white population, while those in-migrants coming from other metropolitan areas are superior to the whites. Controlling for differences in age composition tends to lower the percentages for non-whites and raise those for whites. On an age-standardized basis, the non-white in-migrants to Northern and border cities are slightly below the resident white population in educational status, but in-migrants of metropolitan origin are very much like the whites.

TABLE 42

ACTUAL AND AGE-STANDARDIZED PERCENTAGE OF HIGH SCHOOL
GRADUATES, FOR NON-WHITE IN-MIGRANTS TO CITIES, 1955–60,
AND TOTAL WHITE POPULATION OF CITIES, 1960°

City	Actual			Age-Standardized		
	White, City Total	Non-white In-Migrants		White, City Total	Non-white In-Migrants	
		Total	From Other SMSA		Total	From Other SMSA
Detroit............	37.1	33.8	41.8	40.5	28.9	35.0
Cleveland	30.9	36.9	40.4	32.0	30.1	32.9
Philadelphia....	32.9	35.1	38.8	34.6	28.4	31.3
St. Louis	27.1	30.7	41.9	29.9	25.1	32.6
Washington	61.1	45.1	54.5	71.4	45.1	54.3
Baltimore........	31.8	29.4	37.6	33.7	24.6	31.3
New Orleans ...	42.1	21.9	34.6	44.0	19.0	28.4
Atlanta............	50.7	26.0	34.7	52.9	24.0	31.2
Birmingham ...	46.4	21.9	31.0	47.2	20.3	28.1
Memphis	53.1	16.0	31.7	53.7	15.3	28.7

° Standardized by the indirect method, using the age-sex-specific percentages for the white population of each SMSA as the standard set of rates to be applied to the age-sex composition of non-white in-migrants and the total white population of the city.

In the four Southern cities, the status comparisons have a some-what different pattern. Both the total non-white in-migrants and those of metropolitan origin are substantially below the white population in educational attainment levels; age-standardization tends to widen this gap. Educational levels among non-white in-migrants from metropolitan areas, however, are similar to those among the same segment of in-migrants to Northern and border cities. Still, the total in-migrant group remains of lower educational status, whatever the comparison, because of the preponderant influence in the Southern cities of the low-status in-migrants of non-metropolitan origin.

If these comparisons between non-white in-migrants and resident whites were made for the total metropolitan population rather than the city population, the status levels among whites would generally be slightly raised, while the figures for non-whites would be little affected. If these comparisons were made for occupational levels rather than educational levels, all of the non-white groups would clearly be of lower status. Nevertheless, the figures we have presented demonstrate that the in-migrant non-whites, at least in Northern and border cities, resemble in educational levels the whites among whom they live.

Early Evidence: Migration, 1935–40 and 1940–50. — The socio-economic status of Negro in-migrants between 1955 and 1960 was substantially higher on the average than that of the 1960 resident Negro population. Does this represent a relatively recent development, or was it true of the migrants in earlier periods? Though data for earlier years are scanty, available material for the periods 1935–40 and 1940–50 shed some additional light on the matter.

From the 1940 census, information is available on the character-istics of migrants during the five-year period between 1935 and 1940. These data are very similar to the 1955–60 data analyzed above. Special tabulations of these data were used by Freedman in an ex-tensive analysis of in-migrants to Chicago. Considering all migrants (who were more than 90 per cent white),

> The stereotype of migrants as a distressed group of low social and economic status on the fringe of the urban labor reserve was found to be applicable only to a small part of the total stream of migrants to Chicago . . . mainly to rural migrants from the South.[5]

While white migrants to Chicago were markedly superior to non-migrants in a wide variety of social and economic characteristics, Negro migrants deviated sharply from this pattern.

5. Ronald Freedman, *Recent Migration to Chicago* (Chicago: University of Chicago Press, 1950), p. 210.

At least with reference to the period 1935–40 the [white] migrants tended to be relatively well-educated young adults on the
threshold of their productive careers, ready and willing to work and
able to find employment . . . the Negro migrants of the present
period and the earlier foreign migrants are predominantly persons
of low educational status, without capital or financial reserves, unskilled and ready to enter the labor market at the bottom of the
occupational ladder.[6]

A comparison of the occupational status of non-white in-migrants
to the city of Chicago for the two time periods, 1935–40 and 1955–60,
is presented below:[7]

Time Period and Migration Status	Percentage of Employed Males Engaged in White-collar Occupations
1935–40	
Non-migrants	20.1
In-migrants from:	
South – Total	11.0
South – Urban	12.3
South – Rural	7.8
1955–60	
Non-migrants	21.1
In-migrants from:	
Other SMSA	28.3
Non-metropolitan areas	15.7

These data indicate an upgrading of non-white in-migrants relative to non-white non-migrants between 1935–40 and 1955–60. Even
the highest status in-migrants in the earlier period, those from the
urban South, are less well off compared to non-migrants than the
lowest status migrants in the later period, those from non-metropolitan
areas. However, this is an admittedly crude comparison, for there are
as many reservations about the quality of the earlier data as we have
already discussed with regard to the data for 1955–60. In particular,
the data for 1935–40 refer to only a portion of all Negro in-migrants,
mainly to those from the South, who then comprised 78 per cent of all
Negro in-migrants to Chicago. The omission of a sizable group of the
Negro in-migrants, particularly of the group most likely to be the
high-status intermetropolitan type, may have seriously biased the
results.

6. *Ibid.*, pp. 200, 210.
7. Data for 1935–40 are from *ibid.*, Table 78.

For the 1940–50 decade, we must rely upon estimates of net migration. From these data we may obtain estimates concerning some of the net effects of migration upon the resident Negro population, but we are unable to specify the volume and character of the in- and out-migration streams which combined to produce this effect. The data permit a rough assessment of the total impact of migration, but attempts to infer the character of the gross streams comprising this movement can be misleading.

Again the principal relevant study is of Chicago. Using estimates of net migration by educational status, Duncan and Duncan concluded that

> Improvement in the educational status of Chicago's non-white population between 1940 and 1950 was retarded by the absorption of migrants to the city whose educational attainment was less than that of the population living in the city in 1940.[8]

However, since the educational status of the net migrants was higher than that of all non-whites in the South in 1950, the authors tentatively suggest that

> The migrants are probably a favorably selected group, in terms of the population from which they are drawn.[9]

An analysis identical to that carried out by the Duncans for Chicago was undertaken for the ten cities of the present study. Since educational attainment may be regarded as a "fixed" characteristic of an individual (*i.e.*, for the adult population the number of years of school completed is unlikely to change throughout the remainder of any individual's life), census survival ratios specific for age, sex, color, and educational attainment could be applied to the enumerated 1940 non-white population in each city, thus obtaining an estimate of the educational attainment of the resident population which survived to 1950. Some improvement in educational attainment is inherent in the aging of the resident population, due to higher mortality among older persons, who have low average levels of educational attainment. The discrepancy between this "expected" educational attainment of the resident non-white population surviving to 1950 and the actual educational attainment of the total non-white population enumerated in 1950 (which includes in-migrants but not out-migrants during the decade) may be attributed to the net effect of migration.

The results of this procedure, presented in Table 43, indicate that for most cities the net effect of migration during the 1940–50 decade was to retard slightly the improvement in educational status

8. Duncan and Duncan, *op. cit.*, pp. 59–60.
9. *Ibid.*, p. 62.

of the Negro population. For both median numbers of school years completed and the percentage completing one or more years of high school, values for the estimated survivors of the 1940 population are slightly higher in most cases than for the total non-white population as enumerated in 1950. (In every city but Birmingham there was a net in-migration of Negroes in the decade.) In general, then, net migrants were of lower educational status than the enumerated population.

TABLE 43

EDUCATIONAL ATTAINMENT OF THE NON-WHITE POPULATION
AGE 30 AND OVER, BY MIGRATION STATUS, 1940–50

City	Median Number of School Years Completed		Percentage Completing One Year of High School or More	
	1950 Total Enumerated Population	Estimated Survivors of the 1940 Population	1950 Total Enumerated Population	Estimated Survivors of the 1940 Population
Detroit	8.3	8.5	38.0	40.4
Cleveland	8.3	8.5	39.6	41.9
Philadelphia.....	7.9	8.0	32.7	28.7
St. Louis	7.7	8.2	27.9	32.9
Washington	8.5	8.5	42.4	41.5
Baltimore	6.8	6.9	24.2	24.0
New Orleans ...	6.1	6.4	17.4	19.1
Atlanta°	6.4	6.6	25.3	25.9
Birmingham°....	6.3	6.8	21.7	25.1
Memphis°	6.5	6.9	19.4	22.8

°Adjusted for annexations, 1940-50.

The depressing effect of migration was somewhat greater in the four Southern cities and St. Louis than in the remaining cities. Some insight into these intercity variations in the impact of migration upon educational levels can be obtained from estimated net migration rates by educational attainment for the non-white population (Table 44). The four Southern cities and St. Louis are characterized not only by high rates of net in-migration of non-whites at lower educational levels, but by net out-migration of non-whites at higher levels of educational attainment. This is consistent with the data for 1955–60 which showed in-migrants to the Southern cities to be of low educational status, while out-migrants were of much higher status.

On the basis of figures for net migrants, no inference can be made regarding the educational level of in- or out-migrants. Since

TABLE 44

ESTIMATED NET MIGRATION, 1940–50, PER 100 SURVIVORS OF THE
1940 POPULATION, FOR THE NON-WHITE POPULATION AGE 30
AND OVER, BY NUMBER OF SCHOOL YEARS COMPLETED, 1950

City			*Number of School Years Completed*						
	Total	*None*	*Elementary*			*High School*		*College*	
			1-4	*5-6*	*7-8*	*1-3*	*4*	*1-3*	*4+*
Detroit	61	36	79	70	54	50	40	61	49
Cleveland	44	22	58	59	31	34	25	39	46
Philadelphia	25	5	35	24	5	39	51	39	36
St. Louis	19	37	42	20	10	−8	8	−5	−16
Washington	18	24	15	22	6	12	27	18	15
Baltimore	10	0	10	13	3	7	14	13	0
New Orleans	2	11	10	1	−5	−3	−5	−15	−28
Atlanta°	−3	35	4	−11	−11	−2	−3	−14	−14
Birmingham°	−10	8	1	−8	−20	−24	−27	−30	−1
Memphis°	−6	20	9	−8	−8	−16	−22	−19	−25

°Adjusted for annexations, 1940-50.

the volume of in- or out-migration at each educational level is in-determinate from net figures, the over-all educational distribution of in- or out-migrants is also indeterminate. Any pattern of net migration can be produced by a wide variety of numbers of in- and out-migrants at each educational level.

In the absence of reliable data for earlier periods, discussion of past patterns of Negro migration must be largely speculative. Very likely a high-status intermetropolitan stream of Negro migrants always existed, but its relative importance has increased substantially in recent years owing to the rapid urbanization of the Negro popula-tion. While 49 per cent of the Negro population were classified as urban in 1940, this figure had risen by 1960 to 73 per cent—higher than the comparable figure for whites. We have found that in-migrants of non-metropolitan origin most nearly resemble the stereotype of the socioeconomically depressed migrant. It seems reasonable that as this component declines and the intermetropolitan component in-creases in relative importance, the status of the total in-migrant group would rise. As the character of the Negro population has changed from a disadvantaged rural population to a largely metropolitan population of rising social and economic status, its patterns of migra-tion should increasingly manifest the same responses to economic pushes and pulls as are found among the white population. The patterns of Negro migration we have described from the 1955–60 data are very much like those of the white population, which has a substantial high-status intermetropolitan component.[10] We tentatively conclude that although Negro in-migrants in the past generally were of lower socioeconomic status than the resident Negro population, this can no longer be considered an adequate description of current patterns of Negro migration. There is a large and increasingly important high-status intermetropolitan migration in the total movement of Negro population.

☐ RESIDENTIAL DISTRIBUTION OF MIGRANTS

Spatial expansion of Negro residential areas occurs under the impetus of a growing Negro population, and migration is a major cause of this rapidly growing population. From Table 34, we see that the four Southern SMSA's experienced a net loss of Negro population through migration. The result is little expansion of Negro areas. Northern and border SMSA's, with large net gains in Negro population, exhibit greater expansion of Negro residential areas.[11] What is the role of in-migrants in altering the spatial distribution of the Negro population?

Early writers noted a tendency for newcomers to be concentrated in the worst areas of a city. DuBois, writing of Philadelphia in the 1890's, stated that

> The new immigrants usually settle in pretty well-defined localities in or near the slums, and thus get the worst possible introduction to city life.[12]

Freedman, analyzing the 1935–40 migration data for Chicago, found that the "depressed" migrants from the deep South were concentrated in a low-status area. The small number of Negro migrants from the North and West, however, did not manifest as high a degree of concentration in the "Negro Zone."[13] Duncan and Duncan, summarizing a variety of data for Chicago up to 1950, concluded that the bulk of Negro migrants settled in areas of established Negro residence, and

10. Karl E. Taeuber and Alma F. Taeuber, "White Migration and Socio-economic Differences Between Cities and Suburbs," *American Sociological Review*, XXIX, No. 5 (October, 1964).

11. Although the data for the 1955–60 period indicate a net loss of Negro population in two of the Northern and border cities, Detroit and St. Louis, the growth of the Negro population in these cities over the entire decade renders it exceedingly unlikely that this experience characterized the earlier part of the decade. We have previously discussed the possible inaccuracies in these data.

12. W. E. B. DuBois, *The Philadelphia Negro* (Philadelphia: Publications of the University of Pennsylvania, 1899), p. 81.

13. Freedman, *op. cit.*, p. 202.

that movement of Negroes into formerly white areas was led disproportionately by older residents rather than recently arrived migrants.

Knowledge of the extent to which migrants are localized in particular areas of a city and the extent to which expansion of Negro residential areas is led by recent migrants is relevant to an understanding of residential differentiation within the Negro community. In the previous section we have shown that the increasing urbanization of the Negro population and its rising socioeconomic status have profoundly altered the character of Negro migration to cities. These changes lead us to question the continued applicability of the picture of most newcomers to the city being crowded into tenements in the slums.

Data derived from the 1960 census question concerning place of residence in 1955 were published for each census tract separately for whites and non-whites. As a result, it is possible to compare the spatial distribution of migrants (defined as all persons who resided outside the SMSA or abroad in 1955) with that of the total population. The reservations expressed in the previous section with regard to possible defects in the data apply even more forcefully when we focus on small subareas of a city. For example, in census tract 34 in Washington, 30 per cent of the non-white population in 1960 were migrants, as compared to 10 per cent in the city as a whole, owing to the presence of Howard University in this tract. To eliminate such distortions, tracts containing institutions, colleges, or military installations which would seriously affect the migration data were omitted from the following analysis. Individual tracts may also be affected by serious underenumeration or nonresponse, but such tracts remain in the analysis.

Table 45 presents the distribution of migrants, local movers, and the total Negro population among census tracts aggregated into the racial-change types delineated in Chapter 5. In general, Negro migrants and the total Negro population are similarly distributed. The difference between the percentage of migrants and the percentage of the total population who reside in tracts of a particular type of racial change rarely exceeds a few percentage points. The small differences which do appear are in the direction of an underrepresentation of migrants in areas which remained virtually all-Negro throughout the decade (Established Negro Areas) and an overrepresentation in areas which substantial numbers of Negroes were entering for the first time (Invasion tracts). Similar observations hold for local movers compared to the Negro population as a whole. These findings are substantiated if we examine the consistency of these patterns on a tract-by-tract basis within racial-change types. Table 46 shows the

TABLE 45

PERCENTAGE DISTRIBUTION AMONG CENSUS TRACTS OF TOTAL NEGRO POPULATION, LOCAL MOVERS, MIGRANTS, AND PERSONS NOT REPORTING MIGRATION STATUS, 1955–60, BY TYPE OF RACIAL CHANGE

City and Migration Status	Total	Established Negro Areas	Type of Racial Change				
			Succession	Invasion	Growing	Declining	Displacement
Detroit:							
Total population	100.0	13.9	42.0	27.0	......	16.5	0.6
Local movers	100.0	11.0	42.8	32.3	......	13.3	0.6
Migrants	100.0	10.1	42.5	32.4	......	14.7	0.3
Not reported	100.0	14.2	41.0	27.6	......	16.6	0.6
Cleveland:							
Total population	100.0	23.9	45.4	19.8	0.5	8.0	2.4
Local movers	100.0	20.4	46.2	23.6	0.5	7.2	2.1
Migrants	100.0	14.3	53.6	23.7	0.7	6.9	0.8
Not reported	100.0	23.6	42.1	21.2	1.0	9.6	2.5
Philadelphia:							
Total population	100.0	7.1	61.6	7.8	0.7	21.2	1.6
Local movers	100.0	6.2	58.5	12.5	0.9	20.2	1.7
Migrants	100.0	6.3	64.2	10.5	0.8	17.4	0.8
Not reported	100.0	5.4	61.5	6.5	1.3	23.7	1.6
St. Louis:							
Total population	100.0	15.4	38.3	27.4	......	11.8	7.1
Local movers	100.0	13.3	36.8	34.0	......	9.6	6.3
Migrants	100.0	15.5	37.9	32.0	......	10.7	3.9
Not reported	100.0	16.3	34.4	32.4	......	6.7	10.2
Washington:							
Total population	100.0	5.5	65.0	11.1	2.6	14.6	1.2
Local movers	100.0	5.2	61.9	12.9	3.9	14.9	1.2
Migrants	100.0	3.1	66.0	13.2	3.9	12.2	1.6
Not reported	100.0	7.5	60.8	8.1	1.1	21.3	1.2

City and Migration Status	Total	Type of Racial Change					
		Established Negro Areas	Succession	Invasion	Growing	Declining	Displacement
Baltimore:							
Total population	100.0	24.0	29.8	28.4	0.2	15.5	2.1
Local movers	100.0	22.4	27.3	33.4	0.4	14.8	1.7
Migrants	100.0	19.7	29.2	33.5	0.3	15.2	2.1
Not reported	100.0	24.1	24.4	33.8	0.1	15.3	2.3
New Orleans: °							
Total population	100.0	16.2	55.4	0.7	8.8	11.6	5.7
Local movers	100.0	14.7	58.4	0.9	9.5	10.7	4.4
Migrants	100.0	18.3	51.2	1.4	7.3	13.6	6.9
Not reported	100.0	16.5	56.2	1.5	6.4	12.8	4.9
Atlanta: †							
Total population	100.0	22.0	44.8	1.3	0.4	3.6	6.0
Local movers	100.0	17.2	45.5	2.2	0.4	4.1	5.5
Migrants	100.0	13.9	48.6	3.5	......	5.3	7.4
Not reported	100.0	21.3	48.5	2.4	......	1.4	2.7
Birmingham: †							
Total population	100.0	27.7	40.3	......	8.7	10.2	11.6
Local movers	100.0	30.7	37.5	......	7.8	11.2	11.4
Migrants	100.0	29.4	37.3	......	10.8	10.3	11.3
Not reported	100.0	26.9	38.3	......	7.6	14.1	11.6
Memphis: †							
Total population	100.0	24.7	53.0	......	5.5	14.4	1.6
Local movers	100.0	23.9	54.0	......	4.9	14.8	1.8
Migrants	100.0	19.1	58.9	......	5.2	13.0	2.9
Not reported	100.0	17.1	48.1	......	7.5	23.5	2.1

° Distributions do not add to 100.0 because of the omission of two tracts classified as "Stable Interracial Areas."

† Distributions do not add to 100.0 because of the omission of tracts which were annexed during the 1950–60 decade and thus could not be classified by type of racial change.

TABLE 46

PERCENTAGE OF TRACTS IN WHICH NON-WHITE MIGRANTS,
1955–60, WERE OVERREPRESENTED RELATIVE TO TOTAL
NON-WHITE POPULATION, 1960, BY TYPE OF RACIAL CHANGE

City	Type of Racial Change				
	Established Negro Areas	Succession	Invasion	Declining	Displacement
Detroit..................	17	42	49	30	0°
Cleveland	8	68	50	30	0°
Philadelphia..........	67°	48	64	31	0°
St. Louis	50°	38	75	25°	0°
Washington	0	57	80	20	75°
Baltimore	33	35	55	33	25°
New Orleans	71	44	67°	38	80
Atlanta.	0	40	100°	100°	100°
Birmingham...........	33	42	......	67	27
Memphis...............	27	55	......	40	67°

° Percentage based on fewer than 5 tracts.

percentage of tracts of each type of racial change in which the percentage of all Negro migrants residing in the tract exceeds the percentage of the total Negro population in the tract. More Invasion tracts than other types show an overrepresentation of migrants as compared to the total population, while relatively few Established Negro Areas have an overrepresentation of migrants. Considerable variation within each type of racial change is evident, however, and the principal conclusion is that Negro migrants are not unduly concentrated in census tracts characterized by particular types of racial change.

Ignoring the classification by type of racial change, it is possible to examine on a tract-by-tract basis the degree of unevenness in the areal distribution of migrants as compared to local movers or to the Negro population as a whole. Indexes of.dissimilarity measuring the amount of residential segregation among the three groups are presented in Table 47. For each of the three possible comparisons, index values average about 16, indicating that only 16 per cent of any particular group would have to be reallocated among tracts in order to achieve an identical distribution. These results again suggest overall similarity in the spatial distribution of migrants, local movers, and the total Negro population.[14]

14. Persons who moved 1955–60, but whose residence in 1955 was not reported are nearly as numerous as migrants in some cities. The distribution of these persons over census tracts is not sharply different from the total non-white population, local movers, or migrants — average indexes of dissimilarity are 22, 21, and 24 respectively — and their omission does not affect the conclusion.

TABLE 47

INDEXES OF DISSIMILARITY AMONG NON-WHITE MIGRANTS AND
LOCAL MOVERS, 1955–60, AND TOTAL NON-WHITE
POPULATION, 1960

City	Number of Tracts	Indexes of Dissimilarity		
		Total Population vs. Migrants	Total Population vs. Local Movers	Migrants vs. Local Movers
Detroit......................	178	17.6	18.5	16.6
Cleveland	65	18.2	17.2	14.6
Philadelphia.............	98	14.8	15.9	14.0
St. Louis	37	13.6	16.2	14.9
Washington	65	13.7	11.7	12.2
Baltimore	77	18.1	19.6	13.6
New Orleans	70	22.3	15.2	22.5
Atlanta.....................	42	21.3	16.9	16.7
Birmingham	40	10.4	14.4	12.8
Memphis...................	49	15.1	12.8	15.3

TABLE 48

PERCENTAGE OF WHITE HOUSEHOLDS WHO MOVED INTO
THEIR PRESENT HOUSING UNIT 1958–60, FOR NEGRO RESIDENTIAL
AREAS AND THE REST OF THE CITY, 1960

City	Negro Residential Areas	Rest of City
Detroit...	30.0	22.3
Cleveland...	33.3	29.5
Philadelphia...	24.3	20.8
St. Louis	38.8	31.7
Washington	41.6	33.7
Baltimore	24.9	24.3
New Orleans	35.3	30.6
Atlanta°	40.4	38.8
Birmingham°	34.3	34.7
Memphis°	41.8	31.8

° Annexed areas omitted.

On the basis of evidence for the 1955–60 period, then, we conclude that Negro migrants are not concentrated or overrepresented to
any appreciable degree in any type of area. In few tracts of any type
do migrants comprise as much as 15 per cent of the tract's population.

The data do not reveal the existence of any area that might be considered a "migrant zone." Negro migrants are distributed throughout the city in much the same manner as the total population of which they are a part.

The modest differences we have observed indicate that migrants are relatively fewer in predominantly Negro areas and relatively more numerous in newly invaded areas than the total Negro population. Very likely, housing opportunities are greater in areas in which the normal residential turnover among the Negro population is supplemented by a net out-movement of whites than they are in all-Negro areas. Furthermore, there is considerable residential mobility among the white population remaining in Negro areas. A slightly higher percentage of whites living in Negro areas in 1960 had moved into their present residence during the preceding two years than was true for whites in the remainder of the city (Table 48). Differential volume of housing vacancies may not be the only explanation. We have suggested that Negro migrants of relatively high socioeconomic status comprise a large and increasing share of all in-migrants, particularly in Northern and border cities. Hence, it should not be surprising that such migrants seek residence in all accessible areas of the city compatible with their status rather than settling only in concentrated Negro areas.

7

CONCOMITANTS OF
RESIDENTIAL SUCCESSION

The impact of migration of both white and Negro population on the types of neighborhood racial changes occurring within cities has been examined in Chapter 5, and the characteristics of these migrants and their distribution within cities was considered in Chapter 6. In this chapter, attention is directed toward changes in population and housing characteristics in areas undergoing racial transition. Because residential succession was less common, and the rate of racial change much lower in Southern cities than in Northern cities, emphasis is on Northern cities where these processes are highlighted.

Traditional accounts of the process of racial succession stress the low socioeconomic status of the Negro population entering a neighborhood, the deterioration and overcrowding of housing, and the consequent flight of white residents from the neighborhood. Documenting the fact of racial succession is much easier, however, than describing precisely the process itself, and few accounts are based upon a systematic body of evidence. In their Chicago study, Duncan and Duncan found that the population of areas undergoing succession did not decline in over-all levels of socioeconomic status. National trends, such as the improvement in business conditions after the Depression and the long-term rise in levels of living, more than offset the presumably depressing effect of increasing Negro population in these areas. The present chapter begins with an examination of suburbanization and its influence upon the expansion of Negro residential areas. We then proceed to an examination of the characteristics of the population (both white and Negro) in these areas, and of how these characteristics have been changing in response to suburbanization and other major processes of social change.

□ SUBURBANIZATION

The typical pattern of expansion of cities in the United States has been that of radial growth, with new residential development and population growth occurring on the periphery of the city, along with small population increases or decreases in the central areas. As our large cities became built up, new growth increasingly occurred beyond the city limits. Meanwhile, innovations in transportation technology have altered the time-cost structure influencing residential location. These changes have facilitated the process of decentralization or suburbanization of population.

Though suburbanization has been a discernible trend in the nation's metropolitan areas for many decades, the *pace* of suburbanization has varied from decade to decade in response to the state of the economy as a whole. Long-term trends in housing construction show restricted building activity in wartime and depression, while peak building occurs in times of peace and prosperity. The period 1930–45 was characterized by limited construction of new housing and, despite the high rate of residential building in the late 1940's and 1950's, it was a long time before the postwar scarcity of new housing was overcome.

The movement from the central city to better peripheral residential areas that would normally have accompanied the rising incomes of the war decade was instead "bottled up" by the housing shortage generated by wartime shortages of labor and materials. The intense competition for available housing drove prices up, so that new housing which did become available tended to be taken by high-income groups who could pay inflationary prices.[1]

During the 1950's, the pace of suburbanization was rapid as income levels rose and new credit facilities permitted the increasing numbers of middle-income families to finance home-ownership. As a result, most large cities in the nation underwent absolute declines in population while suburban areas experienced large increases. The magnitude of these changes is indicated in Table 49, which presents rates of suburbanization in the two decades for the ten metropolitan areas of which our cities are a part. The rate of suburbanization is defined as the percentage-point change during a decade in the percentage of the total metropolitan area's population residing in the central city (with adjustments for annexation). In the four Northern metropolitan areas, the rate of suburbanization doubled from 1940–50 to 1950–60, and large increases also occurred in virtually all of the other areas.[2] Although central cities made up over half

1. Lloyd Rodwin, *Housing and Economic Progress: A Study of the Housing Experiences of Boston's Middle-Income Families* (Cambridge: Harvard University Press and The Technology Press, 1961).

2. Comparison between the two decades of the rates for Atlanta, Birmingham, and Memphis results in understatement of the true differences because these cities an-

TABLE 49

RATES OF SUBURBANIZATION FOR METROPOLITAN AREAS,
1940–50 AND 1950–60

SMSA	Percentage City is of SMSA Population		Rate of Suburbanization 1940-50°	Percentage City is of SMSA Population		Rate of Suburbanization 1950-60°
	1940	1950		1950	1960	
Detroit..............	68.3	61.3	7.0	61.3	44.4	16.9
Cleveland.........	69.3	62.4	6.9	62.4	48.8	13.6
Philadelphia......	60.4	56.4	4.0	56.4	46.1	10.3
St. Louis...........	55.7	49.8	5.9	49.8	36.4	13.4
Washington.......	68.5	54.8	13.7	54.8	38.2	16.6
Baltimore..........	75.4	67.6	7.8	67.6	54.4	13.2
New Orleans.....	89.6	83.2	6.4	83.2	72.3	10.9
Atlanta†	54.1	45.2	8.9	45.6	31.1	14.5
Birmingham† ...	58.2	53.2	5.0	58.3	51.7	6.6
Memphis†	81.8	74.4	7.4	82.1	68.3	13.8

° Rate of suburbanization is the difference between percentage in initial year and percentage in terminal year.

† Adjusted for annexations to central city in each decade. Thus, 1950 figures differ slightly depending upon the adjustment procedure for each decade.

the total population of each metropolitan area in 1940, this was true in only four areas by 1960.

The change from the tight housing market of the 1940's to a relatively loose housing market in the 1950's is reflected in the vacancy rates prevailing in these cities over the years. Vacancy rates, presented in Table 50, rose substantially between 1950 and 1960, particularly in Negro areas; housing shortages are reflected in the low vacancy rates prevailing in some cities in 1940 and generally in 1950.

The increased proportion of metropolitan population residing outside the city limits was the result of a greater movement of population to the suburbs from the city than from the suburbs back to the city, and of the failure of the city of capture its proportionate share of in-migrants from outside the metropolitan area.

The population movement out of the city did not draw proportionately from all segments of the population, but was selective of whites of high socioeconomic status. Though white in-migrants to the city were also, on the average, of similarly high status, they were fewer in number than the out-migrants. This exchange of persons of

nexed population in both decades. Though the figures refer to constant city limits within each decade, the constant city during the 1950–60 decade for these cities is not the same as the constant city 1940–50. Data for metropolitan areas for all years are for Standard Metropolitan Statistical Areas (SMSA's) as defined in the 1960 census.

TABLE 50

VACANCY RATES IN NEGRO RESIDENTIAL AREAS AND THE REST OF THE CITY, 1940–50 AND 1950–60 °

| City | 1940–50 Decade | | | | 1950–60 Decade | | | |
| | Negro Residential Areas† | | Rest of the City | | Negro Residential Areas† | | Rest of the City | |
	1940	1950	1940	1950	1950	1960	1950	1960
Detroit	3.5	1.6	3.6	2.0	1.7	10.6	2.1	3.8
Cleveland	3.9	2.0	2.7	1.8	2.0	5.7	1.7	3.8
Philadelphia	5.9	2.8	4.0	2.2	2.7	6.6	2.2	3.7
St. Louis	9.4	1.9	5.4	1.8	1.8	7.2	1.9	4.3
Washington	6.0	2.5	7.1	2.2	2.4	4.2	2.6	3.4
Baltimore	4.1	3.3	3.4	3.3	3.1	6.2	3.6	3.8
New Orleans	2.9	4.8	3.3	3.3	4.2	6.6	4.6	5.6
Atlanta	2.7	1.7	3.9	2.3	1.9	5.0	2.1	4.9
Birmingham	2.6	3.0	2.3	2.5	2.9	6.1	3.2	8.2
Memphis	2.4	2.3	3.3	2.8	2.4	5.2	3.1	3.5

° Vacancies include those currently available, and "other vacant," which includes a variety of units – dilapidated units, seasonal units, units awaiting occupancy, units held for occasional use, and units held off the market for other reasons.

† Negro Residential Areas are defined as all census tracts which contained 250 or more non-whites in the terminal year of a decade (except for "omitted" tracts which were excluded because the non-white population was primarily institutional). Thus, Invasion tracts which were all white in the initial year of a decade but contained Negroes in the terminal year are included in Negro Residential Areas. The 1950 vacancy rates differ slightly because the two sets of tracts (one for each decade) are different.

high levels of educational attainment and occupational status widened the gap between whites in cities and in suburbs on a variety of socio-economic characteristics.[3]

□ CHARACTERISTICS OF NEGRO RESIDENTIAL AREAS

We turn now to the impact of these basically demographic changes on the situation of the Negro population which, for the most part, remained confined to the central cities of metropolitan areas. In the discussion which follows, each of the ten cities in our study is divided into two major parts: *Negro Residential Areas*, defined as all census tracts with 250 or more non-whites in the terminal year of a decade; and the *Rest of the City*, those census tracts which remained virtually all-white throughout the decade. Tracts that Negroes entered for the first time during the decade will be treated separately

3. Karl E. Taeuber and Alma F. Taeuber, "White Migration and Socio-economic Differences between Cities and Suburbs," *American Sociological Review*, XXIX (October, 1964).

from other Negro Residential Areas, since their transition from near-zero Negro population at the beginning of a decade to a significant number of Negroes at the end of a decade makes them of special interest. These "Invasion tracts" include not only Invasion tracts as defined in Chapter 5, but also those few tracts in which Negro entry during the decade was not accompanied by a departure of whites.[4]

The aggregate characteristics of whites and Negroes living in each of the three areas (Negro Areas excluding Invasion tracts, Invasion tracts, and the Rest of the City) in the initial and terminal years of the two decades are presented in Tables 51 to 58.[5] The four characteristics are (1) educational attainment, the percentage of the total population age 25 years or more completing one or more years of high school; (2) white-collar employment, the percentage of employed males engaged in white-collar occupations (professional, managerial, clerical, and sales occupations); (3) home-ownership, the percentage of dwelling units owner-occupied; and (4) room-crowding, the percentage of multiple-person households with more than one person per room.

These tables contain a mass of data, but our discussion can be brief. We consider first the white population, and compare the characteristics of whites living in each area—Negro Areas, Invasion tracts, and the Rest of the City. We then examine the characteristics of Negroes in the two areas of Negro residence—Negro Areas and Invasion tracts—and compare them with whites in these areas.

A common conception of the invasion process is that it involves movement by Negroes into the worst areas of the city:

> Obsolete and run-down areas inhabited by whites are the most susceptible candidates for the sequence of desertion, infiltration, and influx by nonwhites.[6]

However, the data for the six Northern and border cities indicate that, in the initial year of each decade, the average educational and

4. For the number of such tracts for each city, see figures in parentheses in Appendix B.

5. Although for each decade the universe of tracts designated as Negro Residential Areas includes all tracts with at least 250 non-whites in the terminal year, characteristics are not always available for all of these tracts because of a change in the cut-off point used by the Bureau of the Census in selecting tracts for which to publish data for non-whites. In 1940 and 1950, education, occupation, and room-crowding data were available for all tracts with 250 or more non-whites. In 1960, education and occupation statistics are available for all tracts with 400 or more non-whites, while room-crowding figures are available for all tracts with 100 or more non-white housing units. In all three census years, home-ownership data by color are available for all tracts regardless of the number of non-white residents. These changes in census procedures are not of sufficient importance to alter the results obtained.

6. Charles Abrams, *Forbidden Neighbors: A Study of Prejudice in Housing* (New York: Harper and Brothers, 1955), p. 276.

TABLE 51

PERCENTAGE COMPLETING ONE OR MORE YEARS OF HIGH
SCHOOL, BY COLOR AND PLACE OF RESIDENCE, 1940–50

City and Place of Residence	Whites			Negroes		
	1940	1950	Change	1940	1950	Change
Detroit						
Negro Areas	34.0	45.5	11.5	29.4	41.9	12.5
Invasion Tracts	41.0	51.1	10.1	......	48.1	......
Rest of City	50.0	61.3	11.3	......	......	......
Cleveland						
Negro Areas	40.8	55.5	14.7	30.0	43.5	13.5
Invasion Tracts	45.3	55.1	9.8	......	60.3	......
Rest of City	38.4	53.8	15.4	......	......	......
Philadelphia						
Negro Areas	33.7	48.9	15.2	20.2	37.4	17.2
Invasion Tracts	37.3	53.0	15.7	......	42.7	......
Rest of City	36.2	53.1	16.9	......	......	......
St. Louis						
Negro Areas	24.1	35.8	11.7	23.4	30.3	6.9
Invasion Tracts	33.1	45.8	12.7	......	50.7	......
Rest of City	32.5	43.7	11.2	......	......	......
Washington						
Negro Areas	60.2	72.8	12.6	32.0	47.4	15.4
Invasion Tracts	62.2	68.3	6.1	......	54.9	......
Rest of City	72.5	79.0	6.5	......	......	......
Baltimore						
Negro Areas	37.1	45.3	8.2	16.6	26.4	9.8
Invasion Tracts	29.0	38.2	9.2	......	42.4	......
Rest of City	37.3	49.5	12.2	......	......	......
New Orleans						
Negro Areas	36.2	50.0	13.8	12.3	20.4	8.1
Invasion Tracts°	45.9	58.3	12.4	......	22.9	......
Rest of City	45.5	56.5	11.0	......	......	......
Atlanta						
Negro Areas	39.4	46.1	6.7	18.3	29.2	10.9
Invasion Tracts°	47.7	69.0	21.3	......	12.5	......
Rest of City	68.9	73.4	4.5	......	......	......
Birmingham						
Negro Areas	59.3	66.6	7.3	16.6	26.0	9.4
Invasion Tracts	......	......	......	......	......	......
Rest of City	64.4	72.1	7.7	......	......	......
Memphis						
Negro Areas	59.5	66.6	7.1	15.6	22.8	7.2
Invasion Tracts°	42.1	91.8	49.7	......	33.0	......
Rest of City	69.7	78.4	8.7	......	......	......

° Based on fewer than 5 census tracts.

occupational level of the white population in Invasion tracts was
usually higher than that of the white population in Negro Areas and
often higher than that in the all-white Rest of the City. Negro invasion, then, was not limited to deteriorated areas, but occurred in

TABLE 52

PERCENTAGE COMPLETING ONE OR MORE YEARS OF HIGH
SCHOOL, BY COLOR AND PLACE OF RESIDENCE, 1950–60

City and Place of Residence	Whites			Negroes		
	1950	1960	Change	1950	1960	Change
Detroit						
Negro Areas	49.7	44.4	−5.3	43.6	49.0	5.4
Invasion Tracts	58.3	51.4	−6.9	......	61.4	......
Rest of City	61.7	63.0	1.3	......	......	......
Cleveland						
Negro Areas	55.5	52.9	−2.6	45.7	52.8	7.1
Invasion Tracts	56.9	53.6	−3.3	......	63.8	......
Rest of City	53.1	55.8	2.7	......	......	......
Philadelphia						
Negro Areas	50.2	50.2	0.0	37.6	48.8	11.2
Invasion Tracts	54.4	55.3	0.9	......	65.9	......
Rest of City	52.1	57.7	5.6	......	......	......
St. Louis						
Negro Areas	40.3	42.8	2.5	32.3	40.6	8.3
Invasion Tracts	46.4	40.2	−6.2	......	55.8	......
Rest of City	42.6	46.1	3.5	......	......	......
Washington						
Negro Areas	72.5	72.7	0.2	47.9	54.2	6.3
Invasion Tracts	76.3	75.3	−1.0	......	74.2	......
Rest of City	78.2	81.0	2.8	......	......	......
Baltimore						
Negro Areas	41.4	45.6	4.2	27.9	36.3	8.4
Invasion Tracts	53.4	54.3	0.9	......	54.4	......
Rest of City	48.4	52.8	4.4	......	......	......
New Orleans						
Negro Areas	48.7	53.6	4.9	20.4	31.2	10.8
Invasion Tracts°	36.9	54.4	17.5	......	58.5	......
Rest of City	59.7	64.7	5.0	......	......	......
Atlanta						
Negro Areas	48.8	49.9	1.1	29.2	38.8	9.6
Invasion Tracts°	71.8	68.4	−3.4	......	37.5	......
Rest of City	71.5	69.0	−2.5	......	......	......
Birmingham						
Negro Areas	62.7	64.7	2.0	25.8	37.0	11.2
Invasion Tracts	......	......	......	......	......	......
Rest of City	73.3	74.0	0.7	......	......	......
Memphis						
Negro Areas	65.7	64.1	−1.6	22.7	32.6	9.9
Invasion Tracts	......	......	......	......	......	......
Rest of City	76.4	75.5	−0.9	......	......	......

° Based on fewer than 5 census tracts.

some of the better white areas. However, levels of owner-occupancy
were lower, and levels of room-crowding were higher among whites
in Invasion tracts than in the Rest of the City. Improvement in the
four socioeconomic characteristics during each decade was usually

TABLE 53

PERCENTAGE OF EMPLOYED MALES ENGAGED IN WHITE-COLLAR
OCCUPATIONS, BY COLOR AND PLACE OF RESIDENCE, 1940–50

City and Place of Residence	Whites			Negroes		
	1940	1950	Change	1940	1950	Change
Detroit						
Negro Areas	23.2†	23.3	0.1†	10.2†	10.4	0.2†
Invasion Tracts	30.9	31.3	0.4	......	10.8	......
Rest of City	35.4	38.4	3.0	......	......	......
Cleveland						
Negro Areas	37.8†	35.0	−2.8†	13.6†	12.0	−1.6†
Invasion Tracts	38.6	32.4	−6.2	......	21.1	......
Rest of City	29.5	30.8	1.3	......	......	......
Philadelphia						
Negro Areas	38.3†	37.2	−1.1†	12.6†	15.0	2.4†
Invasion Tracts	39.9	40.5	0.6	......	13.2	......
Rest of City	38.7	40.9	2.2	......	......	......
St. Louis						
Negro Areas	32.7†	28.8	−3.9†	11.3†	13.4	2.1†
Invasion Tracts	42.0	38.8	−3.2	......	23.6	......
Rest of City	41.6	41.4	−0.2	......	......	......
Washington						
Negro Areas	50.4	54.5	4.1	14.6	23.2	8.6
Invasion Tracts	56.4	55.3	−1.1	......	27.5	......
Rest of City	70.7	71.1	0.4	......	......	......
Baltimore						
Negro Areas	41.7	38.8	−2.9	9.1	11.6	2.5
Invasion Tracts	34.9	34.6	−0.3	......	17.2	......
Rest of City	41.8	45.0	3.2	......	......	......
New Orleans						
Negro Areas	46.2	49.2	3.0	9.4	11.6	2.2
Invasion Tracts°	57.3	57.5	0.2	......	7.6	......
Rest of City	54.6	57.8	3.2	......	......	......
Atlanta						
Negro Areas	40.8	36.7	−4.1	8.8	11.3	2.5
Invasion Tracts°	44.6	55.6	11.0	......	4.3	......
Rest of City	62.5	62.8	0.3	......	......	......
Birmingham						
Negro Areas	48.6	47.1	−1.5	6.0	7.8	1.8
Invasion Tracts	......	......	......	......	......	......
Rest of City	50.2	51.8	1.6	......	......	......
Memphis						
Negro Areas	50.2	47.0	−3.2	7.6	9.2	1.6
Invasion Tracts°	32.0	74.3	42.3	......	9.4	......
Rest of City	59.6	60.0	0.4	......	......	......

° Based on fewer than 5 census tracts.

† These figures are estimates, since data on occupation by color for census tracts were not
published for Northern cities in 1940. Estimate was made by assuming all Negroes lived in Negro
Areas. The number of non-white males in white-collar occupations in the city as a whole was subtracted from the total number of males in white-collar occupations in tracts classified as Negro
Areas. The figure for whites, then, is a residual, while the figure for Negroes is the city total for
non-whites.

TABLE 54

PERCENTAGE OF EMPLOYED MALES ENGAGED IN WHITE-COLLAR
OCCUPATIONS, BY COLOR AND PLACE OF RESIDENCE, 1950–60

City and Place of Residence	Whites			Negroes		
	1950	1960	Change	1950	1960	Change
Detroit						
Negro Areas	29.2	26.5	− 2.7	10.6	13.4	2.8
Invasion Tracts	37.9	34.0	− 3.9	......	19.3	......
Rest of City	38.1	41.9	3.8	......	......	......
Cleveland						
Negro Areas	33.7	32.1	− 1.6	13.2	14.9	1.7
Invasion Tracts	35.4	30.9	− 4.5	......	19.1	......
Rest of City	29.7	29.5	− 0.2	......	......	......
Philadelphia						
Negro Areas	38.6	39.2	0.6	15.1	18.3	3.2
Invasion Tracts	45.7	43.3	− 2.4	......	27.3	......
Rest of City	39.1	43.2	4.1	......	......	......
St. Louis						
Negro Areas	33.5	35.5	2.0	14.6	17.0	2.4
Invasion Tracts	41.6	30.1	− 11.5	......	20.2	......
Rest of City	40.6	38.4	− 2.2	......	......	......
Washington						
Negro Areas	54.5	58.9	4.4	23.6	26.4	2.8
Invasion Tracts	65.8	63.5	− 2.3	......	46.2	......
Rest of City	72.1	79.8	7.7	......	......	......
Baltimore						
Negro Areas	36.7	38.3	1.6	12.2	14.6	2.4
Invasion Tracts	51.9	55.1	3.2	......	20.3	......
Rest of City	42.2	45.3	3.1	......	......	......
New Orleans						
Negro Areas	47.6	49.0	1.4	11.6	12.7	1.1
Invasion Tracts°	33.2	49.3	16.1	......	36.3	......
Rest of City	61.7	62.1	0.4	......	......	......
Atlanta						
Negro Areas	39.3	37.7	− 1.6	11.3	11.4	0.1
Invasion Tracts°	60.5	54.0	− 6.5	......	8.2	......
Rest of City	60.7	56.3	− 4.4	......	......	......
Birmingham						
Negro Areas	41.1	41.7	0.6	7.8	9.9	2.1
Invasion Tracts	......	......	......	......	......	......
Rest of City	55.7	55.3	− 0.4	......	......	......
Memphis						
Negro Areas	45.2	46.8	1.6	9.2	10.3	1.1
Invasion Tracts	......	......	......	......	......	......
Rest of City	57.3	54.0	− 3.3	......	......	......

° Based on fewer than 5 census tracts.

less for whites residing in Invasion tracts than for whites residing in
the Rest of the City. As a result of these changes, whites in the Rest
of the City were more likely to rank highest on each of the status measures at the end of each decade than at the beginning. These changes

TABLE 55

PERCENTAGE OF HOUSING UNITS OWNER-OCCUPIED, BY COLOR
AND PLACE OF RESIDENCE, 1940–50

City and Place of Residence	Whites			Negroes		
	1940	1950	Change	1940	1950	Change
Detroit						
Negro Areas	35.8	43.2	7.4	13.9	30.2	16.3
Invasion Tracts	28.4	35.4	7.0	......	46.7	......
Rest of City	46.4	62.6	16.2	......	......	......
Cleveland						
Negro Areas	27.5	31.8	4.3	10.0	22.6	12.6
Invasion Tracts	22.4	26.9	4.5	......	47.9	......
Rest of City	38.6	48.8	10.2	......	......	......
Philadelphia						
Negro Areas	34.6	47.4	12.8	10.0	29.3	19.3
Invasion Tracts	31.7	44.6	12.9	......	19.7	......
Rest of City	49.1	69.9	20.8	......	......	......
St. Louis						
Negro Areas	16.1	20.1	4.0	6.8	16.2	9.4
Invasion Tracts	23.7	29.5	5.8	......	39.0	......
Rest of City	32.4	40.9	8.5	......	......	......
Washington						
Negro Areas	23.2	20.5	−2.7	19.4	30.0	10.6
Invasion Tracts	35.0	35.0	0.0	......	50.7	......
Rest of City	48.6	50.0	1.4	......	......	......
Baltimore						
Negro Areas	33.5	40.2	6.7	8.1	21.0	12.9
Invasion Tracts	45.8	57.1	11.3	......	47.8	......
Rest of City	53.3	64.1	10.8	......	......	......
New Orleans						
Negro Areas	27.5	37.4	9.9	10.8	21.7	10.9
Invasion Tracts°	3.3	9.2	5.9	......	0.0	......
Rest of City	31.8	40.9	9.1	......	......	......
Atlanta						
Negro Areas	22.4	37.5	15.1	13.0	24.7	11.7
Invasion Tracts°	45.8	74.1	28.3	......	34.5	......
Rest of City	35.2	50.0	14.8	......	......	......
Birmingham						
Negro Areas	37.0	52.2	15.2	15.0	30.0	15.0
Invasion Tracts	......	......	......	......	......	......
Rest of City	46.4	59.5	13.1	......	......	......
Memphis						
Negro areas	30.5	40.6	10.1	20.4	32.1	11.7
Invasion Tracts°	40.6	53.7	13.1	......	12.3	......
Rest of City	51.7	69.0	17.3	......	......	......

° Based on fewer than 5 census tracts.

are consistent with the assumption that the movement to the suburbs
included disproportionate numbers of high-status whites from Invasion tracts and Negro Areas, as compared to the all-white areas of
the city.

TABLE 56

PERCENTAGE OF HOUSING UNITS OWNER-OCCUPIED, BY COLOR
AND PLACE OF RESIDENCE, 1950–60

City and Place of Residence	Whites			Negroes		
	1950	1960	Change	1950	1960	Change
Detroit						
Negro Areas	38.2	42.3	4.1	34.3	36.8	2.5
Invasion Tracts	37.9	37.1	−0.8	......	45.3	......
Rest of City	70.6	73.2	2.6	......	......	......
Cleveland						
Negro Areas	29.1	31.4	2.3	25.5	27.2	1.7
Invasion Tracts	37.9	38.8	0.9	......	36.9	......
Rest of City	51.0	53.7	2.7	......	......	......
Philadelphia						
Negro Areas	47.0	49.0	2.0	29.1	40.7	11.6
Invasion Tracts	61.3	62.0	0.7	......	71.5	......
Rest of City	71.0	75.4	4.4	......	......	......
St. Louis						
Negro Areas	22.5	18.6	−3.9	18.2	23.0	4.8
Invasion Tracts	31.0	28.1	−2.9	......	37.6	......
Rest of City	42.8	46.3	3.5	......	......	......
Washington						
Negro Areas	21.9	16.0	−5.9	30.6	27.3	−3.3
Invasion Tracts	50.8	38.6	−12.2	......	72.5	......
Rest of City	45.2	41.0	−4.2	......	......	......
Baltimore						
Negro Areas	44.5	42.6	−1.9	23.8	25.5	1.7
Invasion Tracts	64.2	63.9	−0.3	......	58.5	......
Rest of City	62.2	66.8	4.6	......	......	......
New Orleans						
Negro Areas	35.6	39.5	3.9	21.7	24.6	2.9
Invasion Tracts	25.9	42.1	16.2	......	65.5	......
Rest of City	44.4	48.7	4.3	......	......	......
Atlanta						
Negro Areas	40.5	41.4	0.9	24.9	23.7	−1.2
Invasion Tracts°	42.6	34.1	−8.5	......	27.1	......
Rest of City	50.1	45.9	−4.2	......	......	......
Birmingham						
Negro Areas	54.5	60.9	6.4	31.8	36.4	4.6
Invasion Tracts	......	......	......	......	......	......
Rest of City	55.6	60.3	4.7	......	......	......
Memphis						
Negro areas	42.5	41.7	−0.8	33.3	35.3	2.0
Invasion Tracts	......	......	......	......	......	......
Rest of City	66.3	69.8	3.5	......	......	......

° Based on fewer than 5 census tracts.

In the four Southern cities, where Invasion tracts were uncommon, the white population living in Negro areas was lower in educational and occupational status, less likely to be home-owners, and more likely to be crowded, than whites living outside these areas.

TABLE 57

PERCENTAGE OF MULTIPLE-PERSON HOUSEHOLDS WITH 1.01 OR
MORE PERSONS PER ROOM, BY COLOR AND PLACE OF RESIDENCE,
1940–50

City and Place of Residence	Whites			Negroes		
	1940	1950	Change	1940	1950	Change
Detroit						
Negro Areas	19.1	13.8	−5.3	27.1	26.2	−0.9
Invasion Tracts	15.9	11.5	−4.4	......	23.4	......
Rest of City	11.8	8.1	−3.7	......	......	......
Cleveland						
Negro Areas	14.2	10.8	−3.4	23.5	25.3	1.8
Invasion Tracts	13.8	11.1	−2.7	......	16.3	......
Rest of City	11.5	8.2	−3.3	......	......	......
Philadelphia						
Negro Areas	14.1	11.8	−2.3	24.9	25.1	0.2
Invasion Tracts	12.3	10.5	−1.8	......	30.9	......
Rest of City	9.3	6.2	−3.1	......	......	......
St. Louis						
Negro Areas	36.5	35.7	−0.8	40.6	42.2	1.6
Invasion Tracts	23.9	23.3	−0.6	......	27.7	......
Rest of City	20.4	18.8	−1.6	......	......	......
Washington						
Negro Areas	22.7	14.8	−7.9	40.8	30.9	−9.9
Invasion Tracts	17.3	9.9	−7.4	......	25.0	......
Rest of City	7.5	5.2	−2.3	......	......	......
Baltimore						
Negro Areas	14.4	15.0	0.6	24.7	27.8	3.1
Invasion Tracts	13.8	13.3	−0.5	......	26.3	......
Rest of City	11.1	7.9	−3.2	......	......	......
New Orleans						
Negro Areas	25.9	19.2	−6.7	48.1	44.6	−3.5
Invasion Tracts°	62.9	18.3	−44.6	......	72.9	......
Rest of City	19.1	13.5	−5.6	......	......	......
Atlanta						
Negro Areas	36.9	28.0	−8.9	51.1	42.4	−8.7
Invasion Tracts°	19.6	10.1	−9.5	......	53.7	......
Rest of City	15.9	9.9	−6.0	......	......	......
Birmingham						
Negro Areas	20.7	13.0	−7.7	46.6	43.2	−3.4
Invasion Tracts	......	......	......	......	......	......
Rest of City	13.6	8.7	−4.9	......	......	......
Memphis						
Negro Areas	27.7	22.2	−5.5	47.3	44.1	−3.2
Invasion Tracts°	40.0	5.0	−35.0	......	35.1	......
Rest of City	14.0	8.8	−5.2	......	......	......

° Based on fewer than 5 census tracts.

Changes in status during each decade were unsystematic and insufficient to alter the large differences between whites living in
Negro Areas and those living in all-white areas.

Turning to the characteristics of Negroes living in Invasion

TABLE 58

PERCENTAGE OF MULTIPLE-PERSON HOUSEHOLDS WITH 1.01 OR
MORE PERSONS PER ROOM, BY COLOR AND PLACE OF RESIDENCE,
1950—60

City and Place of Residence	Whites			Negroes		
	1950	1960	Change	1950	1960	Change
Detroit						
Negro Areas	11.8	10.7	−1.1	25.4	19.8	−5.6
Invasion Tracts	9.1	9.2	0.1	......	17.4	......
Rest of City	8.2	6.7	−1.5	......	......	......
Cleveland						
Negro Areas	10.9	10.8	−0.1	24.2	23.5	−0.7
Invasion Tracts	7.7	9.4	1.7	......	19.1	......
Rest of City	8.4	8.5	0.1	......	......	......
Philadelphia						
Negro Areas	11.5	8.2	−3.3	25.1	20.1	−5.0
Invasion Tracts	7.2	6.3	−0.9	......	11.5	......
Rest of City	6.5	4.7	−1.8	......	......	......
St. Louis						
Negro Areas	31.6	27.1	−4.5	40.9	36.7	−4.2
Invasion Tracts	20.9	23.0	2.1	......	29.0	......
Rest of City	18.8	14.7	−4.1	......	......	......
Washington						
Negro Areas	14.2	12.0	−2.2	30.6	28.4	−2.2
Invasion Tracts	6.0	5.4	−0.6	......	12.0	......
Rest of City	6.8	2.7	−4.1	......	......	......
Baltimore						
Negro Areas	14.7	12.3	−2.4	27.5	26.7	−0.8
Invasion Tracts	6.0	5.5	−0.5	......	18.6	......
Rest of City	9.1	6.6	−2.5	......	......	......
New Orleans						
Negro Areas	19.8	15.2	−4.6	44.6	42.0	−2.6
Invasion Tracts°	28.1	17.9	−10.2	......	34.8	......
Rest of City	11.7	8.9	−2.8	......	......	......
Atlanta						
Negro Areas	26.7	22.6	−4.1	42.4	39.1	−3.3
Invasion Tracts°	10.9	9.8	−1.1	......	32.3	......
Rest of City	10.9	9.1	−1.8	......	......	......
Birmingham						
Negro Areas	14.8	9.7	−5.1	43.1	39.3	−3.8
Invasion Tracts	......	......	......	......	......	......
Rest of City	9.5	7.0	−2.5	......	......	......
Memphis						
Negro areas	22.6	12.3	−10.3	44.2	41.8	−2.4
Invasion Tracts	......	......	......	......	......	......
Rest of City	11.2	7.5	−3.7	......	......	......

° Based on fewer than 5 census tracts.

tracts and Negro Areas in the six Northern and border cities, two
general observations may be made: (1) Negroes in Invasion tracts
are of higher educational and occupational status, are more likely to
be home-owners, and less likely to be crowded than Negroes in Negro

Areas. Movement of Negroes into previously all-white areas is clearly led by high-status Negroes. (2) Negroes in Invasion tracts are often of higher educational status and more likely to be home-owners than whites in these tracts, both before and after invasion. Not only are high-status Negroes the first to enter all-white neighborhoods, but owner-occupancy is apparently a major avenue of entry into the new neighborhood. That incoming Negroes are not of higher occupational status than the white population they displace reflects the fact that Negro occupational levels are not consistent with their levels of educational attainment, in large part because of job discrimination. Negroes display higher levels of room-crowding, but this is affected by age of the family head and stage in the family life-cycle; without more detailed data, it cannot be ascertained just how much "overcrowding" exists, or what form it takes. The aggregate findings on the higher levels of educational attainment and home-ownership of Negroes compared with whites are not the result of a few deviant situations, but occur in the majority of Invasion tracts. These results are in agreement with a recent case study which has shown for Chicago that of all white areas peripheral to Negro areas, Negroes tended to enter the best areas.[7] These findings support an obviously plausible supposition that high-status persons of whatever color tend to seek out the best available areas of residence.

The previous findings on the acceleration in the pace of suburbanization during the 1950's as compared to the 1940's, the tight housing market of the war decade as compared to the relatively loose housing market of the 1950's, and the selectivity of the movement of population to suburbs, and the above findings on the tendency for high-status Negroes to enter the better white residential areas, all fit into a generalized Burgess model of urban growth. White out-movement from Invasion tracts (and other Negro Areas) has been disproportionately selective of high-status whites seeking better residential locations. This out-movement leaves behind vacancies which are filled, in part, by Negroes whose demand for adequate housing has never been fully met. This general pattern prevailed during both decades, but was much more pronounced during the freer housing market situation of the 1950's.

What happens in the white community apparently creates the context or sets the conditions within which the Negro community can change, given the prevailing patterns of segregation. During the tight housing market conditions of the war decade, the Negro com-

7. This unpublished study is based on data only for 1950–60. See also E. F. Schietinger, "Real Estate Transfers During Negro Invasion" (unpublished Master's thesis, University of Chicago, 1948), pp. 18 and 92.

munity was particularly impacted residentially. During the 1950's, however, in response to the increased rate of suburbanization among whites and the rising vacancy rates in the cities, there was (in Northern cities) a greatly increased spatial expansion of Negro residential areas (see Tables 25 and 26).

A general implication of the preceding discussion is that it is virtually impossible to isolate specific concomitants of racial succession, because expansion of Negro residential areas appears to be an integral part of the normal processes of urban growth. Neighborhoods in large cities tend to be broadly differentiated according to distance from the city center, with high-status areas located at greater distances than low-status areas, and there is a familiar pattern of gradients evident in a variety of social and economic characteristics according to distance from the center. Negro areas have generally originated near the center of cities and expanded outward from these initial locations, encroaching upon the higher-status white areas towards the periphery of the city. Any distinctively racial aspects of these processes are exceedingly difficult to isolate.

Examination of the maps in Appendix D can facilitate this discussion. Negro areas in a number of cities now extend to the city limits, and it is thus not surprising that Negroes are displacing high-status whites. Furthermore, it appears that the classification of tracts by type of racial change roughly corresponds to a classification by distance from the city center. Growing tracts tend to be distant from the center, have more new residential building, and contain higher-status population. Declining tracts and Established Negro Areas, by contrast, are more centrally located and contain lower-status population. In many ways, then, the movement of Negro population out of the poorer areas into better areas is not only facilitated by the tremendous suburbanization of white population, but is analogous to this out-movement of whites. Even the existence of Displacement tracts is less anomalous when their location is considered. Where they occur, they tend to be distant from the city center in areas still desirable to white population. The new pattern of Displacement by centrally located urban renewal projects may alter this pattern, but is not yet much in evidence.

Decentralization, then, characterizes both Negro and white populations. What are observed to be the results of racial transition may well be consequences of broader changes in the national economy and of nearly universal patterns of differentiation and change in cities and metropolitan areas. In the following paragraphs, we examine the impact of these changes on (1) the degree of congestion of the Negro population; and (2) the over-all characteristics of areas containing Negroes. Again attention is focused on Northern cities since they have experienced the greatest growth of Negro population and the greatest change in Negro residential areas.

□ PILING-UP

One of the major findings of the Chicago study was the increased congestion of the Negro population at each stage of succession. Increases in population occurred without corresponding increases in the amount of housing space. "Excess" Negro population was housed in converted dwelling units or crowded into existing units.

In the 1940–50 decade, the situation observed in Chicago was duplicated in a somewhat less extreme form in the Northern and border cities being analyzed here. Despite out-movement of white population from Negro areas in these cities, the increase in Negro population greatly exceeded the loss in white population. Construction of new dwellings was negligible in these cities during the war decade (Table 59). Conversions added to the number of rooms, and levels of room-crowding of the Negro population changed little during the 1940's. As noted in Chapter 5, Southern cities had a different pattern of population changes. Pressure of population on the housing supply in Southern cities during the 1940's was much less and new construction was more common. Consequently, the levels of room-crowding among Negroes frequently decreased.

The situation changed markedly in both North and South when tight housing market conditions relaxed during the 1950's. The net loss of white population in Negro Residential Areas (including Invasion tracts) greatly exceeded the gain in Negro population in most of the ten cities, and there was considerably more new residential construction, resulting in general declines in levels of room-crowding among Negroes.

In Northern and border cities these changes in Negro room-crowding were typical of a majority of the census tracts in which Negroes resided (Table 60). In Southern cities the share of tracts increasing in levels of room-crowding was not systematically different in 1950–60 than in 1940–50.

As a result of these changes, during the 1940's the levels of room-crowding in Northern and Southern cities tended to converge. The Southern cities, which initially had the highest levels of crowding, experienced the greatest improvement during the 1940's. During the 1950's, however, this situation was reversed as housing conditions improved generally. Northern cities with their initially lower levels of Negro room-crowding made the greatest improvement during this

TABLE 59

NET POPULATION CHANGE, NEW CONSTRUCTION, AND LEVELS OF
ROOM-CROWDING BY COLOR: NEGRO RESIDENTIAL AREAS,
1940–50 AND 1950–60 °

City and Color	Net Change in Population (in 000's)		New Construction† (in 000's of units)		Percentage Room-crowding		
	1940–50	1950–60	1940–50	1950–60	1940	Change, 1940–50	Change, 1950–60
Detroit							
White	− 137.3	− 363.1	1.8	2.0	13.4	− 4.4	− 1.7
Negro	148.5	189.9	4.0	6.5	26.8	− 1.2	− 6.4
Cleveland							
White	− 44.1	− 127.8	0.8	2.0	12.0	− 3.3	0.0
Negro	62.5	102.8	2.0	3.3	23.3	1.0	− 1.7
Philadelphia							
White	− 83.4	− 306.4	3.7	4.9	11.1	− 3.0	− 2.6
Negro	125.5	159.1	2.6	4.6	24.9	0.4	− 5.9
St. Louis							
White	− 25.2	− 128.6	0.3	2.3	22.7	− 1.7	− 4.7
Negro	45.1	62.4	1.2	4.0	40.1	0.9	− 6.3
Washington							
White	3.3	− 171.2	15.7	15.9	16.6	− 6.1	− 3.1
Negro	94.7	137.9	18.4	15.1	40.6	−10.0	− 4.4
Baltimore							
White	− 29.6	− 154.9	3.1	4.3	12.1	− 2.4	− 2.5
Negro	57.6	104.8	6.0	4.7	24.6	3.0	− 3.3
New Orleans							
White	31.2	− 6.1	13.7	15.5	22.7	− 6.1	− 4.2
Negro	33.1	52.2	9.7	11.4	47.9	− 3.4	− 2.8
Atlanta‡							
White	− 3.2	− 30.1	0.0	2.0	22.1	− 7.1	− 1.9
Negro	18.4	26.5	6.2	7.1	51.4	− 8.9	− 3.4
Birmingham‡							
White	8.9	− 17.3	6.4	9.1	18.5	− 6.9	− 4.0
Negro	10.7	4.9	4.0	5.9	46.6	− 3.5	− 3.7
Memphis‡							
White	13.1	− 31.8	4.2	5.7	22.5	− 6.6	− 7.3
Negro	17.7	38.1	6.9	10.3	47.4	− 3.2	− 2.7

° Negro Residential Areas are defined as all census tracts which contained 250 or more non-whites in the terminal year of the decade.

† Number of new dwelling units by color for 1940–50 was estimated using the total number of new units given in the 1950 Census Tract Bulletin and the number of units built 1940–50 by color presented in the 1960 Census Tract Bulletin.

‡ Adjusted for annexations to central city in each decade.

decade, thus increasing once again the differences between Northern and Southern cities.

Negroes, of course, do not have access to all vacancies opening up within a city. But even though they are confined to existing Negro

TABLE 60

PERCENTAGE OF CENSUS TRACTS IN WHICH NEGRO LEVELS OF
ROOM-CROWDING INCREASED, 1940–50 AND 1950–60

City	Percentage of Tracts Increasing in Room-crowding		Number of Census Tracts	
	1940–50	1950–60	1940–50	1950–60
Detroit......................	47.8	29.3	69	116
Cleveland.................	78.4	53.2	37	47
Philadelphia	52.9	20.7	104	82
St. Louis...................	68.0	33.3	25	27
Washington...............	14.8	38.1	61	63
Baltimore	66.7	41.8	51	55
New Orleans.............	32.9	27.3	85	77
Atlanta	10.5	24.2	38	33
Birmingham..............	24.4	22.0	41	41
Memphis..................	28.8	33.3	52	51

° Based on all census tracts for which data for non-whites were available in both initial and terminal years of a decade. Invasion tracts are omitted by this procedure since they had insufficient numbers of non-whites at the beginning of a decade.

areas and their immediate vicinity, the degree of congestion and crowding in these areas seems clearly to be in large part a function of the general housing market situation. If a tight housing market exists, then few vacancies even in areas near Negro residential areas will be made available to Negroes, while a loose housing market brought about by prosperity and accompanied by substantial new construction in the suburbs will presage improvement in housing opportunities for Negroes.

An analogous situation existed during and after World War I. Drake and Cayton describe the transition in Chicago from a small prewar Negro population concentrated in the service occupations to a sizable Negro population making up a significant share of the wartime industrial labor force. With the cessation of residential construction at the beginning of the war, doubling up of families, overcrowding of existing dwellings, and increases in rent were inevitable. But then, in what the authors of *Black Metropolis* call the "Fat Years" of the 1920's, suburban growth accelerated after a wartime lull, and the city was left to the poor, the Negroes, and the immigrants. The improvement in socioeconomic status of Negroes brought about by the war and postwar boom was halted and even reversed with the onset of the Depression.[8]

With the outbreak of World War II, the cycle was repeated. Mi-

8. St. Clair Drake and Horace R. Cayton, *Black Metropolis: A Study of Negro Life in a Northern City* (New York: Harcourt, Brace, and Co., 1945), Part I.

gration of Negroes to Northern industrial cities increased, but new residential construction ceased and the demand for housing became acute. As a result, congestion of both white and Negro population was a necessary concomitant of the succession process. During the post-war period and the 1950's, suburbanization resumed as it had in the 1920's, leaving more than enough vacancies behind to accommodate the expanding Negro population. The result again was a period of general improvement in housing conditions for both Negroes and whites.

What first appears to be a typical consequence of the succession process – an increase in crowded living conditions among Negroes – can thus be seen as a result of the general housing market situation and the pace of white suburbanization, which together largely determine whether or not housing opportunities will be ample to meet Negro housing demand.

□ SOCIOECONOMIC CHANGES

Since Negroes, in the aggregate, have been of lower status than the white population (though differences in educational attainment are now slight in Northern cities), it seems reasonable to expect that areas undergoing racial transition will decline in the general socioeconomic status of their population as the proportion Negro increases. The Chicago study found that this simple inference was not supported. Although some socioeconomic measures for the population of such areas tended to decline, others tended to increase. These increases could be explained by the nationwide rise in levels of living of both whites and Negroes. Educational status was perhaps the clearest example of the impact of these forces. Despite substantial increases in the proportion of Negroes in the population of many census tracts during the 1940–50 decade, the educational level of the total population increased in virtually every tract during this period.

> The general rise in educational level in the population as a whole was more than sufficient to counterbalance the presumably depressing effect of population turnover on the educational level of tracts undergoing succession.[9]

This was also true for levels of home-ownership (which rose) and levels of unemployment (which declined) in tracts undergoing succession.

On the other hand, declines in white-collar employment and

---

9 Duncan and Duncan, *The Negro Population of Chicago, op. cit.,* p. 241.

increases in room-crowding levels were also typical of these areas, reflecting in part the extremely large differences between the races in these characteristics. In conclusion, Duncan and Duncan observe:

> A review of the changes in population and housing character-
> istics occurring along with racial succession discloses no evidence
> that any given type of change is unique to a particular stage of suc-
> cession. Moreover, it demonstrates that changes which presumably
> would accompany succession in an otherwise static situation may
> not be evidenced because of the quantitatively greater effect of social
> and economic changes that are essentially independent of succes-
> sion. This finding has both theoretical and practical importance. It
> emphasizes the fact that for any study of, or social action with re-
> spect to, modifications of residential patterns to be realistic or effec-
> tive, it must take account of the dynamic social setting of these
> modifications.[10]

Examination of similar data for our ten cities for two decades underlines the importance of this statement. We have already shown that changes in room-crowding among the Negro population were largely a function of trends in white suburbanization and the loose-ness of the general housing market. Additional confirmation is given in Tables 61 and 62 which present, for our ten cities in both decades, the percentage of census tracts containing Negroes that increased in three measures of socioeconomic status — educational attainment, white-collar employment, and home-ownership. The data are pre-sented separately for whites and Negroes. In the overwhelming majority of tracts, both white and Negro population increased in socioeconomic status between 1940 and 1950, with usually well over three-fourths of the census tracts showing these increases. The chief exception is that tracts were about evenly divided as to increases and decreases in the level of white-collar employment among the white population.

The figures for the 1950–60 decade present a striking contrast to the picture for the 1940's. In most cities, sharp declines occurred for both races in the proportion of tracts (containing non-whites) that increased in socioeconomic status. To illustrate the difference between the two decades we may cite Detroit: between 1940 and 1950 there were increases in the educational level of the Negro residents in 95 per cent of tracts in which Negroes resided, but in 1950–60 this occurred for only 56 per cent of such areas. For whites, 96 per cent of the tracts showed gains in the educational level during the 1940's, while the figure dropped to 18 per cent for the 1950's. During both decades, the Negro and white populations as a whole in Detroit and the other cities increased on virtually all of these meas-

10. *Ibid.*, p. 243.

TABLE 61

PERCENTAGE OF CENSUS TRACTS WITH INDICATED CHANGES IN
CHARACTERISTICS OF NEGRO POPULATION, 1940–50 AND 1950–60 °

City	Educational Attainment		White-collar Employment		Home-ownership	
	1940–50	*1950–60*	*1940–50*	*1950–60*	*1940–50*	*1950–60*
	Percentage of Census Tracts Increasing in:					
Detroit	97.1	55.6	− †	57.3	95.7	27.9
Cleveland	97.3	64.6	− †	50.0	89.2	34.0
Philadelphia	98.1	92.7	− †	65.9	100.0	78.3
St. Louis	88.0	61.5	− †	50.0	96.0	40.7
Washington	96.7	66.1	93.4	45.2	82.0	20.3
Baltimore	98.0	87.5	80.4	60.7	98.0	16.9
New Orleans	96.5	97.1	82.4	55.7	94.1	60.3
Atlanta	92.1	94.1	71.1	38.2	94.7	33.3
Birmingham	97.6	95.0	87.8	72.5	97.6	68.3
Memphis	84.6	89.6	76.9	45.8	96.2	22.6
	Number of Census Tracts					
Detroit	69	117	− †	117	69	122
Cleveland	37	48	− †	48	37	50
Philadelphia	104	82	− †	82	104	83
St. Louis	25	26	− †	26	25	27
Washington	61	62	61	62	61	64
Baltimore	51	56	51	56	51	59
New Orleans	85	70	85	70	85	78
Atlanta	38	34	38	34	38	36
Birmingham	41	40	41	40	41	41
Memphis	52	48	52	48	52	53

° Based on all census tracts for which data for non-whites were available in both initial and terminal years of a decade. Invasion tracts are omitted by this procedure since they had insufficient numbers of non-whites at the beginning of a decade.

† Information not available. Census tract data on occupation separately for whites and non-whites were not published for Northern cities in 1940.

ures, but for both races the amount of improvement was less in 1950–60 than in 1940–50.

In attempting to account for the much smaller share of tracts showing increases in socioeconomic status of whites and Negroes during the 1950's as compared to the 1940's, we may consider the races separately. We have already discussed the more rapid suburbanization of whites during the 1950's, and have indicated that the out-migration of high-status whites from Negro areas was disproportionately heavy. Apparently this selective out-migration more than offset the over-all increases in status measures during the 1950's among whites in Negro Residential Areas.

As for the trends in status among Negroes, a crucial factor appears to be the relatively greater spatial expansion of Negro Residential

TABLE 62

PERCENTAGE OF CENSUS TRACTS WITH INDICATED CHANGES IN
CHARACTERISTICS OF WHITE POPULATION, 1940–50 AND 1950–60°

| City | Percentage of Census Tracts Increasing in: | | | | | |
| | Educational Attainment | | White-collar Employment | | Home-ownership | |
	1940–50	1950–60	1940–50	1950–60	1940–50	1950–60
Detroit	96.2	18.1	−†	48.6	79.2	69.3
Cleveland	97.6	33.3	−†	38.5	73.2	52.2
Philadelphia	97.3	39.0	−†	45.1	85.5	63.6
St. Louis	100.0	48.3	−†	27.6	80.8	51.6
Washington	96.7	32.7	51.7	38.5	28.3	30.9
Baltimore	90.6	40.8	32.1	36.7	67.9	27.8
New Orleans	96.1	73.8	76.6	40.0	88.3	37.0
Atlanta	86.2	33.3	41.4	16.7	93.1	5.0
Birmingham	94.1	66.7	55.9	56.7	91.2	74.2
Memphis	90.7	23.3	37.2	33.3	79.1	11.4
	Number of Census Tracts					
Detroit	106	138	−†	138	106	150
Cleveland	41	39	−†	39	41	46
Philadelphia	110	82	−†	82	110	88
St. Louis	26	29	−†	29	26	31
Washington	60	52	60	52	60	55
Baltimore	53	49	53	49	53	54
New Orleans	77	65	77	65	77	73
Atlanta	29	18	29	18	29	20
Birmingham	34	30	34	30	34	31
Memphis	43	30	43	30	43	35

° To insure reliability of data for the white population of census tracts containing Negroes, all tracts over 90 per cent non-white were omitted from the analysis. Invasion tracts are included.

† Information not available. Census tract data on occupation separately for whites and non-whites were not published for Northern cities in 1940.

Areas during the 1950's than during the 1940's. We have described the Negro community as being impacted during the war decade. All Negroes, migrants or not, high status or low, had to take whatever housing they could find within existing Negro areas. There was little expansion of those areas to augment the quantity and variety of housing available, despite great increases in Negro population. With the easing of the housing market in the 1950's, much additional housing became accessible, and it became increasingly possible for Negroes to relocate in accord with their income and their tastes. The normal processes of sifting and sorting of population in residential areas according to their socioeconomic characteristics resumed with great force during the 1950's. For whites, there was a large suburbanization of those who could afford new housing. For Negroes, there was a similar sharpening of the patterns of residential differentiation, but it involved racial succession and took place largely within the city limits. The results were similar to those already described for whites: selective out-migration of higher-status Negroes from many portions of the Negro Residential Areas more than offset the effects of over-all socioeconomic upgrading.

Our findings in this chapter concerning the manner in which racial succession proceeds are in substantial agreement with the results of a detailed case study of a single neighborhood undergoing succession in Detroit.[11] This study, based on interviews with a large sample of residents in the neighborhood, found that neither the degree of prejudice nor a stated intention to move was a reliable indicator of who actually moved during the course of invasion. Instead, actual movers were persons who possessed the resources to move: they were more likely to be renters, to have incomes over $10,000, and to be self-employed rather than wage or salary workers. Negroes moving into the neighborhood were of relatively high socioeconomic status. Whites moving into the neighborhood, as compared to the long-term residents, were younger, of lower income, more likely to be renters, and more likely to hold blue-collar occupations. Although the maintenance of residential segregation affects the location, quantity, and quality of housing available to Negroes, the behavior of whites and Negroes in the housing market appears to be very similar, within the limits set by discrimination. Whether the focus is on a neighborhood in Detroit, or any of a number of large cities, the prevailing processes of residential change appear to involve for both races a continual series of adjustments of housing to need and capacity to pay.

The foregoing analysis of concomitants of racial succession has indicated the virtual impossibility of separating neighborhood changes due to racial transition from changes wrought by "normal" processes of social and residential mobility. What happens to a neighborhood seems to depend less upon changes in its racial composition than upon how it fits into the general pattern of residential differentiation. Rather than remaining preoccupied with the task of isolating concomitants of racial succession, our focus shifts in the next chapter to a more direct concern with patterns of residential differentiation within the Negro community.

11. The study referred to is a five-year study of the Russel Woods area in Detroit, under the direction of Albert J. Mayer of Wayne State University.

8

□

RACE AND RESIDENTIAL DIFFERENTIATION

Socioeconomic status is an important basis for residential differentiation of urban populations. Central city slums and middle-class suburbs are commonplace examples of this type of differentiation, and careful research has documented that persons of high occupational status are residentially segregated from persons of lower occupational status, less likely to live in low-rent areas,[1] and less closely bound to their places of work.[2] In our discussion of the concomitants of racial succession, we concluded that changes in the characteristics of an area's housing and population result primarily from forces that produce areal differentiation in the metropolitan community as a whole, rather than from forces specific to the fact of racial change.

Race, however, is independently an important basis for residential differentiation. We have shown previously that racial segregation does not depend only on the lower economic status of Negroes, and that it is more pronounced than segregation along class or ethnic lines. Thus, we are faced with a complex set of relationships between racial differentiation and socioeconomic differentiation of urban areas. On one hand, racial differentiation appears to be influenced by socioeconomic differentiation, but on the other, socioeconomic factors alone are not sufficient to account for racial differentiation. In this chapter, we approach the task of sorting out these relationships further by means of a more detailed investigation of patterns of residential differentiation within Negro residential areas.

□ STABILITY OF AREA CHARACTERISTICS

In Northern and border cities, and in some areas of Southern

1. Otis Dudley Duncan and Beverly Duncan, "Residential Distribution and Occupational Stratification," *American Journal of Sociology*, LX, No. 5 (March, 1955).
2. Beverly Duncan and Otis Dudley Duncan, "The Measurement of Intra-City Locational and Residential Patterns," *Journal of Regional Science*, II, No. 2 (Fall, 1960);

cities, Negroes live in buildings and neighborhoods that were once occupied by whites. When these areas were white-occupied, they formed part of a general pattern of socioeconomic differentiation among residential areas. With residential succession from white to predominantly Negro occupancy, is the position of an area in this general pattern altered? Is the change in racial occupancy accompanied by other radical changes in socioeconomic characteristics of the area and its relationship to other areas? Or is the general residential character of the area the major determinant of the character of the occupying population? If the latter is true, Negroes might be expected to be distributed among the areas of a city in much the same manner as were the whites before them, so that, over time, a substantial degree of stability should be evident among areas undergoing racial change. Stability can be interpreted to mean that, in a "before-and-after" comparison, areas which rank high in the initial year on a variety of socioeconomic measures also rank high in a later year.

The pattern of residential use of a built-up area is largely predetermined by the age and type of structures, the accessibility to transportation and places of work, and the character of nonresidential land uses in the area. The physical character of the area and basic patterns of land use are little affected by racial turnover. A high degree of stability in housing patterns and socioeconomic characteristics might therefore be expected. In a "before-and-after" correlation analysis for Chicago, the Duncans found this to be the case. In areas undergoing racial succession during the decade, coefficients of correlation between tract characteristics in 1940 and 1950 were high. These high coefficients indicate, for the various housing and socioeconomic variables, that tracts tended to maintain their positions relative to other tracts undergoing racial change. The constants for the linear regression of 1950 on 1940 characteristics can be used to specify more precisely the nature of the relationship between tract characteristics at the beginning and end of the decade. The change in the mean value for a given characteristic for a given set of tracts indicates whether tracts tended to increase or decrease in average status during the decade. The slope of the regression line indicates whether change occurred more or less evenly in all tracts regardless of initial level ($b = 1.0$); whether increases in status were greater in tracts of initially low status ($b < 1.0$); or whether increases were smaller in tracts of initially low status ($b > 1.0$).

Regression analyses of this type were undertaken for nine of our en cities, comparing characteristics of census tracts in 1940 with the

and Beverly Duncan, "Factors in Work-Residence Separation: Wage and Salary Workers, Chicago, 1951," *American Sociological Review*, XXI, No. 1 (February, 1956).

same characteristics in 1960. (Philadelphia was omitted because changes in census tract boundaries made it difficult to effect a suitable degree of comparability over the 20-year period.) All census tracts with 250 or more non-whites in 1960 were used in the analysis, and four socioeconomic measures were included—measures of educational attainment, white-collar employment, home-ownership, and room-crowding (as defined in Chapter 7).

The regression technique is illustrated in Fig. 5, which presents the scattergram for educational attainment, 1940 and 1960, for Detroit census tracts with 250 or more non-whites in 1960. The educational status of these tracts tended to increase during the two decades despite large increases in percentage non-white (an average change of 47 percentage points). In 1940, the average (unweighted) percentage completing some high school was 39.7, while by 1960 it had reached 48.0. The regression equation is $\hat{Y} = 24.3 + .60X$, where

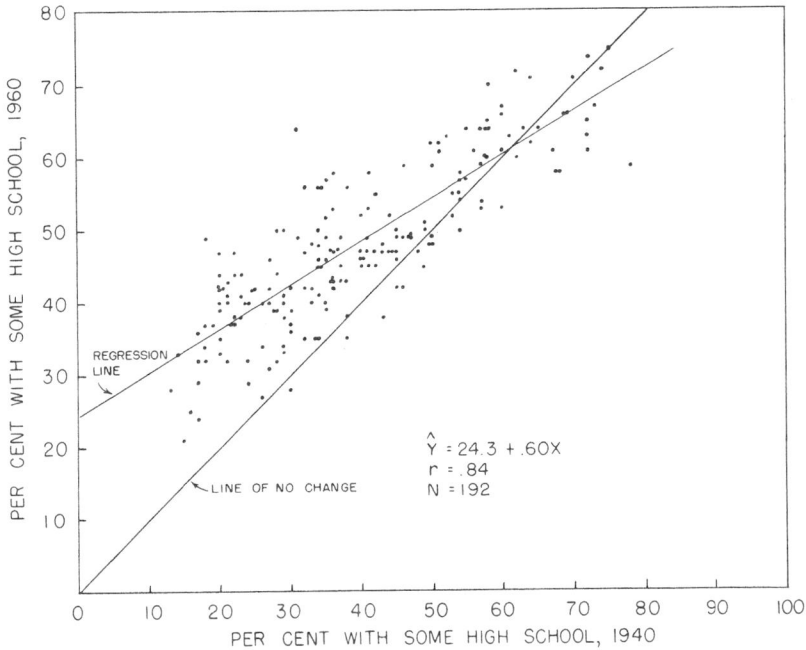

FIGURE 5.—*Detroit: Scattergram and Regression Line Showing Relationship of 1960 to 1940 Percentages of the Population Completing One or More Years of High School, for Census Tracts with 250 or More Nonwhites in 1960*

Y is the percentage of the tract population in 1960 completing some high school, and X is the corresponding percentage in 1940. The regression coefficient being less than unity indicates that improvement in educational status was greatest in tracts of initially low status. The high correlation coefficient (.84) indicates a strong tendency for tracts to maintain their rank in this group for educational status over this 20-year period. The results of the regression analyses for all four variables for the nine cities are summarized in Tables 63 and 64.

The degree of stability in areal characteristics might be expected to vary with the amount of racial change. In cities with substantial growth of Negro population, tracts that have undergone a complete replacement of white by Negro population are common; such tracts are rare in cities experiencing low rates of Negro population growth. The average change in percentage non-white in the census tracts included in the analysis is shown in the first column of each table. Between 1940 and 1960, three of the four Southern cities had an average increase of less than 10 percentage points in percentage non-white in these tracts, whereas the average increase in tracts in the five Northern and border cities was more than 32 percentage points. Thus the question of maintaining pre-existing patterns of residential differentiation despite changing racial composition is less meaningful for the Southern cities, and greater stability might be anticipated. In fact, however, the correlation coefficients for Northern and Southern cities are all high, and sizable regional differences in the degree of areal stability are not in evidence.

In most cities, the mean levels of educational attainment and home-ownership in these tracts increased between 1940 and 1960, while mean levels of room-crowding decreased. On each of these measures, Negroes measured lower than whites in both 1940 and 1960. Between 1940 and 1960, however, there was considerable upgrading of both races on these socioeconomic measures. Thus, it was possible for increases in tract levels to occur despite substantial increases in percentage non-white. In occupational levels, however, disparities between whites and Negroes were too great for a similar result. In the Northern and border cities with large increases in percentage non-white, declines in the mean levels of occupational status were the rule. In the Southern cities, changes in occupational levels were slight.

The high correlation coefficients indicate that areas undergoing racial change have maintained their relative positions on the four measures despite the sometimes large changes in average levels. The greatest stability is apparent for home-ownership. Correlation coefficients for the nine cities range from .89 to .98. Home-ownership

TABLE 63

SUMMARY OF 1940–60 REGRESSION ANALYSIS FOR EDUCATION AND OCCUPATION[a]

City and Measure	Average Change in Percentage Non-white, 1940–60	Mean, 1940	Mean, 1960	Regression Constants			Number of Tracts
				Intercept a	Slope b	Correlation r	
Educational Attainment							
Detroit	47.4	39.7	48.0	24.3	0.60	.84	192
Cleveland	42.8	38.5	52.5	31.1	0.56	.73	71
St. Louis	37.9	29.3	41.8	21.1	0.71	.85	41
Washington	32.4	53.5	60.9	26.8	0.64	.76	77
Baltimore	36.1	31.2	41.8	19.6	0.71	.91	83
New Orleans	6.8	27.3	43.2	22.5	0.76	.83	79
Atlanta	18.2	30.9	41.6	22.2	0.63	.84	38
Birmingham	4.1	32.9	46.8	21.9	0.76	.90	37
Memphis	8.0	32.7	41.9	17.2	0.76	.87	50
Occupational Status							
Detroit	47.4	27.3	20.0	7.7	0.45	.77	192
Cleveland	42.8	30.4	20.3	9.8	0.34	.50	71
St. Louis	37.9	33.4	23.1	4.5	0.56	.78	41
Washington	32.4	43.0	39.7	9.0	0.71	.74	77
Baltimore	36.1	35.2	25.1	3.8	0.61	.78	83
New Orleans	6.8	33.6	33.1	3.4	0.88	.89	79
Atlanta	18.2	25.4	18.4	2.7	0.62	.79	38
Birmingham	4.1	22.2	23.7	5.9	0.80	.89	37
Memphis	8.0	24.7	23.4	1.8	0.88	.88	50

[a] Correlations are based on all census tracts containing 250 or more non-whites in 1960. Philadelphia is omitted because of extensive changes in census tract boundaries between 1950 and 1960.

TABLE 64

SUMMARY OF 1940–60 REGRESSION ANALYSIS FOR HOME-OWNERSHIP AND ROOM-CROWDING [a]

City and Measure	Average Change in Percentage Non-white, 1940–60	Mean, 1940	Mean, 1960	Regression Constants		Correlation r	Number of Tracts
				Intercept a	Slope b		
Home-ownership							
Detroit	47.4	30.4	40.1	3.3	1.21	.97	192
Cleveland	42.8	24.6	31.0	1.7	1.19	.98	71
St. Louis	37.9	17.7	25.2	4.3	1.18	.94	41
Washington	32.4	29.0	27.9	0.9	0.93	.90	77
Baltimore	36.1	33.3	39.0	1.4	1.13	.90	83
New Orleans	6.8	22.5	29.5	5.2	1.08	.89	79
Atlanta	18.2	20.5	27.4	3.2	1.18	.92	38
Birmingham	4.1	26.6	42.8	6.0	1.38	.96	37
Memphis	8.0	29.5	33.3	5.6	0.94	.92	50
Room-crowding							
Detroit	47.4	17.2	16.1	6.6	0.55	.65	192
Cleveland	42.8	16.5	19.6	6.7	0.78	.70	71
St. Louis	37.9	30.3	31.4	10.7	0.68	.88	41
Washington	32.4	24.9	21.4	3.9	0.70	.84	77
Baltimore	36.1	15.5	19.7	5.3	0.92	.78	83
New Orleans	6.8	35.2	27.4	-1.6	0.82	.83	79
Atlanta	18.2	42.4	35.5	4.8	0.72	.78	38
Birmingham	4.1	36.8	27.6	-7.2	0.94	.90	37
Memphis	8.0	39.4	31.9	-0.9	0.83	.77	50

[a] Correlations are based on all census tracts containing 250 or more non-whites in 1960. Philadelphia is omitted because of extensive changes in census tract boundaries between 1950 and 1960.

levels depend upon the types of structures prevailing in an area, and on the average were not greatly altered by the structural conversions sometimes accompanying racial transition. These results confirm the conclusion of the Duncans that physical characteristics of areas affect Negroes and whites similarly.

For educational attainment, white-collar employment, and room-crowding, the regression slopes for each city are substantially below unity, demonstrating that tracts initially low on these three measures tended to experience the greatest increases (or the smallest decreases) in status during the 20-year period. This tendency was more pronounced in Northern and border than in Southern cities. For home-ownership, regression slopes were usually near or above unity, demonstrating some tendency for areal differentiation in home-ownership to increase during the 20 years.

To summarize, an analysis of changes over a 20-year period in socioeconomic characteristics of areas changing in racial composition has revealed a high degree of stability. Even substantial changes in racial composition do not greatly alter pre-existing patterns of residential differentiation. Two limitations on this mode of analysis may be noted. First, we obviously cannot say what might have happened to these areas in the absence of racial change. Although it seems likely that a high degree of stability would still have been maintained, the regression slopes and the direction and amount of change in means might have been quite different. Second, the analysis has been concerned only with those tracts that contained 250 or more non-white residents in 1960. No account has been taken of how these tracts changed relative to tracts in the rest of the city. Within this areal universe, patterns of differentiation have remained stable, but we cannot say from these data how areas experiencing racial change compare with areas remaining white-occupied throughout the 20-year period.

□ CLASS SEGREGATION
IN THE NEGRO COMMUNITY

That patterns of residential differentiation are little changed by the impact of racial change suggests the presence of class segregation within the Negro community. This contrasts with the views of many earlier writers, particularly when describing small communities. Powdermaker, for example, observed that

> Side by side live the respectable and the disreputable, the moderately well-to-do and the very poor, the pious and the unsaved, the

college graduates and the illiterates, the dusky blacks, the medium browns, the light creams, all thrown together because all are Negroes.[3]

Does residential segregation by race inhibit the development of segregation by socioeconomic status within Negro areas in large cities? To examine the extent of class segregation within the Negro community, we use indexes of dissimilarity in residential distribution among Negro males in eight major occupational groups. The index measures the extent to which one occupational group is residentially segregated from another. A low value between the residential distributions of any two occupational groups indicates little segregation, while a high value indicates a tendency for the two groups to live apart. This procedure produces 28 index values for each city for each census year, one for each occupational group against each other. The detailed results are presented in Appendix C.

The increased suburbanization among whites during the 1950's and the attendant loosening of the housing market led us to hypothesize an increase in class segregation in the Negro community between 1950 and 1960. Wartime housing shortages had impeded the normal sorting of persons into residential areas according to socioeconomic status, but this process resumed during the 1950's, permitting whites to move to the suburbs and allowing areas of Negro residence to expand considerably. That segregation among occupational groups within the Negro community did increase between 1950 and 1960 is evident from the average indexes for each census year.

City	Average Index of Dissimilarity Among Occupational Groups	
	1950	1960
Detroit	18.9	28.4
Cleveland	20.4	26.0
Philadelphia	16.8	24.2
St. Louis	18.9	21.2
Washington	19.2	22.8
Baltimore	20.0	26.9
New Orleans	21.1	28.3
Atlanta	19.2	32.3
Birmingham	22.1	28.8
Memphis	16.8	26.9

3. Hortense Powdermaker, *After Freedom: A Cultural Study in the Deep South* (New York: The Viking Press, 1939), p. 13.

Judging from fragmentary sources, it appears that the amount of class segregation in the Negro community is, on the whole, less than that found among the white population. Similar analyses for whites in Cleveland and Chicago indicate not only a greater amount of occupational differentiation for whites in these cities, but also little change in the level of differentiation between 1950 and 1960.[4] The lesser average degree of class segregation among Negroes is probably due not only to the limitations on the housing supply imposed by racial residential segregation, but also to the lesser degree of occupational diversity among the Negro population. The stability of patterns of class segregation observed for whites over the decade contrasts with the marked increases for Negroes. This difference may be a function of the continuing rise in socioeconomic status of the Negro population, compared to the minor gains experienced by whites *in cities* over the 1950–60 decade. In the preceding decade, Negro gains in class differentiation could not be translated into residential distinctions because of the tight wartime housing market. Small declines in class segregation in the Negro community between 1940 and 1950 are apparent in the following data, which are available only for Southern cities (the complete occupation-by-occupation indexes are given in Appendix Table C-2):

City	*Average Index of Dissimilarity Among Occupational Groups*	
	1940	*Change, 1940–50*
Washington.............	22.4	−3.2
Baltimore	22.6	−2.6
New Orleans...........	23.4	−2.3
Atlanta	21.9	−2.7
Birmingham...........	25.1	−3.0
Memphis...............	23.3	−6.5

Certain occupations showed greater changes in residential distribution between 1950 and 1960 than others. The main features of these changes are summarized in Table 65. In general, persons in white-collar occupations became more segregated both from each other and from blue-collar workers, while there was little change in the amount of segregation among members of the various blue-collar

4. Eugene S. Uyeki, "Residential Distribution and Stratification, 1950–1960," *American Journal of Sociology*, LXIX, No. 5 (March, 1964). See also Duncan and Duncan, "Residential Distribution . . .," *op. cit.*, and *The Negro Population of Chicago, op. cit.*, Table 69; and Arthur H. Wilkins, "The Residential Distribution of Occupation Groups in Eight Middle-sized Cities of the United States in 1950 (unpublished Ph.D. dissertation, University of Chicago, 1956).

TABLE 65

AVERAGE INDEXES OF DISSIMILARITY IN RESIDENTIAL DISTRIBUTION AMONG WHITE-COLLAR AND BLUE-COLLAR WORKERS, FOR EMPLOYED NON-WHITE MALES, 1950 AND 1960

City	White-collar vs. White-collar			White-collar vs. Blue-collar			Blue-collar vs. Blue-collar			Number of Tracts	
	1950	1960	Change	1950	1960	Change	1950	1960	Change	1950	1960
Detroit	18.3	31.8	13.5	20.6	31.1	10.5	15.1	17.8	2.7	131	183
Cleveland	20.1	30.0	9.9	22.5	28.6	6.1	14.9	15.0	0.1	54	66
Philadelphia	17.3	27.3	10.0	17.7	26.6	8.9	14.0	14.7	0.7	122	137
St. Louis	21.1	25.6	4.5	20.5	23.2	2.7	12.6	11.6	-1.0	33	38
Washington	18.5	24.2	5.7	21.6	25.8	4.2	13.4	13.6	0.2	69	74
Baltimore	22.8	31.0	8.2	21.0	29.6	8.6	14.4	15.4	1.0	67	80
New Orleans	23.1	34.6	11.5	22.1	29.9	7.8	16.4	18.0	1.6	89	77
Atlanta	19.6	31.5	11.9	21.5	38.4	16.9	12.8	16.9	4.1	41	48
Birmingham	23.2	34.3	11.1	23.9	32.1	8.2	16.1	14.4	-1.7	45	42
Memphis	17.8	34.2	16.4	17.5	28.1	10.6	13.9	16.4	2.5	58	50

Source: Appendix Table C-1.

occupations. These results are consistent with an assumption that persons with higher incomes are more likely to take advantage of new opportunities to upgrade their housing. In the major white-collar occupations, Negro managerial and sales workers made the greatest changes during the decade, followed by professional workers, while clerical workers changed little in their segregation relative to other white-collar or blue-collar workers. These broad trends are influenced by complex patterns of change in the distribution of Negroes among specific detailed occupational categories, which in turn are interrelated with improving levels of education and income.[5]

□ RELATIONS BETWEEN WHITES AND NEGROES IN MIXED AREAS

In the preceding section, we have demonstrated the existence of residential segregation according to socioeconomic status within the Negro community. How do patterns of residential differentiation in the Negro community relate to those in the white community? If, in fact, "...the residential structure of an urban community is in good part independent of the racial makeup of the community's inhabitants,"[6] we would expect that at any given point in time there should be a positive correlation between the characteristics of whites and Negroes living in mixed areas. The finding in the earlier section that neighborhoods retain their character despite racial change supports this expectation. On the other hand, writing in 1903, DuBois observed that

> Segregation by color is largely independent of that natural clustering by social grades common to all communities. A Negro slum may be in dangerous proximity to a white residence quarter, while it is quite common to find a white slum planted in the heart of a respectable Negro district. One thing, however, seldom occurs: the best of the whites and the best of the Negroes almost never live in anything like close proximity. It thus happens that in nearly every *Southern* town and city, both whites and blacks see commonly the worst of each other.[7]

Our strategy is to compute correlations between the characteristics of whites and non-whites residing in racially mixed tracts, for each city and each census year. A high correlation indicates that tracts with white populations of high socioeconomic status relative to white

5. A discussion of trends in detailed occupations is forthcoming in a census monograph by Daniel O. Price of the University of North Carolina.

6. Duncan and Duncan, *The Negro Population of Chicago, op. cit.*, p. 18.

7. W. E. B. DuBois, *The Souls of Black Folk* (Chicago: A. C. McClurg, 1904), pp. 166–167. (Italics added.)

populations in other mixed tracts also contain Negro populations of high socioeconomic status relative to Negro populations in other mixed tracts. Areas which are exclusively white-occupied are excluded from consideration, as are tracts greater than 90 per cent non-white.[8] This analysis was carried out for tracts of mixed racial composition in each of our ten cities for each of the three census years, 1940, 1950, and 1960. Table 66 presents the Spearman rank correlations for these tracts between white and non-white values on each of the four measures of socioeconomic status for the three dates.

TABLE 66

RANK CORRELATION (SPEARMAN) BETWEEN WHITE AND NEGRO CHARACTERISTICS FOR "MIXED" TRACTS: 1940, 1950, AND 1960 †

Characteristic and Year	Detroit	Cleveland	Philadelphia	St. Louis	Washington	Baltimore	New Orleans	Atlanta	Birmingham	Memphis
Educational attainment:										
1940	.67°	.61°	.56°	.58°	.41°	.65°	.50°	.28	.32°	.22
1950	.57°	.50°	.50°	.60°	.42°	.61°	.36°	.07	.26	.16
1960	.46°	.26	.62°	.09	.15	.70°	.39°	.29	.39°	.11
White-collar occupation:										
1940	‡	‡	‡	‡	.32°	.36°	.25°	.31	.18	−.38°
1950	.63°	.57°	.33°	.60°	.33°	.66°	.44°	−.01	.19	.08
1960	.47°	.24	.66°	−.05	.25°	.55°	.39°	.21	.10	−.07
Home-ownership:										
1940	.61°	.47°	.53°	.69°	.61°	.43°	.81°	.65°	.78°	.75°
1950	.67°	.48°	.62°	.76°	.62°	.71°	.76°	.58°	.88°	.75°
1960	.78°	.76°	.54°	.80°	.83°	.74°	.80ᶜ	.72°	.81°	.77°
Room-crowding:										
1940	.51°	.36°	.54°	.40°	.55°	.59°	.56	.02	.44°	.37°
1950	.74°	.69°	.67°	.78°	.55°	.55°	.67°	.20	.62°	.50°
1960	.74°	.61°	.77°	.79°	.71°	.76°	.73°	.48°	.61°	.44°
Number of tracts:										
1940	60	31	102	19	54	44	80	28	36	43
1950	106	41	110	26	60	53	79	29	38	46
1960:										
Education, occupation	138	39	82	29	52	49	65	28	30	32
Home-ownership	150	46	88	31	55	54	73	31	31	37
Room-crowding	138	39	82	29	53	48	72	27	31	35

° Statistically significant at the .05 level. Although the assumptions underlying the significance test are not fully satisfied by these data, the test provides a rough means of distinguishing high and low coefficients.

† Based on all census tracts in a given year with 250 or more non-whites, less than 90 per cent non-white, and with data available.

‡ Not available, since occupational data were not published separately for non-whites in Northern cities in 1940.

8. Aggregate comparisons of the socioeconomic status of whites and Negroes in white, mixed, and Negro areas were presented in Chapter 7.

In a similar analysis for Chicago, quite high correlation co-efficients were obtained between white and non-white levels of home-ownership and room-crowding, and moderately high coefficients between whites and non-whites on educational attainment and white-collar employment. It was concluded that Negroes were areally differentiated in much the same manner as whites, presumably as a result of general factors operating independently of race.[9]

The correlations between white and non-white values on home-ownership and room-crowding in all ten cities are moderately high, and generally increased between 1940 and 1960, providing further support for the notion that both whites and Negroes respond similarly to the physical characteristics of areas. This is true for Southern cities as well as for Northern and border cities.

For educational attainment and occupational status, however, Northern and border cities differ from Southern cities. Looking first at the six Northern and border cities, in 1940 and 1950, correlations between white and non-white levels of educational and occupational status are positive and significant in every case. Between 1940 and 1950, changes in correlations were generally slight. Between 1950 and 1960, however, sizable declines occurred in the correlations for both educational and occupational status. By 1960, several of the correlations were not much different from zero. Thus, in Northern and border cities, the processes of racial succession were often accompanied by a lessened tendency for the whites and Negroes in mixed areas to resemble one another in educational and occupational status. From the data (presented in Chapter 7) showing the average status of whites and Negroes residing in Negro residential areas, it appears that by 1960 Negroes had moved from a situation in which they were markedly inferior to whites to one where color differentials had narrowed. In fact, in the case of measures of education and home-ownership, Negroes now tend to surpass whites living in these areas. These findings from the correlation analysis and the analysis of aggregative status measures can be shown to be general tendencies, and not solely the result of a few extreme tracts. In Cleveland, for example, non-white levels of educational attainment in 1940 exceeded white levels in 32 per cent of mixed tracts, whereas in 1960 they were higher in 69 per cent of mixed tracts.

Our interpretation of these changes again attributes much importance to the accelerated trend of suburbanization in 1950–60 as compared to the tighter housing market of the wartime decade. During 1940–50, the normal tendency for housing changes to accompany increasing income and increasing family size was impeded.

9. Duncan and Duncan, *The Negro Population of Chicago, op. cit.*, p. 277.

Despite considerable residential mobility, restricted housing opportunities interfered with the processes of rapid adjustment of housing to means and desires. Patterns of areal differentiation within mixed areas remained relatively constant during the decade. But during 1950–60, high-status whites living in mixed areas, who desired and could afford alternative housing, took advantage of newly available opportunities. The "catching-up" period of adjustment of housing to changing needs and incomes depleted racially mixed areas of much of their high-status white population. Whites living in mixed areas became a more homogeneous low-status group, so that correlations between white and Negro status measures for these mixed tracts diminished.

In three of the four Southern cities, by contrast, there has been little relationship in any year between the educational and occupational status of whites and Negroes residing in mixed tracts. (New Orleans is an exception, resembling the Northern and border cities in displaying positive correlations between white and Negro characteristics.) These results indicate that race has a more dominant role in the socioeconomic differentiation of residential areas in Southern cities than in Northern and border cities.

Thus, we have an apparent regional difference in patterns of residential differentiation. In Northern and border cities, whites and Negroes residing in mixed areas tend to resemble each other in socioeconomic status, while there is a general lack of relationship in Southern cities. What factors might be responsible for this observed North-South difference? As a first consideration, we suggest that there may be regional differences in the character of the "mixed" tracts just analyzed and the character of those tracts over 90 per cent nonwhite, which were excluded. Residence in neighborhoods in which Negroes comprise a high proportion of the population tends to be viewed as undesirable by whites in both North and South. Whites of high socioeconomic status, who have a wide choice of residential areas, generally elect to live in areas almost exclusively white. Is there, however, a regional difference in where high-status Negroes live? We have seen (in Chapter 7) that in Northern and border cities, Negroes in Invasion tracts are generally of relatively high status, in many cases higher than the whites in these tracts. We may hypothesize for these cities that residential areas with a high-status Negro population tend to be mixed neighborhoods with a lower percentage Negro than other Negro residential areas. There were too few Invasion tracts in Southern cities for us to pursue this mode of analysis, so another procedure was utilized in an effort to examine these possible regional differences more systematically.

All census tracts were considered for which data were available separately for non-whites — all tracts comprising what we previously designated Negro Residential Areas. Within each city, these tracts were ranked from high to low according to the educational or occupational status of their non-white population. The top fifth of tracts on educational attainment of non-whites was designated "high-status" tracts, and the bottom fifth as "low-status" tracts. Top and bottom fifths were similarly designated for occupational status. The median percentage non-white for each of these groups of tracts is presented in Table 67. In Cleveland in 1960, for example, the top fifth of tracts

TABLE 67

MEDIAN PERCENTAGE NON-WHITE OF CENSUS TRACTS
CONTAINING THE HIGHEST AND LOWEST FIFTH OF TRACTS
RANKED ACCORDING TO NON-WHITE EDUCATIONAL AND
OCCUPATIONAL STATUS, 1940 AND 1960°

City and Year	Number of Tracts	Educational Status†		Occupational Status‡	
		High	Low	High	Low
1960					
Detroit.....................	180	70.3	91.0	71.0	63.7
Cleveland	65	43.4	83.4	32.6	69.3
Philadelphia.............	100	35.6	33.8	37.6	33.7
St. Louis	39	63.9	80.8	67.2	83.8
Washington	74	52.6	73.7	52.4	81.3
Baltimore	80	50.5	71.3	73.4	67.8
New Orleans	74	31.6	36.0	34.2	37.0
Atlanta.....................	47	87.4	43.9	84.6	40.1
Birmingham	40	84.8	50.4	73.4	67.4
Memphis..................	50	79.0	36.1	77.5	27.2
1940					
Detroit.....................	69	54.6	55.2	§	§
Cleveland	38	18.5	64.7	§	§
Philadelphia.............	104	27.1	17.0	§	§
St. Louis	25	48.6	33.0	§	§
Washington	61	39.4	45.0	34.7	45.0
Baltimore	49	7.5	48.5	10.4	38.5
New Orleans	85	39.6	19.4	29.8	19.6
Atlanta.....................	38	96.9	14.9	92.9	16.0
Birmingham	42	84.4	25.1	63.3	8.8
Memphis..................	52	74.3	42.5	81.8	16.0

° Includes all census tracts (including annexed area) for which data were available separately for whites and non-whites.

† The measure of educational status is the percentage of persons age 25 and over completing one or more years of high school.

‡ The measure of occupational status is the percentage of employed males age 14 and over engaged in white-collar occupations.

§ Not available, since occupational data were not published separately for non-whites in Northern cities in 1940.

in terms of non-white educational status had a median percentage non-white of 43, as compared with a median percentage non-white of 83 in those tracts in the lowest fifth. This is the hypothesized pattern for Northern and border cities: residential areas containing high-status Negroes are more racially mixed than residential areas containing low-status Negroes.

Although there are several exceptions, the general pattern in the Northern and border cities is that areas where the Negro population is of high occupational or educational status are also those where Negroes comprise a relatively lower proportion of the population. Areas where the Negro population is of low socioeconomic status tend to have a higher proportion non-white. In Southern cities, it is more common for areas with high-status Negroes to be predominantly Negro areas, while low-status Negroes live in racially mixed residential areas. Therefore, where we based our correlation analysis only on the population in mixed tracts, we omitted from the analysis in Southern cities many of the tracts containing high-status Negroes, and thus reduced the already limited range of variation in tracts according to non-white status. In the Northern and border cities, omitting those tracts with very high percentages non-white excluded only a portion of all low-status tracts, while retaining most of the high-status non-white tracts in the analysis, and thus allowing the full range of variation in tracts according to non-white status. We are still confronted, however, with an apparent regional difference in Negro residential structure. Some possible historical explanations for it are explored in the next section.

□ REGIONAL DIFFERENCES

In every city except Atlanta, Birmingham, and Memphis, there is a positive relationship between the status of whites and Negroes living in racially mixed tracts, as well as a tendency for high-status Negroes to live in mixed areas rather than in predominantly Negro areas. It is tempting to seek a regional interpretation of the distinctive patterns observed in these three cities. Frazier is among the many writers who have stressed the importance of historical factors in distinguishing residential patterns in Southern cities:

> Small Negro settlements, comprised mostly of servants, have grown up close to the houses of the whites in which Negroes served. These settlements thus took root before the spatial pattern of the cities was affected by the economic forces which have shaped the pattern of our modern industrial and commercial cities. ... The light

scattering of Negroes over a large area is attributable . . . to historical factors, while the large concentrations of the Negro population reflect the increasing influence of economic and social forces inherent in the growth of the modern city.[10]

Any simple regional explanation, however, is tempered by the necessity of explaining why Atlanta, Birmingham, and Memphis differ
not only from Northern cities but also from the other Southern cities,
New Orleans, Washington, and Baltimore.

Differences among Southern cities in the relative importance of
"the light scattering of Negroes" and "the large concentrations"
appear to be determined by whether the city grew up before or after
the Civil War. Important and continuing differences among Southern
cities in current racial patterns can be traced to this distinction between "old" and "new" cities. Southern cities that were large prior
to the Civil War, such as New Orleans, Washington, Baltimore, and
Charleston, tended to have the "back-yard" or "alley dwelling"
pattern of Negro residence described by Frazier. New cities that grew
up after the Civil War never developed to any great extent a similar
pattern of residential intimacy. The survival of pre-Civil War patterns
of racial residential intermixture was documented earlier in discussing the historically low level of residential segregation in Charleston,
S. C. Demolition and rehabilitation of the older mixed areas of
Charleston are partially responsible for sharp increases in segregation in recent decades. By contrast, we have seen how increases in
residential segregation in Augusta, Georgia (an "old" Southern city)
over the decades resulted from the creation of new all-Negro areas
rather than from changes in residential patterns within existing areas.
Examination of the population and racial composition of our ten cities
in 1850, shown in Table 68, indicates that Atlanta, Birmingham, and
Memphis are "new" Southern cities, while Washington, Baltimore,
and New Orleans are "old" Southern cities.

One interesting feature distinguishing old and new Southern
cities is the large ante-bellum free colored population in the old cities.
While the effect of the presence of this group on Negro residential
patterns in these cities can only be speculated on, we have seen
earlier that the free colored population of Charleston in 1861 was
residentially segregated to the same degree from both whites and
slaves, while the latter two groups tended to have similar residential
distributions. It seems likely that the free colored population contributed to greater diversity among the Negro population, and that
this diversity in turn contributed to greater residential differentiation
in the Negro community.

10. E. Franklin Frazier, *The Negro in the United States* (New York: The Macmillan Co., 1957), p. 237.

TABLE 68

POPULATION BY RACE, 1850

City	Total	White	Free Colored	Slave	Percentage Negro
Detroit............	21,019	20,432	587	....	2.8
Cleveland	17,034	16,810	224	....	1.3
Philadelphia ...	121,376	110,640	10,736	....	8.8
St. Louis	77,860	73,806	1,398	2,656	5.2
Washington	51,687	37,941	10,059	3,687	26.6
Baltimore........	169,054	140,666	25,442	2,946	16.8
New Orleans ...	116,375	89,459	9,905	17,011	23.1
Atlanta............	2,572	2,060	19	493	19.9
Birmingham°...	....	....	....	....	......
Memphis.........	8,841	6,355	126	2,360	28.1

Source: United States Census, *The Seventh Census of the United States, 1850* (Washington: Robert Armstrong, Public Printer, 1853), Table II for each state. Data for Birmingham are from United States Census Office, *Compendium of the Eleventh Census: 1890*, Part I, *Population* (Washington, D. C.: Government Printing Office, 1892), Table 17.

° The first census in which data by race are available for Birmingham is 1890, when the city had a total population of 26,178, of which 14,909 were white and 11,269 were Negro. The percentage Negro was 43.0. Birmingham first appears in the census as a city in 1880, with a total population of 3,086.

Changing urban patterns during the Reconstruction period in Georgia are described in one account:

> This new or greatly augmented class of black inhabitants changed the character of negro dwellings in towns, which had formerly been small houses in the rear of white people's houses. Later, separate negro tenements were built in a distinct section of the city, the beginning of the "Shermantown" or "darktown" settlements of Southern cities.[11]

A study of the residential development of Memphis revealed an older central area of Negro residence, while new Negro areas were found on the periphery of the city.

> The rigid building restrictions of the City Planning Commission ...will not permit any more isolated negro islands to spring up in the higher types of residential communities. It is to be hoped that those now existing in the better communities will gradually decrease in size until they finally disappear from the map.[12]

Woofter, describing the Negro settlements of Athens, Georgia (a new city), in the early part of the twentieth century found that Negroes

11. C. Mildred Thompson, *Reconstruction in Georgia* (New York: C. Mildred Thompson, 1915), pp. 56–57.

12. Rayburn Whitson Johnson, "Land Utilization in Memphis" (unpublished Ph.D. dissertation, University of Chicago, 1936), p. 62.

> Live in several different localities, and yet there are very few
> blocks in which both white and colored people live, for the reason
> that the whites do not like such neighborhoods and the average
> negro cannot afford any other.[13]

Housing to accommodate increasing Negro population in the
post-Reconstruction period was confined to the worst areas of the city.
In Athens,

> The negro settlements are found in the low places between
> the ridges, and on the outskirts of the town.[14]

In Memphis,

> They follow along the small creeks and bayous, and along the
> margins of the Wolf River Swamps. A recent report released by the
> Slum Clearance Committee points out a very high correlation be-
> tween the distribution of bad drainage areas and negro residential
> communities.[15]

Clearly, the Negro areas in these cities had never undergone succession from white to Negro occupancy, but were Negro-occupied from
their inception. It would seem, then, that additional Negro population in post-Civil War cities and in pre-Civil War cities *after* the War
tended to be housed in all-Negro areas developing in the least desirable sections of town.

The residential intermingling characteristic of the older cities
before the War diminished gradually in succeeding decades, and the
relative importance of these older areas in the total housing picture
of a city depends upon the rate of post-Civil War growth in Negro
population. The six Northern and border cities experienced large-
scale in-migration of Negroes in the two decades from 1910 to 1930
and again from 1940 to 1960. Atlanta, Birmingham, and Memphis
had some Negro in-migration 1910–30, but none of the recent rapid
growth that has characterized Northern and border cities. The Negro
population of New Orleans has followed a unique pattern, growing
slowly every decade since the turn of the century, with no periods
of heavy influx.

Consider the situation in the Northern and border cities during
periods of rapid increase in Negro population. In these older, larger
cities, land suitable for residential development was becoming increasingly scarce, and additional land could not be acquired through
annexation. High-status Negros seeking good housing were excluded

13. T. J. Woofter, *The Negroes of Athens, Georgia*, Bulletin of the University of
Georgia, XIV, No. 4 (Phelps-Stokes Fellowship Studies, No. 1: December, 1913), p. 9.

14. *Ibid.*, pp. 9–10.

15. R. W. Johnson, *op. cit.*, pp. 50, 53.

from the new housing on the periphery of the city. These cities, however, contained much old housing in central areas which was gradually being given up by whites as their incomes rose and their families
expanded. Housing in these cities was made available to Negroes
through a filter-down process. By contrast, the newer, smaller Southern city is still growing and annexing territory. The housing stock
as a whole in these cities is fairly new, so there is only a small supply
of old housing to be filtered down to either whites or Negroes. These
cities still contain vacant land in ample supply for new residential
construction. Consequently, the best housing available to Negroes in
these cities is housing newly built specifically for Negroes, an alternative permitted these cities by the slow growth of Negro population
and the ready availability of land.

Our historical interpretations cannot be documented systematically, but we can show for recent decades that increases in the Negro
demand for housing in the newer Southern city have been met largely
through new residential construction, while in the Northern and
border cities the most important source of new Negro housing is the
transmission of existing dwellings from white to Negro occupancy.
Table 69 shows, for the 1950–59 period, the amount of new construction for Negroes and the number of Negro-occupied units formerly
occupied by whites, in those of our ten cities included in the 1959

TABLE 69

NUMBER OF NON-WHITE — OCCUPIED DWELLING UNITS BUILT
1950–59 AND NUMBER OF NON-WHITE — OCCUPIED DWELLING UNITS
OCCUPIED BY WHITES IN 1950: SELECTED SMSA'S, 1959

SMSA	*Non-white — occupied Dwelling Units, 1959*	
	Built 1950–59	*White-occupied in 1950*
Detroit	7,613	71,786
Cleveland	2,957	35,581
Philadelphia	8,293	49,859
St. Louis	6,505	23,832
Washington	9,010	34,536
Baltimore	12,256	29,160
Atlanta	17,458	5,419

Source: U. S. Bureau of the Census, *U. S. Census of Housing: 1960,* Vol. IV, *Components of Inventory Change,* Final Report HC(4), Part 1A (Washington: U. S. Government Printing Office, 1962), Tables 1 and 4.

National Housing Inventory. In Atlanta, the only one of our "new" Southern cities included in the Inventory, new construction is a much more important source of housing than the transfer of existing dwellings from white to Negro occupancy. In Dallas, the only other "new" Southern city included in the Inventory—though not one of our ten —Negroes in 1959 occupied 18,396 units which had been constructed during the decade, compared to only 5,743 units which had been occupied by whites in 1950. Thus, neighborhood racial change in "new" Southern cities is primarily a function of new construction. Declines in tract percentages Negro (Displacement tracts) are the result of new construction for whites or selective demolition, not the transfer of existing units from Negro to white occupancy. Similarly, succession or increases in tract percentages Negro in these cities are primarily the result of new construction for Negroes.

Baltimore and Washington, "old" Southern cities with a substantial stock of old housing, have been subjected to large increases in Negro population in recent decades, and the Inventory shows that the transfer of existing dwellings from white to Negro occupancy is the most important source of additional dwellings for Negroes. In this they resemble the Northern cities.

The initial residential differentiation of the newer, smaller Southern city incorporated within it an adaptation to the presence of a large Negro population, and the subsequent slow growth of the Negro population has permitted this adaptation to persist. The present residential patterning of the Negro community in these cities, then, is not "...the product of a long process of succession from white to Negro occupancy."[16] By contrast, older, larger Southern cities resemble Northern cities in that housing patterns for rapidly growing Negro populations were superimposed upon pre-existing patterns of residential differentiation.

16. Duncan and Duncan, *The Negro Population of Chicago, op. cit.*, p. 237.

THE MEASUREMENT OF RESIDENTIAL SEGREGATION

☐ THE CONCEPT OF RESIDENTIAL SEGREGATION

A distinction between residential segregation as *process* through time and as *pattern* at a point in time was made in Chapter 3, and one measure was described for indexing the residential pattern of a city at a point in time. The segregation index presented there may be viewed as a measure of the over-all unevenness of white and non-white residential distributions. There are, however, alternative measures of the over-all unevenness of two spatial distributions, and there are additional aspects or dimensions of residential segregation which might be measured.

Within the framework of either traditional urban studies or of studies in race relations, a number of aspects of a city's pattern of racial residential segregation might be of relevance to an intercity comparative analysis. First are the population parameters. The relative proportions of whites and non-whites may be mentioned, along with the number of residents of each color. One would expect differences in residential patterns and their impact on other aspects of community organization between New York City, with more than 1,000,000 Negro residents, and another large city, Boston, with but 63,000 Negro residents in 1960. Similarly, where Negroes make up less than 9 per cent of the population, as in Milwaukee, residential patterns might be expected to differ from those in a city such as Washington, D.C., where Negroes comprise 54 per cent of the population. Other things being equal, the number of all-Negro neighborhoods will depend on the size and proportion of the Negro population. However, size and relative proportion of Negro population do not serve to specify the residential pattern, but only to set limits on it.

The term "clustering" may be used to refer to the residential concentration of Negroes into predominantly Negro areas. Such clusters may be as large as New York's Harlem, or as small as any arbitrary lower limit set for the size of a cluster. A given city may have one Negro residential area in which nearly all of the city's Negroes live, or it may have several such clusters of varying size and racial homogeneity. Examination of maps of Negro residential patterns in various cities has led to several attempts to characterize patterns according to the nature of the clusters[1] but, as we shall see, these attempts have not been very satisfactory, and no reliable basis has been developed for delineating the boundaries of a cluster, or for assessing the difference in impact of two smaller clusters as opposed to one large cluster.

The clustering of Negro residences is the most frequently noted aspect of racial residential patterns. If there are sizable racially homogeneous clusters, then public institutions such as schools, libraries, and parks, as well as stores, theaters, and other places of business, may serve only one racial group solely because of the residential segregation. This is not necessarily the case if there is a high degree of over-all unevenness, as we shall demonstrate below — if every third city block were set aside for Negro occupancy, there would be a high degree of residential segregation in the sense of unevenness, but little clustering and the associated consequences for social organization. Unevenness without clustering is, however, hypothetical and not to be found in U.S. cities. Nonetheless, it is possible that the development of separate facilities of a type not heavily dependent upon location, such as Negro undertaking services, may depend primarily on the size and proportion of the Negro population, rather than on the specific nature of its intracity distribution. The situation with respect to entertainment facilities is less clear, for the development of separate Negro establishments is certainly enhanced by a high degree of clustering. In political activity, the potential consequences of overwhelming Negro majorities in a small number of precincts are clearly different from the effects of small proportions of Negroes in each of a large number of precincts.

Another identifiable aspect of residential patterning is the location of Negro residents within the city, whether highly clustered or not. The zonal theory of city structure, for instance, suggests a general tendency for Negroes to live closer to the city center than whites. Orientation to the city center is not the only relevant locational feature. For example, in describing Negro residential patterns in Chicago, it is necessary to take into account the location of such things as the lake shore, the rapid transit lines, the tenements erected to

1. T. J. Woofter, Jr., *Negro Problems in Cities* (Garden City, N.Y.: Doubleday, Doran, 1928); Robert C. Weaver, *The Negro Ghetto* (New York: Harcourt, Brace, 1948); Charles S. Johnson, *Patterns of Negro Segregation* (New York: Harper Brothers, 1943).

house low-income immigrants after the fire of 1871, the stockyards and manufacturing plants, and so on.

The various aspects of residential patterning are not completely independent dimensions. It is obvious that if all the Negroes in a city are concentrated in a "Black Belt" extending south of the central business district, then there is a high degree of unevenness in the over-all distribution. Nonetheless, delineation of these various aspects does indicate the complexity of the problem of comparing residential patterns in different cities, and clarifies the text statement that any single index of such a complex phenomenon is an arbitrary over-simplification of reality, and is useful in the same way that any other average or summary measure is useful.

It is clear, therefore, that no single-valued "segregation index" can be superior to all others for all purposes. Although the various dimensions of residential segregation are interrelated, no one determines another, and an index of one may not adequately represent another. Aside from what we believe to be insurmountable problems of measurement, it seems preferable, for both methodological and conceptual reasons, to undertake some study of variations in residential patterns along particular dimensions before making any concerted effort to analyze variations in all aspects taken together. Any composite index would require or imply some arbitrary weighting of the separate components, and if interpretation were to be carried very far, it would be necessary to break down the composite index into these components.

☐ LITERATURE ON THE MEASUREMENT OF RESIDENTIAL SEGREGATION

The measurement of Negro residential segregation is methodologically similar to many other problems in the measurement of segregation, location, concentration, and other geographic and distributional phenomena. The "segregation indexes" developed in sociology have been set in the context of these broader problems in a recent monograph, *Statistical Geography*, which also contains extensive bibliographic references to this literature.[2] There is no need here to duplicate that useful effort. Nonetheless, there has been a rather independent sociological literature on the measurement and intercity comparison of racial residential segregation, and various issues recur persistently in sociological discussions. The remainder of

2. Otis Dudley Duncan, Ray P. Cuzzort, and Beverly Duncan, *Statistical Geography: Problems in Analyzing Areal Data* (Glencoe, Ill.: The Free Press, 1961).

this appendix is devoted to explicit discussion of methodological considerations in the quantitative sociological study of residential segregation. By bringing some general statistical principles to bear on this specific problem, and by giving a variety of empirical demonstrations and assessments of theoretically pertinent issues, we hope not only to defend our own choice of procedures, but also to help settle some of the controversies and misconceptions among sociologists who are unfamiliar with the technical statistical literature.

A straightforward review of the sociological literature, more or less an annotated bibliography, will indicate the general nature of the methodological concerns. This will be followed by a unified overview of the various specific measures proposed as indexes of residential segregation.

The first important comparative study of residential segregation was that supervised by T. J. Woofter, Jr., in the mid-1920's, *Negro Problems in Cities*.[3] Firsthand observations of housing, recreation, and schools were undertaken in Negro neighborhoods in 16 cities. To illustrate the generality of residential segregation and the concentration of Negroes in undesirable residential areas, areas with high proportions of Negro residents were shown in a series of maps. A classification of city segregation patterns was developed from inspection of the maps, but there was no attempt to use the classification for systematic comparative study. This early study also presented a long list of city characteristics presumed to affect the pattern of racial segregation, but there was no supporting analysis.

Weaver's investigation of *The Negro Ghetto*[4] in Northern cities (1947) was also more concerned with demonstrating the fact of widespread residential segregation than with comparing cities. Weaver developed another classification of patterns of "Black Belts," based on inspection of maps, but again used as a descriptive device rather than as a tool for comparative analysis. Casual inspection of the maps and his category of patterns indicates the subjectivity inherent in this approach.

Hoyt's study of *The Structure and Growth of Residential Neighborhoods in American Cities* (1939)[5] was the first to present objective data in a direct analysis of intercity variations in residential segregation. Examining the distribution of Negro population among areas (enumeration districts or blocks) classified as to percentage Negro, Hoyt concluded:

3. T. J. Woofter, Jr., *op. cit.*

4. Robert C. Weaver, *op. cit.*

5. U.S. Federal Housing Administration, Homer Hoyt, *The Structure and Growth of Residential Neighborhoods in American Cities* (Washington: U.S. Government Printing Office, 1939).

We may, therefore, suggest the generalization that "the degree of nonwhite concentration in any city increases directly with the number and proportion of nonwhite persons in the population." Either a large nonwhite population in absolute numbers, or a high proportion of nonwhite persons in the total population is necessary to produce concentrated nonwhite areas.[6]

Nance (1951)[7] used a procedure similar to Hoyt's in a study of residential segregation in five Northern cities. Census tracts in each city were grouped according to percentage Negro, and the five cities were ranked on "concentration" of Negroes. Some relationships between this ranking and rankings on other city characteristics were presented.

Hatt (1945)[8] studied the spatial patterns of residence of several ethnic minorities in the central residential area of Seattle, chosen because of its ethnically diverse character. He used a rough measure of ethnic association within blocks, comparing the actual frequency of group members in each block with the number expected on the basis of a random allocation. By this index, Negroes were the most "isolated" of the ethnic groups. Hatt suggested that city blocks were somewhat unsatisfactory units for such an analysis, and that data for the two sides of a street might be preferable.

Jahn, Schmid, and Schrag (1947)[9] inaugurated the series of sociological articles explicitly concerned with the construction of "segregation indexes." They presented four alternative indexes, giving a computational formula and a verbal description of each. Several criteria for a good index were suggested, and it was demonstrated that each index met several of the criteria. Unfortunately, they failed to give explicit attention to the degree to which their indexes met their criterion that the measure should "not be distorted by the size of the total population, the proportion of Negroes, or the area of a city."[10] Census tract data from the 1940 census were used in the computation of index values for a number of cities, and relationships with region and other variables were reported.

The data are intended to be merely suggestive of the explanations and relationships that might be found between these measures of ecological segregation and certain other social conditions. A

6. *Ibid.*, p. 68.

7. Frederic D. Nance, "Patterns of Negro Residential Segregation in Five Selected Northern Cities" (unpublished Master's thesis, Syracuse University, 1951).

8. Paul Hatt, "Spatial Patterns in a Polyethnic Area," *American Sociological Review*, X, No. 3 (June, 1945).

9. Julius A. Jahn, Calvin F. Schmid, and Clarence Schrag, "The Measurement of Ecological Segregation," *American Sociological Review*, XII, No. 3 (June, 1947).

10. *Ibid.*, p. 294.

precise, quantitative definition makes it possible to test any hypothesis relating segregation to other specified variables.[11]

Hornseth replied to this article, demonstrating various interrelationships among the four indexes, and claiming that all four
measured essentially the same thing and therefore three of them were
redundant. "The subtle distinctions between them have no correlates
in the sociological problem of segregation."[12] Jahn, Schmid, and
Schrag rejoined that although the four indexes were similar, they were
not simple functions of one another and did not correlate perfectly
when applied to the same data. Two general criteria, prediction and
reproducibility, were elaborated as a suggested basis for choosing an
index for any particular purpose.

Williams also replied to this article, attempting "to simplify the
problem of selecting an index, without oversimplifying it."[13] She
recognized that the problem of defining segregation indexes resembled many other measurement problems, and likened it to the definition of "measures of association for a contingency table with two columns; that is, where one of the attributes, like Negro and non-Negro, is
dichotomous."[14] She discussed the proposed indexes within the
framework of chi-square analysis, concluding that there is no generally
"best" index and suggesting numerous criteria other than prediction
and reproducibility.

Jahn later (1950) offered still another index, differing "particularly in the use of 'reproducibility' as an explicit assumption in its
derivation."[15] At this time, Jahn agreed that many possible indexes
could be developed, even with reproducibility as the principal
criterion.

Cowgill and Cowgill (1951) were critical of all previously suggested segregation indexes because of their presumed dependence
on census tract data.[16] Only data for city blocks, it was argued, reveal
the true extent of residential segregation, and an index was presented
designed explicitly for use with block data. Values of this index were
calculated for 1940 for 187 cities, and a brief analysis of variations by

11. *Ibid.*, p. 303.

12. Richard A. Hornseth, "A Note on 'The Measurement of Ecological Segregation'
by Julius Jahn, Calvin F. Schmid, and Clarence Schrag," *American Sociological Review*, XII, No. 5 (October, 1947), p. 604.

13. Josephine J. Williams, "Another Commentary on So-Called Segregation
Indices," *American Sociological Review*, XIII, No. 3 (June, 1948), p. 299.

14. *Ibid.*, p. 298.

15. Julius A. Jahn, "The Measurement of Ecological Segregation: Derivation of an
Index Based on the Criterion of Reproducibility," *American Sociological Review*,
XV, No. 1 (February, 1950), p. 101.

16. Donald O. Cowgill and Mary S. Cowgill, "An Index of Segregation Based on
Block Statistics," *American Sociological Review*, XVI, No. 6 (December, 1951).

region, city size, percentage non-white, and functional type of city was reported. Cowgill later presented scores on this index for 209 cities, using block data from the 1950 census,[17] and a set of aggregated index values for cities within a common metropolitan area.[18] He recently repeated his fundamental criticism of all other segregation indexes,[19] and we shall subsequently give considerable attention to the merit of city blocks as opposed to census tracts as an areal unit for the computation of segregation indexes.

Shevky and Williams (1949) attempted a distinction between isolation and segregation, segregation being "the position of a group beyond a certain critical point of isolation." The isolation index "indicates the number of times the average concentration is greater than the group's percentage in the total population of the area studied."[20] The measure apparently could be utilized for intercity comparisons, but was used only for comparisons of ethnic groups within one city. In the course of his revision of the Shevky-Williams scheme of social area analysis, Bell developed an index based on a model specifying the probability that the next person one might meet in his residential neighborhood would be a Negro. "The chief advantage of the probability model for the measurement of ecological segregation is that it provides a context for the direct interpretation of scores at all points along the continuum from 'no segregation' to 'complete segregation.'"[21] This index was utilized in "social area" studies of Los Angeles and San Francisco.[22] Willis used the index for an intercity comparative study of residential segregation as of 1950.[23] A multiple regression and covariance analysis was undertaken, with region, size of Negro population, and percentage Negro as independent variables for explaining values on the segregation index.[24]

Bell, commenting on the second Cowgill paper, attacked Cowgill's contention that block data were more useful for the study of residential segregation, and went on to a more far-reaching criticism:

17. Donald O. Cowgill, "Trends in Residential Segregation of Nonwhites in American Cities, 1940–1950," *American Sociological Review*, XXI, No. 1 (February, 1956).

18. Donald O. Cowgill, "Segregation Scores for Metropolitan Areas," *American Sociological Review*, XXVII, No. 3 (June, 1962).

19. *Ibid.*

20. Eshref Shevky and Marilyn Williams, *The Social Areas of Los Angeles* (Berkeley: University of California Press, 1949), p. 49.

21. Wendell Bell, "A Probability Model for the Measurement of Ecological Segregation," *Social Forces*, XXXII, No. 4 (May, 1954), p. 357.

22. Eshref Shevky and Wendell Bell, *Social Area Analysis* (Stanford: Stanford University Press, 1955).

23. Ernest Moore Willis, "A Comparative Study of Negro Segregation in American Cities" (unpublished Master's thesis, Northwestern University, 1956).

24. Wendell Bell and Ernest M. Willis, "The Segregation of Negroes in American Cities," *Social and Economic Studies*, VI, No. 1 (March, 1957).

Dr. Cowgill's article is an important contribution to the study of residential segregation. However, his conclusions, which he states "conclusively," and his conviction that we have "adequate operational definitions of the term segregation" as well as "valid and sensitive measures" of it need to be tempered by the explicit recognition of the fact that the use of alternative procedures and data might result in different, even contradictory, findings and that many methodological problems remain to be solved.[25]

In a detailed unpublished report and a briefer published article (1955), Duncan and Duncan reported a number of "Contributions to the Theory of Segregation Indexes."[26] Most of the previously suggested indexes were related to a common frame of reference, and their interrelations and various other properties were noted. The Duncans gave explicit consideration to problems in using the indexes for inter-city comparative analyses. These contributions drew on a variety of literature on related measurement problems in other fields, and helped clarify many of the methodological issues. Our subsequent methodological discussions bring new empirical material to bear on these issues, but rely heavily on the Duncans' theoretical analysis.

Finally, one case study of "Residential Concentration of Negroes in Chicago" may be noted for its use of a segregation index computed for five different years to quantify a discussion of long-term trends.[27] Wallace drew on the Duncans' analysis in his choice of an index, and developed a unique compromise between reliance on census tracts or city blocks as areal units.

□ SOME INDEXES

The summary methodological article by Duncan and Duncan presented definitions of six segregation indexes within a common framework and notation. They utilized an adaptation of a Lorenz curve for graphical representation. We will sketch their approach here, but much more detail and alternative definitions are presented in the published article, their unpublished report, and the original articles proposing segregation indexes.

25. Wendell Bell, "Comment on Cowgill's 'Trends in Residential Segregation of Nonwhites,'" *American Sociological Review*, XXII, No. 2 (April, 1957), p. 222.

26. Otis Dudley Duncan and Beverly Duncan, "A Methodological Analysis of Segregation Indexes," *American Sociological Review*, XX, No. 2 (April, 1955); "Contributions to the Theory of Segregation Indexes," Urban Analysis Report, No. 14, Prepared under Contract with the Human Resources Research Institute, Air University, Maxwell Air Force Base, Montgomery, Alabama (hectographed preliminary report, Chicago Community Inventory, University of Chicago, February, 1953).

27. David A. Wallace, "Residential Concentration of Negroes in Chicago" (unpublished Ph. D. dissertation, Harvard University, 1953).

Arrange the areal units of a city in order from high to low on the basis of the percentage non-white. With this ordering, for each unit compute X, the cumulative percentage of the city's non-whites residing in that unit and all preceding units, and Y, the cumulative percentage of the city's whites residing in that unit and all preceding units. These cumulative percentages may be plotted in the form of a Lorenz curve to make a "segregation curve." Table A-1 and Fig. A-1 present illustrative data for a hypothetical city with five areal units. If the distribution of whites and non-whites is perfectly even, then every areal unit has an equal percentage non-white, every unit has the same rank order, the cumulative percentages X and Y will be equal, and the segregation curve will follow the diagonal $X = Y$.

If the distribution of whites and non-whites is completely uneven (each areal unit is either 100 per cent non-white or 100 per cent white), then reading down the X column, 100 per cent of the non-whites will be cumulated with 0 per cent of the whites. The segregation curve will follow the X axis to the point (100,0) and then rise along the line $X = 100$. For distributions intermediate between these two extremes, the greater the deviation of the segregation curve from the diagonal $X = Y$, the greater the segregation. Most segregation indexes can be regarded as alternative ways of measuring the deviation of the curve from the diagonal.

The Gini index (identified in subsequent discussion as Gi) is a ratio of the area between the diagonal and the segregation curve to the total area of the triangle beneath the diagonal. The index of dissimilarity (D), which we described in an alternative fashion in Chapter 3, is equal to the maximum vertical distance between the segrega-

TABLE A-1

ILLUSTRATIVE COMPUTATION OF A SEGREGATION CURVE WITH HYPOTHETICAL DATA

Areal Unit	Population (Number) Total	White	Non-white	Percentage Non-white	Cumulative Number White	Non-white	Cumulative Percentage White	Non-white
City total	750	500	250	33.3	......	......	......	......
1	100	10	90	90.0	10	90	2.0	36.0
2	200	90	110	55.0	100	200	22.0	80.0
3	200	155	45	22.5	255	245	51.0	98.0
4	100	95	5	5.0	350	250	70.0	100.0
5	150	150	0	0.0	500	250	100.0	100.0

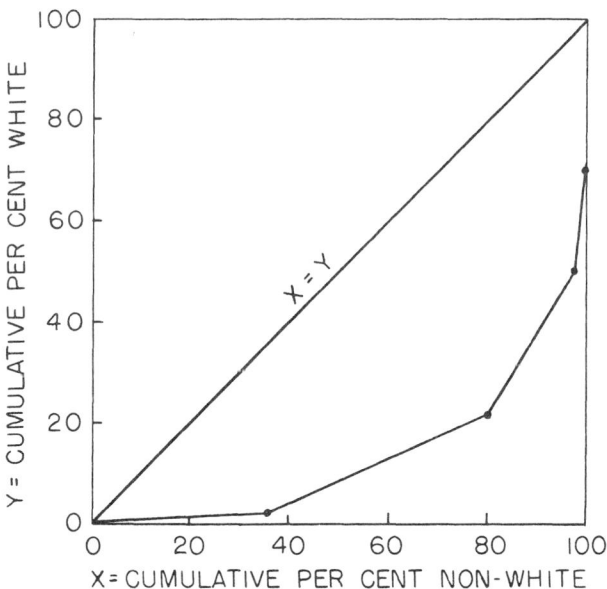

FIGURE A-1. — *Illustrative Segregation Curve, Based
on Hypothetical Data*

tion curve and the diagonal. The index used by Cowgill cannot be
related directly to the segregation curve, but a slight modification
gives an index (Co) that is equal to the length of that portion of the
segregation curve coinciding with the line $X = 100$. Co thus represents the percentage of the city's whites who live in areal units that
are exclusively white. By analogy, an index may be defined equal to
the percentage of the city's non-whites living in areas exclusively
non-white; this index (Oc) is equal to the length of that portion of the
segregation curve coinciding with the line $Y = 0$. These four indexes
— Gi, D, Co, and Oc — utilize only the information contained in the
segregation curve. For several other indexes it is also necessary to
take into explicit consideration the city's non-white percentage (q).

The ghetto index (Gh), like the index of dissimilarity, is a measure
of the displacement of the segregation curve from the diagonal, but
at a point dependent on the city non-white percentage rather than at a
point of maximum displacement. Jahn's reproducibility index (Rep)
is a measure of the extent to which the observed areal distribution of
whites and non-whites can be reproduced solely from the known
total numbers of whites and non-whites and the total populations of
the areal units. Bell's index (Bell) was developed as a probabilistic

interpretation, but is equal to the square of a standard statistic, the correlation ratio of color on areal unit. Several of the segregation indexes, in fact, are equivalent to, or only minor variants of, statistical measures in common use for other purposes.

Hoyt's index, the percentage of non-whites living in areal units that are more than 50 per cent non-white, is directly obtainable from the computations for the segregation curve. The original Cowgill index (Cwg) is analogous to Co, but cannot be defined in terms of the segregation curve. In the subsequent discussion it is shown to have different criteria of minimum and maximum segregation than do indexes dependent on the curve. The indexes identified by Jahn, Schmid, and Schrag as I-1, I-2, I-3 and I-4 have already been mentioned: I-1 = Gh, I-3 = Gi, I-4 = D, and I-2 is approximately equal to the square root of Bell.

□ CRITERIA FOR CHOICE OF AN INDEX

All the indexes mentioned are primarily measures of unevenness in the areal distribution of whites and non-whites. Whether by intent or not, none has been a measure of clustering or location or other aspects of segregation. Thus, none of the indexes distinguishes situations which might be obviously different to the observer relying on maps of racial distributions. Consider the hypothetical example of a city with 25 square areal units, 5 occupied entirely by non-whites and 20 entirely by whites (Fig. A-2). Neither the segregation curve,

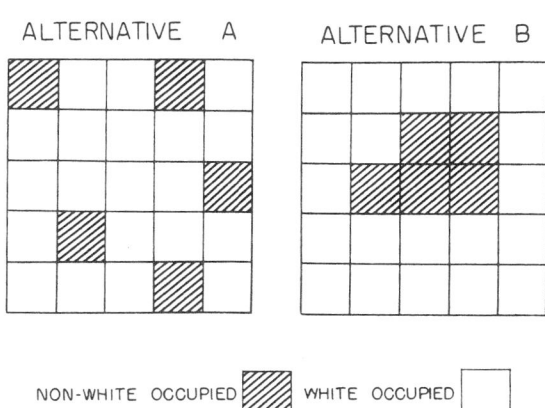

FIGURE A-2. — *Schematic   Locations   of   5*
Blocks Occupied by Non-whites
in a City with 25 Blocks

nor any of the proposed indexes, nor any other measure of unevenness as represented by the segregation curve, can distinguish the two
situations represented in the alternative spacings of the five non-white
residential areas. Again we emphasize that any single measure of a
complex phenomenon must abstract some tiny portion of that complexity. With regard to the two alternatives shown in Fig. A-2, however, we can assume for U.S. cities that under circumstances where
whites and non-whites are highly segregated from each other, it is
more likely that the distribution will be closer to the clustered pattern
than to the scattered one.

Although the possibility of describing an index verbally may be
useful in explaining the index, we see no reason to list this as an
important criterion in the choice of a segregation index. In some cases,
a verbal index may be misleading. Williams, for instance, christened
index I-1 proposed by Jahn, Schmid, and Schrag the "Ghetto index,"
arguing as follows:

> The first index, "I-1," was defined as the difference between the
> proportion of all Negroes, and the proportion of all whites, in a
> certain area, called "area I." The area is in the heart of the Negro
> community and is just large enough to accommodate all the Negroes
> of the city. We can visualize it as the area where the Black Ghetto
> would be if there were one. I shall accordingly refer to it as the
> Ghetto, and to the first index as the Ghetto index.[28]

In the computation of the Ghetto index, however, no account is
taken of the location of Negro residential areas or whether there is a
"ghetto." Both Alternative A and Alternative B in Fig. A-2 would have
the same value on this index. In a similar vein, Williams christened
index I-4 the "Section index," because of an analogous relationship
to the "Negro section." The computation of the index takes no account
of the degree of clustering of Negroes into a "section."

Another blind alley in the verbal discussion of segregation
indexes is the attempt to distinguish between segregation, concentration, isolation, and so on. All these terms have a variety of meanings,
and distinctions between them are arbitrary. We do not share the
opposite extreme, however, of reliance on statistical properties only
in choice of an index. We endorse the plea by Duncan and Duncan
for a closer articulation in this field between concept and method:

> A difficult problem of validation is faced by the proponent of a
> segregation index formula. The concept of "segregation" in the
> literature of human ecology is complex and somewhat fuzzy, i.e.,
> the concept involves a number of analytically distinguishable
> elements, none of which is yet capable of completely operational
> description. Yet it is a concept rich in theoretical suggestiveness

28. Williams, op. cit., p. 301.

and of unquestionable heuristic value. Clearly we would not wish to sacrifice the capital of theorization and observation already invested in the concept. Yet this is what is involved in the solution offered by naïve operationism, in more or less arbitrarily matching some convenient numerical procedure with the verbal concept of segregation. The problem must be faced of considering a variety of possible selections of data and operations on these data in an effort to capture methodologically what is valuable in the work done with the concept prior to the formulation of an index. As we have suggested, it may be that no single index will be sufficient, because of the complexity of the notion of segregation, involving as it does considerations of spatial pattern, unevenness of distribution, relative size of the segregated group, and homogeneity of sub-areas, among others. In short, we are emphasizing the distinction between the problems of (a) working from a limited set of data to a mathematically convenient summary index, and (b) working from a theoretically problematic situation to a rationale for selecting and manipulating data.[29]

Let us for the moment accept a concern with unevenness of distribution as the basic aspect of residential segregation we desire to measure, and inquire into some criteria that have been proposed for evaluating an index of unevenness, and the degree to which the various indexes meet these criteria. Two basic criteria have been generally accepted, specifying that an index should have a value of 0 for a situation of "no segregation" and 100 for a situation of "complete segregation." With respect to unevenness, these criteria may perhaps best be specified with reference to the segregation curve. Coincidence of the curve with the diagonal represents complete evenness; and coincidence with the X-axis and the line $X = 100$ represents complete unevenness. Nearly all of the indexes discussed above conform to these criteria. The original Cowgill index is an exception. Indexes of the type used by Hoyt, taking the percentage of a city's non-whites who reside in areas where non-whites comprise more than a certain percentage of the population, will conform to the criteria provided the specified percentage is above the non-white percentage in the city as a whole.

Curiously, Cowgill and Cowgill claimed to be conforming to these criteria, but at the same time indicated a different criterion of "no segregation."

At this juncture the authors devised their own operational index which meets the basic specifications originally set forth by Jahn and his associates for their indices, viz., complete lack of segregation, operationally defined as maximum of distribution among blocks of

29. Duncan and Duncan, *op. cit.*, p. 217.

the city, will result in an index of zero; and complete segregation will produce an index of 1.000.[30]

Minimum segregation is thus defined as occurring when non-whites reside in the maximum number of blocks:

> This is equivalent to one of two figures; it is either the total number of blocks in the city or the total number of dwellings occupied by nonwhites, whichever is the lesser figure. The rationale for this figure is that obviously in a city with only 20 nonwhite dwelling units, these dwelling units cannot be distributed in more than 20 blocks, hence, 20 blocks will represent the maximum spread or complete lack of segregation for that city. However, in another city with 3400 nonwhite dwelling units and only 700 blocks, the maximum number of blocks which could be occupied by nonwhites is not the number of nonwhite dwellings units, but the total number of blocks. Complete nonsegregation in the latter case would be achieved, for purposes of this index, when there is at least one nonwhite dwelling unit in each block.[31]

We are not concerned here with the arbitrary decision to scale the maximum value at 1.00 or 100, but rather with the differing concepts of minimum segregation. These concepts may be illustrated, first with an actual example and then with a hypothetical situation. This issue has caused some sharp controversy, and a full discussion is necessary.[32]

. The first case to be considered, that of Oak Park (Ill.), in 1950, illustrates the type of situation that the Cowgills argue would be misclassified by the segregation curve criterion indicated above. There were 25 dwelling units occupied by non-whites, each in a different block (Fig. A-3). By the Cowgills' definition, this represents the maximum possible scatter of non-white dwelling units, and the city receives an index of 0 for no segregation. But by the segregation curve criterion, the residential distribution is quite uneven. Of 513 blocks, 488 are occupied exclusively by whites. The other 25 blocks have non-white percentages ranging from 0.6 to 100, all of which are considerably higher than the over-all city percentage, 0.1. The index of dissimilarity for this situation is 95.0, which is high in the range of observed values for cities in 1950.

The difference between the two criteria of minimum segregation may be illustrated with further consideration of the Oak Park situation. Assuming that the 25 non-white dwellings are located in different blocks and that the value of the Cowgill index is therefore zero, what

---

30. Cowgill and Cowgill, *op. cit.*, p. 827.

31. *Ibid.*, pp. 827–829.

32. See, for example, the correspondence in the *American Sociological Review*, by Bell, *op. cit.*; by Duncan and Duncan in XXVIII, No. 1 (February, 1963); and by Cowgill and Taeuber in XXVIII, No. 3 (June, 1963).

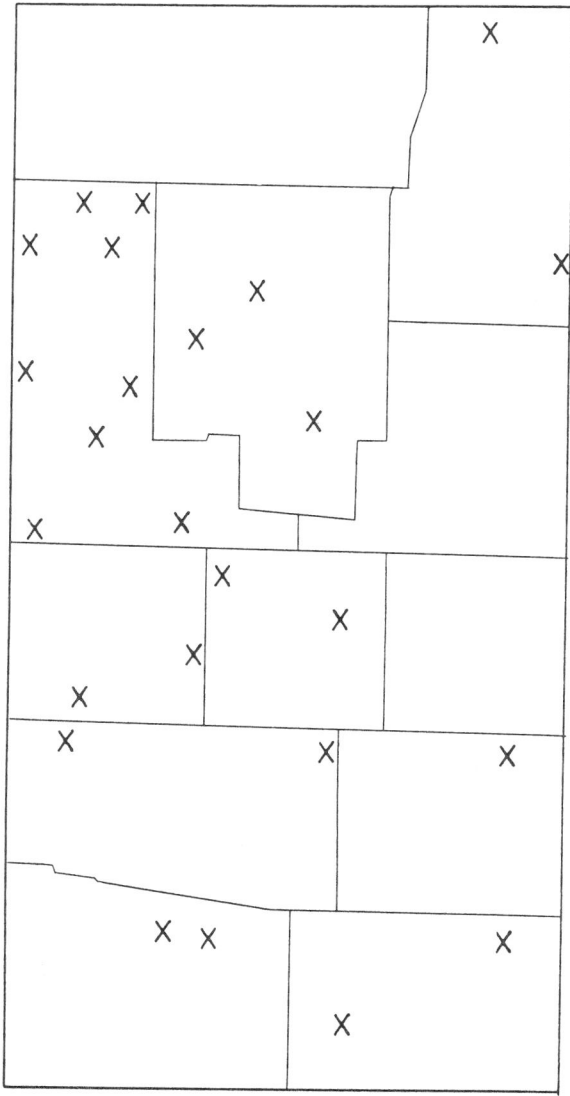

NOTE: THE CENSUS TRACT BOUNDARIES ARE
OUTLINED. EACH X REPRESENTS THE APPROXI-
MATE LOCATION OF A BLOCK CONTAINING ONE
NON-WHITE-OCCUPIED DWELLING UNIT.

FIGURE A-3.—*Oak Park, Ill.: Location of Dwelling
Units Occupied by Non-whites, 1950*
(Source: *Census Block Bulletin for
Oak Park, Illinois, 1950*)

is the range of possible values for the index of dissimilarity? The maximum obtains if the 25 non-white dwellings are located in the 25 smallest blocks, in this case, those with fewer than 10 occupied dwelling units. These 25 blocks would then contain 100 per cent of the non-white dwellings, but only 0.5 per cent of the white dwellings, and the index of dissimilarity would have a value of 99.5. If the 25 non-white dwellings were located in the 25 largest blocks (those with 110 to 243 occupied dwelling units), then those 25 blocks would contain 100 per cent of the non-white-occupied dwellings and 17.5 per cent of the white-occupied dwellings, and the index would have a value of 82.5. Thus, we find that for a situation which one segregation index assigns the minimum value of zero, another index assigns a value possibly as high as 99.5, and no lower than 82.5, still very high.

This example demonstrates the fact that an even distribution of whites and non-whites is impossible to attain in practice, particularly where both the number of non-whites and the areal units are small. Complete evenness requires equal proportions of non-whites in each areal unit, and attaining this for small units would ordinarily require fractional persons or dwellings. For cities with sizable non-white populations, these fractions become small relative to the actual numbers in each areal unit, and the index of dissimilarity (or another index of unevenness) can approach its theoretical minimum value of zero. It would be possible to compute for each city the minimum attainable index, and adjust the index of dissimilarity or other segregation index so that its attainable range is 0 to 100. Such an adjustment to an index would alter somewhat its interpretation, and any such adjustment must be made on conceptual as well as methodological grounds.

A second example illustrates hypothetically the difference between perfect unevenness and maximum spread as criteria for minimum segregation. Assume a city in which all the whites live in modern, large apartment houses, each of which occupies one city block. Assume that almost all Negroes live in rundown tenements in a cluster of blocks near the center of the city, except that each white-occupied apartment building employs a Negro janitor who lives in a basement room. Since there is at least one non-white dwelling unit in each block, the Cowgill index would therefore assume a value of 0. Unevenness in the racial distribution, however, is obvious, and an index of dissimilarity would assume a value near 100.

The Cowgill and dissimilarity indexes do not differ solely in their treatment of selected extreme patterns of residential distribution. Other differences between them can perhaps be viewed more easily by considering the modified Cowgill index. The index of dissimilarity is a measure of the maximum deviation of the segregation curve from the diagonal that represents an even distribution. The modified

Cowgill index, Co, is a measure of the length of the portion of the upper right-hand tail of the segregation curve lying on the line $X = 100$. The index of dissimilarity is clearly a superior general index of unevenness, and the modified Cowgill measure is clearly a special-purpose measure focusing on one aspect of unevenness. The index of dissimilarity must be at least as large as the modified Cowgill index, but, as we have seen, can assume almost any value if the modified Cowgill index has a low value. To anticipate our conclusions concerning index choice, we believe that as a first step in analyzing segregation indexes, it is more sensible to choose an index that is a general measure of unevenness. At a later stage, it might be worthwhile to use the modified Cowgill index and other measures of specific aspects of residential distribution to distinguish among cities with similar degrees of over-all unevenness. However, we do not believe that such specific measures can be regarded as general-purpose indexes of residential segregation.

Another general conclusion about the use of segregation indexes may be reached at this point. In terms of the segregation curve, any suburb or other city with only a few Negro residents will almost invariably have a very uneven residential distribution. For such cities, however, the internal evenness of the distribution may be of little interest compared to the racial composition of the city considered in the context of the metropolitan area or region of which it is a part. In a study of Negro suburban movement and the beginnings of residential integration, it might be appropriate to be concerned with whether Oak Park's 25 non-white households were located in a single cluster or scattered more widely in the city. Conceptually, however, it is hard to merge a study of patterns of residential integration of a few Negro residents in a predominantly white suburb with a study of general differences in patterns of residential segregation in cities with large established Negro populations. An index appropriate for the latter study may be inappropriate for the former, and it may be necessary for the latter type of study to restrict its attention to cities with sizable Negro populations.

In addition to criteria specifying minimum and maximum values, other criteria for segregation indexes have been suggested:

> In addition to these two basic stipulations, a satisfactory measure of ecological segregation should (1) be expressed as a single quantitative value so as to facilitate such statistical procedures as comparison, classification, and correlation; (2) be relatively easy to compute; (3) not be distorted by the size of the total population, the proportion of Negroes, or the area of a city; (4) be generally applicable to all cities; and (5) differentiate degrees of segregation in

such a way that the distribution of intermediate scores cover most of the possible range between the extremes of 0 and 100.[33]

Accepting a concern with measuring the general degree of unevenness in the residential distributions of whites and non-whites, we may briefly indicate our feelings about these criteria, and their implications for index choice.

The first criterion is met by all of the proposed indexes. Conceptually, however, more than one dimension of a residential distribution may be of interest, and for some purposes a set of values may be needed to characterize a single city. We have already suggested the possibility of using jointly an index of dissimilarity and a modified Cowgill index. Any measure of segregation, single- or multiple-valued, may be used for comparison and classification.

Correlation and various other statistical techniques, however, may require assumptions about the nature of a segregation index which are hard to justify. Williams, for instance, pointed out some ambiguities in the use of segregation indexes. Proposing for the sake of argument that an index be developed that is proportional to the percentage of all Negroes living in completely Negro areas, she commented:

> It would mean, for instance, that if 50% of the Negroes in one such city and only 25% in another lived in the Negro section, the indices would have the ratio 2 to 1. But are we sure that the first city is "twice as much segregated" as the other? I think not. For if we were to compare the proportions of Negroes who were living in the *unsegregated* area, we should have 50% and 75% respectively, in the two cities, and the ratio would no longer be 2 to 1. This shows, I think, that as far as intuition goes, we simply do not know what we mean by the amount of segregation, even in this very simple case, and that the proposed criterion would be unduly arbitrary.[34]

Williams' example confuses the issue slightly by contrasting an index based on one set of percentages with an index based on a set of percentages obtained by subtracting each of the original set from 100. That those two indexes differ is of more interest conceptually than methodologically, since it smacks of the problem discussed previously in connection with the Cowgill index: should the index focus on the white population in exclusively white areas, the Negro population in exclusively Negro areas, or some other aspect of the residential pattern? The methodological issue is whether or not a segregation index is a true ratio scale for which it is meaningful to make statements such as: "This index value is twice as large as that one." This is

33. Jahn, Schmid, and Schrag, *op. cit.*, p. 294.
34. Williams, *op. cit.*, p. 302.

clearly formally possible, since the indexes under discussion are all continuous over the range 0 to 100. In a formal sense, an index value of 50 can be regarded as being midway between 25 and 75, or as being twice as large as a value of 25. The techniques of correlation, regression, and the like are applicable. Williams is correct, however, in pointing to some substantive questions associated with treating index values in this manner. Is there any substantive meaning in a statement that one city is twice as segregated as another? Is the difference between 80 and 90 equivalent to the difference between 90 and 100? Clearly there is no substantive meaning in such statements independent of the specific index being utilized. Once the concept of residential segregation is operationalized in a particular way, however, such statements have a legitimate meaning, but only with respect to that particular definition of segregation. If we may recall the previously quoted statement of Duncan and Duncan, we would caution once again that we are not calling for "arbitrarily matching some convenient numerical procedure with the verbal concept of segregation," but for "working from a theoretically problematic situation to a rationale for selecting and manipulating data."

The criterion suggested by Jahn, Schmid, and Schrag—that a segregation index should be easy to compute—has less merit in the age of computers than it did when they offered it. We do agree that the economics of research can legitimately dictate reliance on the more easily computed index, if the choice is between two equally valid representations of a concept. For example, it is essentially economy that dictated our reliance on the index of dissimilarity rather than the Gini concentration index, since we regard the two as equally defensible operationalizations of the concept of over-all unevenness, and the index of dissimilarity is more simply calculated. Ease of computation, however, must be secondary to conceptual validity.

That an index of segregation "not be distorted by the size of the total population, the proportion of Negroes, or the area of a city" sounds reasonable, but we share the Duncans' difficulty in understanding what is meant. In general, we believe that the relationship between degree of segregation and a city's population size, Negro proportion, and land area are empirical questions; and it would seem preferable that an index not have a built-in mathematical relationship with any of these variables or any other variables that might be studied as correlates of segregation. Jahn, Schmid, and Schrag reported correlations between one of their four indexes (the Ghetto index) and several variables they thought might be related to the degree of residential segregation. They obtained a moderately high coefficient of correlation between the Ghetto index for a city and the city's crude death rate from tuberculosis. However, crude death rates from tuberculosis are highly correlated with city proportion non-white, which enters directly into the computation of the Ghetto index; and the Duncans showed that the apparent relationship between residential segregation and tuberculosis death rate was greatly reduced if the proportion non-white was held constant by statistical procedures. Using the Gini index, which does not directly involve the non-white proportion in its computation, the correlation between segregation and tuberculosis death rates was insignificant.

If the concept of residential segregation is defined in such a manner that the proportion non-white in a city must enter explicitly into the computation of an index, then any analysis of relationships between segregation and other variables becomes difficult. Many variables are correlated with proportion non-white, and correlations with proportion non-white would be confounded with correlations with residential segregation. Holding constant the proportion non-white would not be an appropriate solution. It would not be legitimate to argue that a partial correlation between some variable and a segregation index, holding constant the proportion non-white, represents the relationship between the variable and residential segregation. It makes little sense to use an index in which the non-white proportion is an integral component, and then to partial out that component and claim that what is left is residential segregation.

Our feeling is that the concept of residential segregation should be distinguished from the proportion non-white and other such characteristics of a city's population. We view residential segregation as a concept suggesting only that the residential distribution of whites differs from that of non-whites. This view of residential segregation seems adequately represented by the segregation curve, and by the alternative terminology of the "unevenness" of the residential distributions. An appropriate measure should be a measure of the deviation of the segregation curve from the diagonal of "perfect evenness." Of the indexes discussed so far, only the Gini, dissimilarity, modified Cowgill, and converse Cowgill (Oc) indexes are invariant so long as the segregation curve remains unchanged. With a given segregation curve, values of the Ghetto, Reproducibility, Bell, and Hoyt indexes can vary, depending on the proportion non-white. The first four indexes, therefore, might be said to be "pure" measures of unevenness, not "distorted" by the proportion non-white. The other four clearly do not meet a criterion that "a satisfactory measure . . . not be distorted by . . . the proportion of Negroes. . . ."

We believe that the above discussion indicates a reasonable solution of the problem posed by the confounding of residential segregation and proportion non-white. It might be objected that the shape of the segregation curve is itself partially dependent on the relationship between the size of the total population, the number and population size of the areal units, and the number and proportion of non-whites. In fact, we demonstrated some of these relationships previously for the case of Oak Park. However, the whole notion of residential segregation is dependent on these same variables, and any metric must have some dependence on them. The distinction that we deem crucial derives from the fact that a specifiable mathematical relationship holds between some proposed segregation indexes and the proportion non-white, whereas for other indexes there is only a loose dependence.

We have focused on the problem of "distortion" of index values by the proportion non-white because this seems a serious problem which has caused difficulties. The criterion proposed by Jahn, Schmid, and Schrag also mentioned the size of the total population and the area of a city. It is not obvious that any of the proposed indexes are "distorted" by these variables in the sense in which they are distorted by the proportion non-white. The suggestion that a segregation index be generally applicable to all cities is either trivial or has reference to sources of data rather than to the concept itself. It seems obvious that a segregation "index" should be conceptualized in terms applicable to all cities, or to all cities meeting certain criteria. This excludes measures (which ordinarily would not be called "indexes") such as the ratio of the number of Negroes living in the area of Chicago bounded by Roosevelt Road, Cottage Grove, 103rd Street, and Halsted to the total number of Negroes living in Chicago.

If the criterion of general applicability refers to the availability of data, then we do not think it relevant at this point, although another version of it recurs in the controversy over the merits of census tracts and city blocks as areal units, to be discussed later. Although most segregation indexes proposed in the literature have been defined in terms of data for a specific areal unit, all of them are applicable to any areal unit. The availability of appropriate data is a problem of cost and feasibility. We prefer to determine first the conceptual validity of an index and to leave for later the question of whether the requisite data can be obtained using one or another set of published data, or whether expensive field operations are necessary to obtain them.

The proposed criterion of "general applicability" of an index can be interpreted to make it more meaningful. An index value of, say, 85.1, should be comparable to any other index value of 85.1. Our purpose in computing segregation indexes is to permit intercity comparisons, and there must be some sense in which equal index values mean equal degrees of segregation. On the one hand, this consideration can lead to methodological questions, such as that of comparability between indexes computed with census tract data and those computed with city block data, which will be discussed later. More relevant here is the conceptual implication. Our preference for indexes depending solely on the segregation curve has been made clear by now, so that attention may be confined to the concept of residential segregation or unevenness represented by the segregation curve. The modified and converse Cowgill indexes measure the deviation of a segregation curve from the diagonal at particular points. Index values are directly translatable into statements about the corresponding segregation curves, and, indeed, can be regarded primarily as descriptions of the right and left tails of the curve. Two cities with identical index values clearly have segregation curves that are identical at the tail.

The Gini and dissimilarity indexes, which are over-all measures of the deviation of the segregation curve from the diagonal, share the property of most averages — differing distributions can have identical average values. Two cities with identical index values do not necessarily have identical segregation curves, and two cities with differing segregation curves do not necessarily have different index values. If two segregation curves do not intersect between the points (0,0) and (100,100), then the Gini and dissimilarity indexes, and any other reasonable measure of over-all unevenness, would rank the two curves in the same order. If, however, the curves do intersect, then the two Gini indexes might rank differently than the two indexes of dissimilarity. If the curves intersect, unambiguous comparison of over-all unevenness is not possible, and the choice of index determines the manner of deciding which curve represents the greater deviation from the diagonal.

The final criterion to be discussed — that a satisfactory segregation index should "differentiate degrees of segregation in such a way that the distribution of intermediate scores covers most of the possible range between the extremes of 0 and 100" — can be disposed of quickly. If all cities for which index values are computed are highly segregated residentially, then it seems reasonable that the obtained values would cluster near the maximum. The distribution of scores for any set of cities is an empirical outcome, not a conceptual or methodological problem. It is always possible to adjust any index in such a way that the values will appear more spread out, but the rationale for such a procedure escapes us, since there is danger that the conceptual meaning of the index could thereby be obscured or altered.

□ EMPIRICAL INTERRELATIONS AMONG INDEXES

We have seen that various measures proposed for the measurement of residential segregation differ in (1) the items of information utilized in their computation and (2) the specific formulas by which values between 0 and 100 are assigned to differing residential distributions. In their analysis relating most of the measures to the common framework of the segregation curve, the Duncans demonstrated certain algebraic interrelations among the indexes. In the preceding discussion, we noted that some of the indexes utilize the proportion non-white in the city for their computation, other indexes depend only on the information in the segregation curve, and still others cannot be directly related to the segregation curve. The general question may be raised as to whether the various conceptual and operational differences between the several indexes are significant in empirical investigation. Aside from extreme cases such as Oak Park, will a city generally be found to have approximately the same degree of residential segregation relative to other cities, regardless of which segregation index is used?

Using data on the distributions of white and non-white households from the 1950 census, values of eight separate segregation indexes have been computed for each of 188 cities.[35] Intercorrelations among the various indexes are presented in Table A-2. The numerous low coefficients indicate that the indexes are not simply minor variants of each other. The conceptual and algebraic differences between the indexes are apparent in the patterning of the intercorrelations.

The first column of the table shows the correlations between each index and the proportion of non-whites in the city population. The coefficients are positive and moderately high for the three indexes (Gh, Rep, Bell) that utilize the proportion non-white in their formulas. Of substantive as well as methodological interest is the lack of association between either of the pure measures of general spatial unevenness (Gi, D) and the proportion non-white. The moderately high correlations obtaining for the two specialized pure measures of unevenness (Co, Oc) reflect an empirical relationship between proportion non-white and the shape of either tail of the segregation curve. In other words, the greater the proportion non-white in a city, the greater the proportion of this non-white population that lives in blocks occupied exclusively by non-whites, and the lower the proportion of the city's white population that lives in blocks occupied exclusively by whites. The original Cowgill index resembles Gi and D in displaying a low association with proportion non-white. The above findings justify our conceptual and methodological concern with the distinction between residential segregation and proportion non-white.

Three indexes, Gh, Rep, and Bell, share a confounding of unevenness and proportion non-white, and their formulas are such that high

35. A later section of this appendix deals with sources and computation procedures for all these indexes.

TABLE A-2

INTERCORRELATIONS AMONG EIGHT SEGREGATION INDEXES
AND THE PERCENTAGE NON-WHITE, 188 CITIES, 1950

Segregation Index†	Segregation Index							
	q	Gi	D	Co	Oc	Gh	Rep	Bell
Gi....................	.19°							
D.....................	−.01	.90°						
Co....................	−.50°	.58°	.75°					
Oc....................	.76°	.51°	.32°	−.13				
Gh	.69°	.49°	.13	.32°	.75°			
Rep..................	.79°	.52°	.22°	−.31°	.85°	.95°		
Bell..................	.72°	.52°	.19°	−.30°	.81°	.99°	.98°	
Cwg	.20°	.55°	.05	−.04	.34°	.70°	.49°	.63°

Source: The indexes were computed from data for city blocks, as described in the section on "Computation Procedures."

° Statistically significant at the .05 level.

† The indexes are identified and defined in the section on "Some Indexes."

intercorrelations would be expected. Empirically this is the case, as indicated by intercorrelations of .95 and above.

Our concern with the conceptual differences between the Cowgill index and other indexes also turns out to be very important in practice. The highest correlation between Cwg and any of the other indexes is .70, indicating that a linear relationship can explain less than 50 per cent of the variance between Cwg and any other index. It is interesting that the apparently slight conceptual shift necessary to develop an index analogous to Cwg, but defined in terms of the segregation curve, resulted in an index whose empirical behavior is radically different. Cwg and Co are virtually uncorrelated. These correlations are based on 188 cities, including many, such as Oak Park, containing few non-whites. It is for such cities that the conceptual distinction is most important. If attention is confined to 47 cities with large Negro populations, the correlation between Cwg and Co rises to .92. Recalling that the index of dissimilarity is always greater than or equal to the modified Cowgill index, it is interesting that for the group of 47 cities, the correlation both between D and Co and between D and Cwg is .81. If there is a high degree of unevenness in the white and non-white residential distributions, the maximum deviation of the segregation curve from the diagonal will occur to the right near the line X = 100. Thus, it is reasonable that D and Co (or Cwg) will be highly correlated, providing there is no prevalent pattern of "token integration" (many blocks with only one or two non-white households) to keep the segregation curve a slight distance away from the line X = 100.

The correlation between Gi and D is .90 for the large group of cities, and .96 for the smaller group. Our earlier discussion of these two indexes as being conceptually similar is now supplemented by their empirical similarity. Our discussion of criteria for a useful segregation index indicated our preference for either of these two indexes, and our choice among them, which is made on the basis of computational economy, has little bearing on the outcome of our investigations.

Although the several segregation indexes are not empirically identical, our conceptual discussion has indicated that they are not eight wholly independent measures. Using tract data, the Duncans have reported that observed values of D and the proportion non-white could be used to obtain quite good estimates of Gi, Gh, Rep, and Bell.[36] It is clear from our empirical intercorrelations that multiple linear regressions could be obtained permitting good predictions of most of the indexes, given values of certain others. The non-white proportion, D, and Cwg are relatively independent of each other, at least among the 188 cities. Without precise evaluation, we can see that linear combinations of these three could be used to estimate values of the other six indexes. At least 60 per cent of the variance in Oc could be accounted for, and better predictions could be obtained for the other indexes.

As a means of quickly assessing and summarizing the inter-correlations of the eight indexes and the proportion non-white, an exploratory factor analysis was undertaken using the Turinsky direct-factor program for Univac. The raw data were used for the full set of 188 cities, and the resulting factors are not readily identifiable. For present purposes, however, it is sufficient to note that the patterning of the factor loadings on the indexes for four extracted factors holds no surprises. Gi and D have similar loadings on each factor, and Gh, Rep, and Bell form a separate cluster of indexes. Cwg resembles Co on two factors, but stands by itself on the other two. Co partially resembles Cwg and partially resembles Gi and D. The proportion non-white and Oc form a final distinctive cluster. In summary, although all the segregation indexes proposed by sociologists can be related to a common conceptual framework, there are empirically important

36. Duncan and Duncan, "A Methodological Analysis . . . ," *op. cit.*, p. 214.

methodological and conceptual differences between them. The results of any substantive analysis utilizing segregation indexes will depend very heavily on the choice of a specific index.

□ CHOICE OF AREAL UNIT: THE PROBLEM

Most investigations of residential segregation have relied on data for wards, census tracts, or other moderately large subareas within cities. For the most part this choice of subareas was made on the basis of availability of data and convenience of handling. Data for individual city blocks were not generally available before the late 1930's, and in any case it is much more difficult to prepare a map, let alone a complicated statistical index, with data for several thousand city blocks than with data for a few dozen tracts or wards. Hoyt noticed that instances of complete non-white occupancy of an areal unit were much more common for city blocks than for enumeration districts, a larger unit.[37] With his Reproducibility index for Seattle, Jahn reported values of 63 when computed from block data and 17 when computed from tract data.[38] Neither he nor any other sociologist had given explicit attention to this large effect of choice of areal unit on the observable degree of residential segregation until the Cowgills criticized all prior work on segregation indexes because of its supposed reliance on tract data:

> The use of census tracts as the unit of measurement invalidates all of the indices cited above. No valid segregation index can be constructed on the basis of districts laid out for any other purpose than delineating ethnic groups. In other words, any valid measure of segregation of an ethnic group will have to start with the realities of ethnic distribution, *i.e.*, the real ethnic area at the moment, or reduce the areal unit to such a small size that distortion resulting from overlapping boundaries is held to a minimum. This suggests that some virtue might inhere in an index based on blocks. Certainly tracts or wards cannot suffice.[39]

There is a serious problem in choosing an areal unit for the measurement of residential segregation, but before undertaking a systematic review of the basic considerations, two misleading points in the Cowgills' critique may be noted. First, the indexes cited by the Cowgills can all be computed from data for census tracts, city blocks, or any other areal unit. The relative merits of the various indexes,

37. U.S. Federal Housing Administration, *op. cit.*
38. Jahn, *op. cit.*
39. Cowgill and Cowgill, *op. cit.*, p. 826.

including the index offered by the Cowgills, must be assessed on the basis of other properties, such as those cited in the preceding section. Second, the Cowgills did not demonstrate that city blocks, any more than census tracts, conform to "the realities of ethnic distribution."

> The problem cannot be solved merely by reducing the size of areal units, *e.g.*, to blocks. The objections made to the census tract basis apply also, *mutatis mutandis*, to blocks. For example, if all nonwhites resided on alleyways and all whites in street-front structures, then even a block index would fail to reveal the high degree of segregation.[40]

The valid point in the controversy inaugurated by the Cowgills is that the magnitude of a segregation index, and even the very concept of residential segregation, depend on the choice of an areal unit. Residential segregation cannot be observed or defined except with respect to the distribution of population among some system of areal units.

Measures analogous to those suggested by sociologists have been used in other disciplines for measuring other aspects of areal distributions. A geographer in 1937 concluded that no two such indexes can be regarded as comparable with one another unless they have both been computed with reference to comparable areal systems. Systems such as tracts, blocks, wards, enumeration districts, and the like he termed "irregular," and "irregular systems are never comparable."[41] Strictly speaking, then, we are not justified in undertaking an intercity analysis of residential segregation, for our measures cannot be computed on a comparable basis for different cities.

The choice of an areal unit on which to base an intercity comparative analysis of residential segregation must be based on an assessment both of the conceptual usefulness of defining segregation in terms of that areal unit, and of the degree to which reliance on that areal unit will minimize the inherent problems of non-comparability.

Some illustrations may help clarify this rather abstract discussion. Fig. A-4 presents three alternative locations for a residential area composed solely of members of the minority group. The city is assumed to be divided into four tracts. The first diagram shows the boundaries of the minority area coinciding with the boundaries of one tract. The second diagram shows the minority area overlapping each of the tracts, with unequal parts in each, and the third diagram shows the minority area evenly split among the four tracts. The index

---

40. Duncan and Duncan, *op. cit.*, p. 216.

41. John K. Wright, "Some Measures of Distributions," *Annals of the Association of American Geographers*, XXVII, No. 4 (December, 1937), p. 201.

A. THE NEGRO RESIDENTIAL
   AREA COINCIDES WITH
   ONE TRACT.

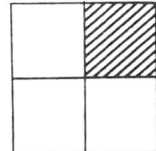

B. THE NEGRO RESIDENTIAL
   AREA OVERLAPS TRACT
   BOUNDARIES.

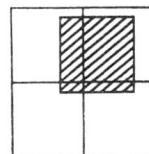

C. THE NEGRO RESIDENTIAL
   AREA OVERLAPS TRACT
   BOUNDARIES, WITH EQUAL
   PARTS IN EACH TRACT.

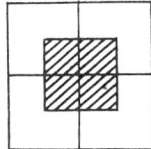

FIGURE A-4. — *Schematic Locations of a Negro Residential Area in a City*

of dissimilarity and most of the other segregation indexes, if computed from data for the four tracts, would assign a value of 100 to the first case, 0 to the third case, and some intermediate value to the second case. The Cowgills used a similar diagram, arguing that census tracts might or might not coincide with minority areas discernible on the basis of more detailed data.

Data for city blocks, however, may similarly fail to demonstrate the maximum degree of residential separation apparent from data on the location of individual households. One study, in fact, utilized data for "linear blocks" (the facing sides of a block-long street segment) rather than the customary "island blocks" in an attempt to get around this problem.[42] Clearly this approach can be pursued to an extreme point where the initial problem is overlooked. Even individual households may not be racially homogeneous. The use of smaller and smaller subareas can increase the observable degree of racial homo-

42. U.S. Federal Works Agency, Work Projects Administration of Georgia, *Population Mobility: A Study of Family Movements Affecting Augusta, Georgia, 1899–1939*, by Glenn Hutchinson and Maurice R. Brewster (Work Projects Administration, 1942).

geneity, but one cannot study residential segregation, defined as the uneven areal distribution of the races, without the use of areas.[43] In fact, it may be far more difficult to locate Harlem on a map showing the percentage Negro for each city block than on one showing the percentage for census tracts or other large areal units. The choice of an areal unit determines whether the data will reveal the "coarse" or the "fine" structure of the residential distribution, and neither course has any inherent superiority.

☐ CHOICE OF AREAL UNIT: CENSUS TRACTS OR CITY BLOCKS

An intercity comparative analysis must utilize available census data unless funds are available for considerable field work. In the national censuses of 1940, 1950, and 1960, data for subareas of cities have been presented principally for two types of areas—census tracts and city blocks. In practical terms, then, there is a choice between using census tracts, using city blocks, or not undertaking the study. Let us review the nature of tracts and blocks, and discuss their relative merits with respect to the twin problems of concept and comparability.

> Census tracts are small areas, having a population usually between 3,000 and 6,000, into which certain large cities . . . have been subdivided for statistical and local administrative purposes, through cooperation with a local committee in each case. Although this subdivision into tracts has been more or less arbitrary, several principles have been followed in laying out the tracts for each city. The tract areas are established with a view to approximate uniformity in population, with some consideration of uniformity in size, and with due regard for natural features. Each tract is designated to include an area fairly homogeneous in population characteristics.[44]

The ordinary city of 50,000 or more population is divided into 15 to 200 census tracts, although the number is much larger for the largest cities, reaching more than 2,000 for New York. In general, this is a convenient number of units for mapping or statistical analysis, and census tracts have been used extensively in urban research as a means

43. It is possible, however, that some techniques tor the study of spatial distributions of (plant and animal) populations which do not depend on areal data might be adapted to the study of residential segregation, but the practical difficulties of obtaining appropriate data seem enormous. See Otis Dudley Duncan, "The Measurement of Population Distribution," *Population Studies*, XI, No. 1 (July, 1957).

44. U.S. Bureau of the Census, *U.S. Census of Population: 1950*, Vol. III, *Census Tract Statistics* (Washington: U.S. Government Printing Office, 1952), p. 1.

of delineating the "coarse" aspects of a city's spatial structure.

The use of census tracts for research in urban sociology has occasionally been criticized on the basis that tracts are not homogeneous subareas. In general, we fail to see the relevance of this sort of criticism. No subarea is homogeneous according to all criteria, and census tracts are more or less homogeneous according to the criterion being considered. Indeed, in a study of residential segregation, it is, of course, the degree of homogeneity with respect to race that would be measured by computing any of the segregation indexes from census tract data. The degree of homogeneity in this case would be an empirical question, the object of study, and not something to be regarded as a methodological nuisance.

There is, however, a more specific aspect of the homogeneity issue that is potentially troublesome when census tracts are the subareas. Local census tract committees are instructed to make tracts somewhat homogeneous in population characteristics. No specific guidance is given, and the extent to which racial composition has been used as one of the criteria for tract homogeneity cannot be ascertained. In their critique of the use of census tracts as a subarea for the computation of segregation indexes, Cowgill and Cowgill argue that the arbitrary and variable degree of racial homogeneity of census tracts destroys their usefulness in studying residential segregation.

> The census tracts of New York City have never had any reference to boundaries of ethnic group settlements. On the other hand, many of the cities tracted at a later date have used race as a criterion for determining tract boundaries. This has two effects with reference to segregation indices based on census tracts: (1) The cities in which race was a determinant of boundaries will evince higher segregation scores than those in which race was not considered. This will happen even if there is no real difference in the degree of segregation. (2) Even among the cities in which race was an original criterion of tract boundaries, the segregation score will tend to be higher for those tracted at a later date, since there will have been less divergence of the ethnic boundaries from the tract boundaries in these recently tracted cities.[45]

The Duncans provided an empirical example of the influence of tract boundaries.[46] Using block data for Augusta (Ga.) for 1950, two sets of quasi-tracts were delineated, each set conforming to the general census procedures concerning size and shape of tracts, but designed to maximize segregation in one case and to minimize it in

45. Cowgill and Cowgill, *op. cit.*, p. 826.

46. "Contributions to the Theory of Segregation Indexes," *op. cit.*, pp. 93–95.

the other. From the actual tract data, a Gini index of residential segregation of 88 was computed; values of 92 and 84 were obtained for the two sets of quasi-tracts. More than one-third of 60 cities for which the Duncans presented Gini indexes computed from tract data (for 1940) had values in the interval 84 through 92. Thus, manipulation of tract boundaries to augment racial homogeneity can in extreme circumstances affect the observed degree of segregation.

Although the racial homogeneity of census tracts is subject to arbitrary manipulation in establishing or revising tract boundaries, the assertions by Cowgill and Cowgill as to its empirical consequences must be treated as undemonstrated hypotheses rather than proven fact. It is likely that most tract committees do pay some attention to race, but not to the overriding extent of the quasi-tracts delineated for Augusta. Furthermore, most cities have been experiencing rapid increases in Negro population, resulting in continually changing boundaries of Negro residential areas. Once delimited, tract boundaries are designed to remain relatively constant from census to census. Tract boundaries are delimited or revised some time prior to any given census, on the basis of the preceding census and any subsequent information available to the committee. It seems unlikely that the straightforward relationships postulated by Cowgill and Cowgill between the committee actions and measures of segregation from census tract data do obtain. Direct data are not available, but it is possible to make a suggestive analysis of the relationship between segregation and the length of time since the delineation of tract boundaries.

Mean scores on several segregation indexes are presented in Table A-3 for cities grouped by the census year at which their tracts were delineated or last revised. For both the Bell and Gini indexes, computed from tract data, the mean scores are lower for cities tracted at dates closer to the measurement date, whereas the hypothesis predicts that they should be higher. To permit some assessment, independent of tract data, of the degree to which the cities tracted at different dates may actually differ in residential patterns, the corresponding segregation indexes computed from block data are shown. On the Bell index for 1950, the block indexes show the same trend as the tract indexes, and the differences do not suggest that the tract indexes depend in any way on the year tracted. On the Gini index for 1940, computed from block data, there is no relationship with year tracted, and there is no reason to doubt the reversal of the predicted pattern shown in the tract data. These brief analyses provide no empirical support for the suggestion of a simple relationship between the year tracted and an observed segregation index computed from tract data.

TABLE A-3

COMPARISON OF SEGREGATION INDEXES COMPUTED FROM TRACT
AND BLOCK DATA, FOR CITIES CLASSIFIED BY YEAR OF LAST
REVISION OF CENSUS TRACT BOUNDARIES

Index	Year of Last Revision of Census Tracts			
	1910	1930	1940	1950
Bell Index (1950 Data):				
Number of cities	1	8	43	20
Mean of tract indexes	71	59	43	38
Mean of block indexes	82	76	64	57
Difference in means	−11	−17	−21	−19
Gini Index (1940 Data):				
Number of cities	2	8	50	......
Mean of tract indexes	92	87	80	......
Mean of block indexes	97	97	95	......
Difference in means	− 5	−10	−15	......

Source: A list of cities showing dates when census tracts were organized and revised was obtained by correspondence from the Bureau of the Census. Source of the indexes is described in the section on "Computation Procedures."

The general nature of city blocks as subareas is so well known that in 1940 and 1950 there was no formal definition in census publications. In 1960, we are told that ". . . a block is a well-defined rectangular piece of land bounded by streets or roads. However, it may be irregular in shape or bounded by railroad tracks, streams, or other features." The question of what constitutes a street rather than an alley is apparently left to the discretion of the mapmakers and enumerators in the field. Although average block populations vary from city to city, and vary from zero to several thousand within cities, most blocks contain fewer than one hundred households. City blocks are thus the smallest readily identifiable subareas for which reliable data can be tabulated.

In general, blocks are arranged in a more or less regular gridwork pattern which is relatively stable over time and not subject to the same types of alteration as tract boundaries. However, we have already indicated our disagreement with arguments that city blocks are necessarily preferable to census tracts as units of analysis because "the city block . . . is a relatively homogeneous and unchanging entity," or because blocks better reveal "the realities of ethnic distribution." The arguments cited by the authors of a study of population mobility in Augusta, favoring "linear blocks" rather than "island blocks," are remarkably similar to those cited by others in favor of "island blocks" over census tracts.

The people in a linear block are likely to be more homogeneous than people in an island block. In Augusta, there are several streets where some of the best white homes are separated by an alley from a row of shacks occupied by Negroes. Likewise, a given amount of encroachment or inharmonious land use is more serious in a linear block than in an island block.[47]

There are some practical considerations respecting the types of data available for tracts and blocks which may influence the choice of subarea for any particular investigation. Prior to the 1940 census, data for blocks were not tabulated, and data for tracts were available for only a few cities. Since 1940, block data have been published for every city reaching 50,000 or more population at the preceding census or at a special census prior to the decennial census. The census tract program, however, has depended to some extent on local initiative. Census tract data are published for cities of 50,000 or more and for as much of the metropolitan area as desired, provided a local committee delineates boundaries and otherwise cooperates with the Bureau of the Census in the program.

Cowgill and Cowgill included in their critique of census tracts a statement that in 1950 block data were available for more cities than were tract data. Bell disputed this, pointing out that many of the tract systems include not only the central city but also other cities within their metropolitan areas, and that the total number of tracted cities greatly exceeds the number of cities for which block data are published.

For the 1960 census, concerted efforts were made to extend the tract program to as many metropolitan areas as possible, and both block and tract data are available for a wide range of cities. Although many suburban cities too small to be included in the block program are tracted, such small cities are divided into only a few census tracts. The influence of location of tract boundaries on the value of a segregation index is generally far more serious when there are only a half dozen tracts than where there are many more.

Only a few characteristics are published for each city block, and the only published characteristic of households has been whether the head of the household was white or non-white. Census tracts are much larger than blocks, and a much wider and more detailed range of tabulations of both population and housing characteristics are published. If any information is necessary other than a simple distribution of white and non-white households among subareas, then block data cannot be used. For some types of analysis, therefore, census tracts are the only available subarea.

47. U.S. Federal Works Agency, *op. cit.*, p. 2.

Segregation indexes computed from block data, then, can only indicate segregation between white and non-white households, while with tract data, indexes can be computed for white and Negro population. Although most non-white groups other than Negroes encounter some discrimination and are somewhat segregated in our society, it is clearly useful for most analyses to distinguish Negroes from other non-whites. Except for a few cities in the Southwest and West, however, Negroes constitute more than 95 per cent of the non-white population, and a segregation index computed between whites and non-whites must necessarily be nearly identical to one computed between whites and Negroes. By eliminating from the analysis or by taking separate account of those few cities in which "other non-whites" are numerous, an analysis of white – non-white segregation can be regarded as virtually equivalent to an analysis of white-Negro segregation. In either case, interpretation of the results must also take some account of the heterogeneity of the white population, which may include many Mexican Americans, Puerto Ricans, and other ethnic minorities, all of whom are subject to distinctive patterns of residential distribution.

Data for city blocks are published as part of the Census of Housing program, and the units identified are not persons or families, but housing units. The distinction between white and non-white is made on the basis of occupied units, or households. The census definitions of what constitutes a housing unit have changed a little with each census. In 1940 and 1950, they were called "dwelling units." For clarification of the concept, we cite the 1950 definition:

> In general, a dwelling unit is a group of rooms or a single room, occupied . . . as separate living quarters, by a family or other groups of persons living together or by a person living alone. . . . Excluded from the dwelling unit count are living quarters with five or more lodgers, institutions, dormitories, and transient hotels and tourist courts.[48]

The changing definitions have affected mainly the dividing line between "separate living quarters" and "large rooming houses." Under conditions of a high degree of residential segregation, it is doubtful that these changes would have much effect on segregation indexes.

Although the segregation indexes presented in the literature based on tract data have been computed from the distribution of persons rather than households, the latter unit seems more appropriate. The household (or "occupied dwelling unit" or "housing unit") is the basic residential unit. Data for persons, as opposed to data for households, include non-white servants and janitors living-in with white households, as well as persons living in prisons, military bases,

48. U.S. Bureau of the Census, *op. cit.*, p. 3.

dormitories, and the like. Omission of these groups in the computation of segregation indexes for an intercity study seems warranted in order to avoid inflating North-South differences by the differing patterns of legal or imposed racial segregation. Residential segregation of households can perhaps be studied best if isolated from patterns of institutional segregation. The distribution of households among subareas is available on both a tract and block basis.

For a few cities, we have computed segregation indexes from tract data for both households and persons. The differences have never been larger than plus or minus one. In an analysis of the relation between income and residential segregation, we have used "families and unrelated individuals" as the population unit, and again there have been no significant differences between indexes computed on this basis and those computed for households. Empirically, then, segregation indexes for a city will be little affected by the choice of population unit. It is likely that these considerations would be important, however, in an analysis of areas smaller than entire cities. In our analyses of residential succession, for instance, it was necessary to pay close attention to the influence of institutional population on the changing population characteristics of subareas.

□ CHOICE OF AREAL UNIT: EMPIRICAL COMPARISONS OF TRACTS AND BLOCKS

In general, segregation indexes computed from block data will not be identical to those computed in a similar fashion from tract data. As we have seen, the smaller the subareas, the greater the degree of identifiable residential segregation, and the larger the values that will be obtained on any given index. In the course of our study, we computed numerous segregation indexes from block data. Already available in the literature were values of corresponding indexes computed from tract data. This afforded an opportunity to make an empirical comparison between segregation indexes computed from block data and those computed from tract data. Granted that the values for block indexes will be higher, is there nevertheless a high correlation between the two sets of indexes? If so, some of the concern with the relative merits of each type of data may be misplaced, as suggested by Duncan and Duncan on the basis of similar comparisons in a study of residential segregation of occupational groups:

> The indexes of segregation and dissimilarity were computed on both a tract basis and a zone-sector segment basis to determine the effect of the size of the area unit on the results. While the indexes for tracts are uniformly higher than for zone-sector segments, this

effect can be disregarded for purposes of determining the relative positions of the occupation groups. . . . The correlation between the two sets of dissimilarity indexes . . . is .98. . . These results indicate that for the kind of problem dealt with here the larger, and hence less homogeneous, unit is as serviceable as the smaller one. This suggests that some of the recent concern about census-tract homogeneity may be misplaced.[49]

We were able to make comparisons for each of six different segregation indexes. For five of the indexes, comparisons are between values computed from tract data and those computed from block data for 60 cities, using data from the 1940 census. For the sixth index, the comparisons are based on 1950 data for 72 cities. Table A-4 presents the product-moment correlation coefficients and the constants for the regressions of block indexes on tract indexes.

The weakest correlation, .63, obtains for the modified Cowgill index. We have already discussed the excessive dependence of this index on size of areal unit. The three indexes Gh, Rep, and Bell share a dependence on the city proportion non-white, which remains the same whether blocks or tracts are used as subareas. This dependence on a common factor may account for the relatively high block-tract

TABLE A-4

COMPARISONS BETWEEN SEGREGATION INDEXES° COMPUTED FROM BLOCK DATA AND FROM CENSUS TRACT DATA

Measure	Index and Year					
	G_t (1940)	D (1940)	Co (1940)	Gh (1940)	Rep (1940)	Bell (1950)
Number of cities	60	60	60	60	60	72
Mean of block indexes ...	96	86	74	70	51	64
Mean of tract indexes......	82	70	8	50	29	44
Correlation of block and tract indexes	.74	.69	.63	.92	.90	.93
Regression of block on tract indexes:						
Slope	18	31	78	70	93	89
Intercept	81	64	68	35	24	25

Source: See the section on "Computation Procedures."

° The indexes are identified and defined in the section on "Some Indexes" in this appendix.

49. Otis Dudley Duncan and Beverly Duncan, "Residential Distribution and Occupational Stratification," *American Journal of Sociology*, LX, No. 5 (March, 1955), pp. 494–495.

correlations obtained for these indexes. Correlations of block with tract values for two "pure" measures of unevenness, the Gini index and the index of dissimilarity, are about .7.

If block indexes are deemed conceptually most satisfactory, but tract data are used to simplify the computational burdens, the indicated regression lines might be used to obtain estimated values of a block index. For Gi and D, the two most useful measures, there would be considerable variation of estimated values around actual block values, and the computational shortcut would not be very helpful. These results suggest that our concern with the conceptual and methodological implications of reliance on tracts or blocks is warranted, and that choice of areal unit will have some effect on the results of an intercity analysis.

□ RANDOM VARIATION OF SEGREGATION INDEXES

In our study, values of the index of dissimilarity computed from block data for 1950 are 88.9 for Augusta (Ga.) and 91.5 for Atlanta (Ga.). Two questions concerning random variation of segregation indexes may be raised, using for illustration these two specific values:

1. Might an index value of 88.9 or above for Augusta occur as the result of a random distribution of white and non-white households?

2. Is the difference between the values for Augusta and Atlanta larger than that likely to occur solely as a result of chance variations in residential distributions?

These questions are similar to the usual questions of statistical significance, but the analogy is only partial. Segregation indexes are computed from complete information on residential distributions within each city, and there is no question of statistical inference from a sample. Similarly, there is no concern with generalizing our results for a specific set of cities to any other universe of cities. Our questions concerning random variation, then, are not posed in order to test the statistical significance of inferences from a sample to a universe, but to point out substantive problems that need to be answered in the course of interpreting our findings.

Part of our study is directed to the analysis of intercity variations in segregation as measured by an index. The index measures deviations of the residential distribution of whites and non-whites from the hypothetical zero point of a perfectly even distribution. For such a perfectly even distribution, the proportion non-white in each block must be equal to the city proportion non-white. Many blocks cannot contain exactly the same proportion of non-whites as in the city as a whole because white and non-white households occur in integer units, and thus some minor deviations from the model pattern are to be expected. Furthermore, there is a continual process of residential mobility, of formation, relocation, and dissolution of households. Suppose these various processes of residential mobility took place independently of the color of the head of the household. There would still be random deviations from the model pattern of an even distribution. A segregation index computed from a random distribution of white and non-white households would not have a value of zero. What, then, can we regard as the likely minimum value to be observed if color did not affect residential location? We shall attempt to answer this question, in the particular form phrased in question 1, by actually carrying out a random distribution, allowing random numbers to represent households.

Our basic data include a table of random numbers and the city block data for Augusta from the 1950 census. Of all occupied dwelling units in Augusta, .392 were occupied by non-whites. Three-digit random numbers from 000 through 391 were regarded as representing non-white households, and from 392 through 999 as representing white households. For each block, as many three-digit random numbers were chosen as the number of occupied dwelling units listed by the census. Depending on the digits, each dwelling unit was regarded as either white or non-white, and the total number of white and non-white households in each block was ascertained. For example, for a block containing 25 occupied dwelling units, 25 three-digit random numbers were examined. If 8 of these were between 000 and 391, the block was recorded as having 8 non-white and 17 white households.

A distribution of white and non-white households by blocks suffices to compute a segregation index for that distribution. From the first allocation, a value of 13.0 was obtained. Since the process is random, other values would be obtained from other sets of random numbers. The whole process of allocation was repeated, following the same procedure except that different portions of the random number table were used each time. The resulting index values from four additional allocations were 14.3, 12.0, 12.8, and 12.8. The mean of these five values is 13.0, and the standard deviation is 0.7. The observed value of 88.9 for Augusta for 1950 is more than 100 standard deviations above the estimated mean value for random residential distributions.

These results permit us to answer question 1 in the negative. The observed values of the segregation index for all cities for all years for which we have computed it are far above the levels likely to occur as a result of residential location occurring independently of the color of the head of the household. As a substantive result, this conclusion is hardly surprising, and its documentation is justified primarily as an aid in understanding how the index of dissimilarity behaves under various conditions. If we had not been able to answer question 1 in the negative, it would hardly have been fruitful to proceed further in trying to relate differences in index values to differences in other variables purported to account for variations in segregation. We may emphasize, however, that a positive answer to question 1 would not affect the value of a study different from this one, in which the indexes would be used as independent variables, with the objective of assessing the effects of a given degree of residential segregation. The deviation of residential distribution from evenness, regardless of whether the deviation is larger than anticipated on the basis of random factors, may have distinct consequences for other aspects of the social position of the segregated group.

What we have undertaken with this random allocation procedure might better have been accomplished in a more direct fashion. For many statistics, there are analytical solutions to the evaluation of index variance, and we would be happy to see a more sophisticated analysis of the index of dissimilarity. In the absence of an analytical solution, we have used an approach which is usually reserved for problems more difficult than ours:

> For more than fifty years, when statisticians have been confronted with a difficult problem in distribution theory, they have resorted to what they have sometimes called "model sampling." The process consists of setting up some sort of urn model or system, or drawings from a table of random numbers, whereby the statistic whose distribution is sought can be observed over and over again and the distribution estimated empirically.[50]

An analytical approximation to our problem is available if we assume that all blocks are of equal size. Then the expected number of blocks with each number of whites and non-whites may be computed by means of the binomial approximation to the normal distribution. From an assumption of a random normal distribution of whites and non-whites in Augusta in 1950, we obtain an index value of 14.4, rather close to the mean value obtained from our random allocation procedure. Because most cities have a very skewed distribution of blocks by size, we were not willing to rely on this analytical approximation without verification of its reasonable fit.

Although our analysis of segregation indexes relies on block data, it took little additional effort to undertake also estimates of random variation for an index based on tract data. Using the data

---

50. John Curtiss, quoted in Herbert A. Meyer, ed., *Symposium on Monte Carlo Methods* (New York: Wiley, 1956), p. vii.

available from the five allocations to blocks, the allocated numbers of white and non-white households by blocks were summed to tract totals, and indexes of dissimilarity then computed. The mean of the five indexes thus obtained is 1.9, with a standard deviation of 0.2, as compared to the observed index value of 74.6 computed from 1950 data for census tracts.

Because the number of tracts is so much smaller than the number of blocks, it was feasible to undertake a "model sampling" approach for tract indexes more quickly than to examine thousands of random digits as was necessary for block indexes. Rather than allocating individual households to tracts, the tract proportion of non-white households could be assigned, taking advantage of the normal approximation to the binomial distribution. Our allocation procedure is a simple binomial one, and the formula for the non-white proportion allocated to tract i on allocation j is:

$$Q_{ij} = Q_i + z_{ij} \left[Q_i (1-Q_i) + N_i \right]^{1/2}$$

where Q_{ij} is the allocated proportion, Q_i is the expected non-white proportion, N_i is the total population of tract i, and z_{ij} is a random normal deviate. For this procedure, the expected non-white proportion for each tract is equal to the proportion for the city, 0.39. This procedure requires that for each allocation one random normal deviate be assigned to each tract. Allocated non-white proportions are obtained by solving the above equation. Indexes of dissimilarity can be computed from the known total populations of tracts and the allocated non-white proportions. For ten separate allocations, we obtained indexes averaging 2.2, with a standard deviation of 0.4.

Whatever procedure we use, and whether segregation indexes are computed from block data or tract data, the conclusion is the same—observed values of residential segregation are far above any that might result from random processes of residential location independent of race.

The second question concerned the magnitude of differences between observed index values, and can be approached by variations of these random allocation models. The allocations already reported might be used for estimating the amount of variation in index values expected from random variation in residential patterns. The models, however, have been shown to produce residential distributions quite different from those actually observed, and it does not seem reasonable to use such poorly fitting models for obtaining estimates of variance. An alternative approach is again to allocate white and non-white households to blocks and tracts, but this time randomly around a segregated pattern rather than on the assumed basis of no relation between race and residence. In particular, consider the observed distribution of whites and non-whites in Augusta in 1950. What values of the index of dissimilarity might be obtained from random fluctuations around this distribution?

The only modification in the allocation procedure is to vary the proportion of non-whites, allowing the expected random value to equal the observed value for each subarea. Thus for a block with 25 households, 20 of which are non-white, two-digit random numbers from 00 to 79 represent non-whites and numbers from 80 to 99 represent whites. The allocated number of non-whites in each block fluctuates around the observed number for that particular block.

Five allocations to blocks were carried out by this procedure. Indexes of dissimilarity for the allocated distributions range from 88.0 to 89.1, with a mean of 88.8 and a standard deviation of 0.4. With this model, summation of results for blocks into results for tracts is not possible, and so a direct allocation of non-white proportions to tracts was carried out. The formula cited above indicates the procedure, with the exception that the expected non-white proportions, Q_i, were set equal to observed tract values rather than to the city proportion. For 10 allocations, the range was from 74.2 to 75.3, with a mean of 74.7 and a standard deviation of 0.3.

These data permit a tentative affirmative answer to the second question: The difference of 2.6 between the segregation indexes computed from 1950 block data for Augusta and Atlanta is larger than any likely to occur solely as a result of chance variations in Augusta's residential distribution. The estimated variances of about 0.4 for a block index and 0.3 for a tract index cannot, however, be generalized to other situations. The allocations were carried out solely with respect to Augusta's observed pattern of residential distribution for 1950. The use of other residential patterns in the model might produce a greater or lesser degree of random variation in the resulting segregation index values. The one set of estimates using Augusta as a model does provide support for an expectation that differences of more than a point or two in block segregation index values are unlikely to arise if both residential distributions are merely random variations around a common underlying pattern. In our analysis of segregation indexes, we paid little attention to such small differences.

□ COMPUTATION PROCEDURES

The segregation indexes used in the bulk of the substantive analysis are indexes of dissimilarity between the distribution of white

and non-white households among city blocks. The ordinary computation procedure for an index of dissimilarity would require percentage
distributions across subareas for white and non-white households, as
illustrated previously with Table A-1. This procedure would be very
burdensome with city blocks used as subareas. Not only would several
thousand percentages have to be computed for each city, but each one
would have to be carried out to several decimal places in order to
retain enough significant digits. Fortunately, another approach to the
computation of an index of dissimilarity avoids some of the labor.

The formula for the index of dissimilarity, D, may be expressed
as:

$$D = 1/2 \text{ (sum of absolute values of } N_i/N - W_i/W)$$

where N_i and W_i are the number of non-white and white households,
respectively, in block i, and N and W are the total non-white and
white households in the city. This formula may be modified if those
differences $N_i/N - W_i/W$ that are positive are distinguished from
those that are zero or negative. Then D equals either the sum of the
positive differences or the sum of the negative differences, and the
zero differences may be ignored or included with either the positive
or negative sum.

The difference, $N_i/N - W_i/W$, will be positive if $N_i/N > W_i/W$.
Algebraic manipulation shows that the sum will be positive if

$$\frac{W}{N} > \frac{W_i}{N_i} \, ,$$

$$\frac{(W + N) - N}{N} > \frac{(W_i + N_i) - N_i}{N_i} \, ,$$

$$\frac{W + N}{N} - \frac{N}{N} > \frac{W_i + N_i}{N_i} - \frac{N_i}{N_i} \, ,$$

$$\frac{W + N}{N} > \frac{W_i + N_i}{N_i} \, ,$$

and

$$\frac{N_i}{W_i + N_i} > \frac{N}{W + N} \, .$$

In other words, if the proportion of non-white households in a
given block is greater than the proportion of non-white households in
the city as a whole, then that block will contribute to the sum of
positive differences. The sum of the positive differences $N_i/N - W_i/W$

equals (sum of N_i/N) minus (sum of W_i/W), if the separate sums are taken over the same values of i, and this in turn equals (sum of N_i)/N minus (sum of W_i)/W.

The first part of the preceding paragraph indicates a way of identifying those blocks which contribute to the sum of positive differences, by identifying those where the non-white proportion is greater than that in the city. The second part shows how to compute the index of dissimilarity by cumulating the numbers of non-white and white households in those identified blocks, and then performing a few arithmetic operations, without any extensive calculation of percentages or ratios for individual blocks.

In practice, the computation of indexes of dissimilarity proceeded as follows. From Table 1 of any 1960 block bulletin, obtain the percentage non-white among occupied housing units in the city as a whole. Then proceed systematically through Table 2, block by block, being careful to ignore the census tract totals. For each block, consider the ratio of the number in the column "Occupied by non-white" to the sum of the number in the "Owner occupied, Total" and "Renter occupied, Total" columns. In most cases, precise calculation of this ratio is unnecessary, since it is only necessary to determine whether this ratio is larger than the city proportion non-white. If it is larger, identify the block by marking a red dot beside the number of non-white units. Most blocks in most cities have no non-white residents, and this procedure permits these blocks to be skipped over rapidly. Once every block has been inspected, and marked if appropriate, go through the bulletin twice, obtaining two sums. The first is the sum of non-white-occupied units in blocks marked with a red dot. The other is the sum of owner-occupied and renter-occupied units in blocks marked with a red dot. For ease of checking and error correction, it is convenient to record these sums page by page, and then obtain the city totals in a separate step.

All the information for computing the index is now at hand. The sum of N_i is simply the sum of non-white-occupied units in blocks marked with a red dot. The total number of non-white-occupied units, N, is given in Table 1 of the bulletin. The sum of W_i is obtained by subtracting N_i from the sum of renter- and owner-occupied units in blocks marked with a red dot. The total number of white-occupied units, W, is obtained by subtracting the non-white total from the city total of occupied units in Table 1 of the bulletin. Compute the two ratios, (sum of N_i)/N and (sum of W_i)/W, difference them, and multiply by 100 to obtain the index of dissimilarity. (The procedures for 1940 and 1950 were identical except for modifications due to changes in the format of the block bulletins.)

Although the operations are simple, the print is small and blocks are numerous, and it is necessary to repeat every step as a check. With an adding machine, a table of percentages to help compute the ratio of non-white to total occupied for marginal cases not obviously too high or low by inspection, appropriate guide cards, and a little experience, it is possible to develop considerable speed at this task. Except for New York and other very large cities, computation of a city index rarely required more than an hour.

For some of the methodological investigations reported in this appendix, values of eight different segregation indexes computed from block data for 188 cities for 1940 and 1950 were utilized. Values of the Cowgill index were obtained from Professor Cowgill. The other seven indexes were calculated on an IBM-650 electronic computer. The basic block data were punched onto cards, and this was done on a sample basis for the larger cities. Because of the skewness of the distribution of blocks by size and by non-white occupancy, sampling errors were relatively large. There were also some punching errors. The index values as computed, therefore, are not always identical to those that would be obtained by an accurate calculation from complete block data. However, for methodological purposes of comparing values of several indexes for a given city, these errors are not of great moment, for all the indexes were computed from the same (possibly inaccurate) distribution of whites and non-whites by blocks. Further details on the computation of these indexes and tables of the index values are available on microfilm.[51]

The segregation indexes computed from census tract data, used in some of the methodological investigations, were taken directly from other sources.[52] Various other segregation indexes and related measures utilized in the substantive analyses were computed directly from the appropriate census data, and necessary particulars are indicated where the measures occur in the text.

□ A NOTE ON ANNEXATIONS

A segregation index computed from census data for city blocks refers to the population living within the city boundaries. If a city changes its boundaries by annexation during the period between

51. Karl E. Taeuber, "Residential Segregation by Color in United States Cities, 1940 and 1950" (unpublished Ph.D. dissertation, Harvard University, 1959), Appendix B.

52. Values of Gi, D, Gh, Rep, and Co for 60 cities, computed from tract data for 1940, are given in "Contributions to the Theory of Segregation Indexes," *op. cit.*, Table 7. Values of the Bell index for a large number of cities and metropolitan areas, computed from tract data for 1950, are given in Bell and Willis, *op. cit.*

censuses, then an index computed for the first census date will refer to a different area than one for the second census date. If the annexed population was numerous, and the degree of residential segregation within the annexed area differed greatly from that within the original city limits, then a different index value would be expected for the two points in time, even in the absence of any changes in racial patterns of residence. In particular, if an area inhabited only by whites were annexed to a city, and no other residential changes occurred, this would increase the computed value of the segregation index for that city.

Annexation to large cities has often been assumed to be much less prevelant in recent decades than during the earlier periods of growth of these cities. It has recently been demonstrated, however, for both the 1940–50 and 1950–60 decades, that annexations are still a frequent occurrence, and failure to take their effect into account can seriously distort an analysis, at least regarding patterns of growth.[53]

The segregation indexes utilized in our study were computed from city block data as published, with no corrections for annexation. For a number of cities which had annexations involving more than a trivial number of residents, however, we undertook an assessment of the impact of annexation on observed changes in index values. Utilizing block data for 1950 and 1960, the city boundaries as of 1950 were located on the 1960 block maps, and segregation indexes for 1960 were recomputed based solely on the population living within the 1950 boundaries. The changes between the 1950 value and the adjusted 1960 value holding constant city boundaries could then be compared with the difference between the 1950 and 1960 unadjusted values. The results for a number of cities are presented in Table A-5.

For only 3 of 24 cities for which adjusted indexes were computed does the adjusted index differ by more than 1.0 from the original unadjusted index. In only one case does the direction of change in segregation between 1950 and 1960 differ when the comparison is between the 1950 index and the adjusted 1960 index rather than the unadjusted 1960 index.

Computation of the adjusted indexes was often laborious, and in view of the limited effect of annexation on values for the first 24 cities for which adjustments were made, a complete set of adjusted indexes was not prepared. Anyone undertaking an intensive analysis of trends in residential segregation in any individual city experiencing a sizable

53. For 1940–50, see Beverly Duncan, Georges Sabagh, and Maurice D. Van rsdol, Jr., "Patterns of City Growth," *American Journal of Sociology*, LXVII, No. 4 anuary, 1962), pp. 427–428. For 1950–60, see Leo F. Schnore, "Municipal Annexa- ons and the Growth of Metropolitan Suburbs," *American Journal of Sociology*, LXVII, No. 4 (January, 1962).

TABLE A-5

ESTIMATED EFFECT OF ANNEXATION ON SEGREGATION INDEXES,
1960, AND CHANGE, 1950–60

City	Segregation Index for 1960			Change, 1950–1960		Annexed
	Original	Adjusted°	Difference	Original	Adjusted	Population
Asheville, N.C.	92.3	92.5	−0.2	3.1	3.3	10,109
Augusta, Ga.............	93.0	92.6	0.4	4.1	3.7	7,971
Austin, Tex..............	93.1	93.1	0.0	1 1	1.1	37,353
Beaumont, Tex.........	92.3	92.7	−0.4	2.7	3.1	8,434
Charleston, W. Va.....	79.0	79.5	−0.5	−0.6	−0.1	18,685
Charlotte, N.C..........	94.3	94.7	−0.4	1.5	1.9	56,706
Chattanooga, Tenn. ..	91.5	91.4	0.1	3.0	2.9	9,433
Cincinnati, Ohio	89.0	88.9	0.1	−2.2	−2.3	7,385
Columbia, S.C..........	94.1	93.5	0.6	6.0	5.4	14,184
Columbus, Ohio.......	85.3	84.4	0.9	−3.6	−4.5	75,635
Dallas, Tex..............	94.6	94.2	0.4	6.2	5.8	192,707
Durham, N.C.	92.7	92.1	0.6	3.9	3.3	9,443
Galveston, Tex.........	82.9	81.6	1.3	4.6	3.3	7,039
Greensboro, N.C.	93.3	94.1	−0.8	−0.2	0.6	36,117
Little Rock, Ark........	89.4	88.5	0.9	4.9	4.0	13,219
Macon, Ga...............	83.7	82.8	0.9	6.6	5.7	4,635
Mobile, Ala..............	91.9	91.9	0.0	2.5	2.5	62,375
Montgomery, Ala......	94.7	94.4	0.3	4.2	3.9	13,757
Port Arthur, Tex.......	90.4	91.1	−0.7	−0.9	−0.2	9,544
Sacramento, Calif.	63.9	67.9	−4.0	−13.7	−9.7	52,672
Savannah, Ga..........	92.3	92.0	0.3	3.5	3.2	25,163
Shreveport, La.	95.9	95.9	0.0	2.⁻	2.7	35,241
Waco, Tex.	90.7	89.3	1.4	3.7	2.3	15,132
Winston-Salem, N.C.	95.0	94.9	0.1	1.2	1.1	20,003

Source: The procedures for obtaining the adjusted indexes are given in the text. The original indexes and
changes are from Table 4. Annexed population is given in U. S. Bureau of the Census, *U. S. Census of Population: 1960*, Vol. 1, *Characteristics of the Population*, Part A, *Number of Inhabitants* (Washington: U. S. Government Printing Office, 1961), Table 9 for states.

° The adjusted index was computed on the basis of the population in 1960 living within the boundaries
of the city as delimited in 1950.

annexation should assess the effect, if any, of that annexation. For our
general analysis of intercity levels and changes in segregation index
values, we felt that the magnitude of the adjustments was not large
enough to justify the effort of completing the estimates.

Several methodological complications were bypassed by the
decision to avoid adjusting for annexation. Consider a city which
annexes a newly developed residential area. If it were possible to
recompute the segregation index for 1950 using the 1960 city boundaries, there might be little effect on the 1950 value because of the
sparse population in the annexed area. Adjusting the other way –
computing a 1960 index for the area within the 1950 city limits – might
present a different picture. This problem of inconsistency among
alternative adjustment procedures is complicated if both the 1940–50

and 1950–60 decades are considered simultaneously. Should all three indexes be adjusted to the 1940 city boundaries, or to the 1960 boundaries? Suppose an adjustment can be made for the effect of annexation on the segregation index, but the necessary data are not available to permit adjusting all the independent variables used in the analysis, such as changes in occupational levels, income, or the like. Should the multivariate analysis utilize some adjusted and some unadjusted measures, or only adjusted measures, or only unadjusted measures? No solution is satisfactory. Incorporated cities, as we have emphasized, are not ideal units for the analysis of urban processes. In general, our data suggest that the effect of annexations is usually small, and we choose to regard the changing boundaries of cities as merely another weakness of city data, but one whose effect on our analysis is minor.

The effect of annexation on measures of population change is not minor, and measures of change in white and non-white population during each intercensal period were based on estimates of the change occurring within the boundaries of the city as delimited at the beginning of the period.

Estimation of the effect of annexation on segregation indexes required several approximations. For the benefit of anyone who chooses to undertake such a task. our procedures for the 1950–60 decade may be outlined. Using the block maps (and tract maps if available), the approximate location of the 1950 city boundary was traced on the 1960 block map. A list was made of all blocks in the annexed area, including very rough estimates of the appropriate fractions for blocks spanning the 1950 city boundary. A tally was then made of the total population, the total and non-white-occupied housing units, and the total and non-white-occupied housing units in blocks marked as having a higher percentage non-white than the city as a whole.

The total population obtained was compared with the total annexed population as reported in the 1960 census, and a ratio estimate was made adjusting all the totals from the tally to be consistent with the published figure. The adjusted segregation index for 1960 was computed by subtracting the totals for the annexed area from the corresponding figures for the entire city, and recomputing the index. Because the percentage non-white in 1960 within the 1950 city limits differed to some degree from the percentage non-white using the 1960 city limits, it would have been more accurate to recompute the index, starting with the first step of identifying those blocks containing more than the city percentage non-white. However, errors in identifying blocks with a non-white percentage close to the city total have little effect on the final index value. This approximation, therefore, is quite good. More disturbing was the fact that for several cities, the total population estimated by us as being in the annexed area was considerably above or below the figure reported by the census. In some of these cases, the determination of the annexed area on the basis of comparing block maps was quite simple, and we can find no reasonable explanation of the discrepancy between the census figure and our estimate.

☐ INDEX CHOICE: A METHODOLOGICAL OVERVIEW

A Chicago newspaper recently headlined a feature story, "Chicago's All-White Areas Greater than Birmingham's." Maps of the two cities were reproduced with shading representing the percentage non-white in each census tract. Unshaded areas, those with less than one per cent non-white, constituted a much higher proportion of the Chicago map than of the Birmingham map. The article neglected to mention an alternative view of the maps: Birmingham's all-Negro areas greater than Chicago's. That Negroes constituted 40 per cent of Birmingham's population and 23 per cent of Chicago's (1960 census), and that this difference might have more to do with the appearance of the maps than did differing patterns of residential segregation, was not mentioned. On the basis of the segregation indexes used in our study, the two cities were virtually identical, with values of 92.8 for Birmingham and 92.6 for Chicago for 1960. It is obvious that unsophisticated inspection of maps cannot provide a reliable basis for intercity comparisons of the degree of residential segregation.

As a first step in attempting to choose a measure for use in an intercity comparative analysis, we reviewed various meanings of "residential segregation," and suggested several dimensions which might be subject to measurement. The notion of over-all unevenness in the distribution of white and non-white households was singled out as a general feature that makes sense conceptually and that underlies most of the methodological work on developing segregation indexes. The segregation curve was used as a graphic device for representing the unevenness, or segregation, of a residential distribution. This mode of analysis of residential segregation was developed by Duncan and Duncan, who noted that the segregation index problem thus became analogous to problems of measuring inequalities of income distributions in economics and of measuring areal concentration in geography.[54] Drawing on the body of statistical

54. Duncan and Duncan, "A Methodological Analysis . . .," *op. cit.*, p. 217.

work in these other fields, considerable methodological clarification was brought to bear on previous efforts by sociologists to develop segregation indexes.

A comparison of the degree of residential segregation in two cities might be made directly by examining the respective segregation curves. If one curve lies above the other at all points, then one city can clearly be designated as less segregated. If the curves intersect, however, then neither city can be designated unambiguously as less segregated. Visual comparison of segregation curves is thus subject to some of the same limitations as visual comparison of maps. Precise, reliable comparisons between two or more cities require an operational means of assigning an index value to each city such that a higher index value indicates a greater degree of segregation than a lower index value.

Several of the segregation indexes which have appeared in the sociological literature, including both of those which have served as the basis for a substantive as well as a methodological analysis, do not conform to the criteria just suggested.[55] The "index of reproducibility" and the "ghetto index" depend not only on the shape of the segregation curve, but also on the city percentage non-white. Bell's index behaves very similarly to those two, and like them must be regarded as a merger of the concepts of unevenness and percentage non-white. Cowgill's index is quite different from any of the others. It bears little direct relationship to the segregation curve, but is more analogous to the newspaper approach of comparing the size of the all-white areas. The basic notion of unevenness is symmetrical: if Negroes are segregated from whites, whites are equally segregated from Negroes. The four measures which deviate from the concept of unevenness, particularly Cowgill's index, are asymmetrical, assigning quite different values to the segregation of Negroes from whites than to the segregation of whites from Negroes. Conceptually, we prefer to focus on the general unevenness of the residential distribution of whites and Negroes.

Four indexes were defined that are pure measures of unevenness in that they depend only on the shape of the segregation curve and require no auxiliary information. Two of these indexes (Co and Oc) are special-purpose indexes, indicating the shape of the curve at either tail. The Gini index and the index of dissimilarity, however, are both central measures of the deviation of the segregation curve from a position of zero segregation. Both these indexes have been

55. The two substantive studies are Cowgill and Cowgill, *op. cit.*, and Bell and Willis, *op. cit.* Some miscellaneous findings are included in an incidental fashion in Jahn, Schmid, and Schrag, *op. cit.*, and Duncan and Duncan, *op. cit.*

widely used in various research contexts, and are known to perform sensibly. We believe that either one of these indexes is a satisfactory measure of residential segregation for general research purposes. Future studies may require measures focusing on special features of segregation patterns, but we wanted a conceptually simple over-all index of a city's residential segregation. Our choice of the index of dissimilarity over the Gini index was made solely for computational ease. As expected on methodological grounds, there is a high empirical correlation between the two indexes when computed for a large group of cities, and an analysis using either index should produce about the same results.

All the segregation indexes can be computed using data for any system of subareas in a city. The conceptual meaning and the numerical value of any index, however, depend on the subareas used. For intercity comparative analysis in the United States, the choice of subareas in practice is a choice between census tracts or city blocks. Our analysis of the relative merits of each unit touched on the following points:

1. Blocks are a finer scale unit than census tracts, and thus indicate the "detailed" rather than the "coarse" texture of the white and Negro residential distributions. Block boundaries are less subject to arbitrary delimitation than are tract boundaries. Although the problems of census tract heterogeneity have been exaggerated in the literature, we believe that segregation indexes computed from block data are methodologically more comparable from city to city.

2. Block boundaries are probably more stable over time than are tract boundaries, and block indexes are therefore more comparable than tract indexes for the study of changes over time.

3. For a study extending from 1940 to 1960, city block data are available for more cities. Many small suburban cities have tract data but not block data, but there are too few tracts for computation of reliable indexes. For 1960 the tract program has been extended to embrace a number of entire metropolitan areas, and this gives tracts an advantage over blocks for the study of segregation on a metropolitan basis.

4. For blocks, the only available relevant data are the numbers of white- and non-white-occupied housing units (households) in each block. For tracts, some choice of population unit is available. However, occupied housing units are an appropriate unit for the study of residential segregation, and a distribution of housing units automatically eliminates consideration of officially segregated institutional population which would affect an index based on the distribution of persons. The white – non-white dichotomy is not always a

useful one in the study of segregation, but for an average measure for a large number of cities it is probably as useful as any other division of the total population.

For a study of trends in residential segregation during the 1940–1960 period for a large number of cities, city blocks seem preferable as subareas for the computation of segregation indexes. Tract data, however, are the only recourse for the analysis of metropolitan segregation, of segregation of other race and ethnic groups, and of the relationships between residential segregation and economic differentials.

SUPPLEMENTARY TABLES ON RESIDENTIAL SUCCESSION

APPENDIX TABLE B-1

DISTRIBUTION OF CENSUS TRACTS HAVING 250 OR MORE NON-WHITES IN 1950 BY TYPE OF RACIAL CHANGE: 10 CITIES, 1940–50

Type of Racial Change	Detroit	Cleveland	Philadelphia	St. Louis	Washington	Baltimore	New Orleans	Atlanta	Birmingham	Memphis
Established Negro Areas …	9	6	2	6	7	7	4	9	6	7
Consolidation	121	47	107	23	49	44	54	21	26	14
Succession	53	27	71	9	32	23	21	12	6	4
Invasion	(57)	(13)	(6)	(5)	(5)	(11)	…	…	…	…
Growing	8(5)	7(3)	21(8)	7(2)	6(2)	6(1)	9(1)	5(1)	16	6
Declining	3	…	9	2	6	4(1)	24	4	4	4
Stable Interracial Areas …	…	…	1	…	…	2	5	3	1	6
Displacement	1	…	8	3	12	11	23	7	8	26
"Pure"	…	…	2	1	5	2	2	3	3	5
Growing	1	…	4	2	6	7	13	3(1)	5	14(1)
Declining	…	…	2	…	1	2	8	1	…	7
Omitted°	…	1	6	2	2	3	1	1	…	1
Total	131	54	124	34	70	67	87	41	41	54

Note: Figures in parentheses indicate the number of tracts in the cell which had fewer than 250 non-whites in the initial year.
° Tracts omitted because the non-white population was primarily institutional.

APPENDIX TABLE B-2

DISTRIBUTION OF CENSUS TRACTS HAVING 250 OR MORE NON-WHITES IN 1960 BY TYPE OF RACIAL CHANGE: 10 CITIES, 1950–60

Type of Racial Change	Detroit	Cleveland	Philadelphia	St. Louis	Washington	Baltimore	New Orleans	Atlanta	Birmingham	Memphis
Established Negro Areas ...	23	13	3	4	7	12	7	11	6	11
Consolidation	165	55	110	32	64	66	65	23	23	35
Succession	63	22	51	13	35	25	42	16	12	20
Invasion	(70)	(21)	(21)	(14)	(12)	(23)	(3)	(2)	...	...
Growing	...	1(1)	6(4)	...	2(1)	3(2)	7(1)	1	4	3
Declining	32	11	32	5	15	15	13	4	7	12
Stable Interracial Areas ...	...	...	...	...	...	...	3	...	...	...
Displacement	4	...	3	5	6	7	7	4	12	8
"Pure"	...	4	3	5	2	...	1	...	2	1
Growing	...	1	1	...	...	1(1)	4	1	5	3
Declining	4	2	2	5	4	6	2	3	5	4
Omitted°	3	1	5	2	1	1	...	...	1	...
Total	195	73	121	43	78	86	82	38	42	54

Note: Figures in parentheses indicate the number of tracts in the cell which had fewer than 250 non-whites in the initial year.

° Tracts omitted because the non-white population was primarily institutional.

247

APPENDIX TABLE B-3

DISTRIBUTION OF CENSUS TRACTS HAVING 250 OR MORE NON-WHITES IN TERMINAL YEAR OF DECADE BY TYPE OF RACIAL CHANGE: FIVE CITIES, 1930–40 AND ONE CITY, 1910–30

Type of Racial Change	1930–40 Decade					1920–30 Decade Cleveland	1910–20 Decade Cleveland
	Detroit	Cleveland	Philadelphia	St. Louis	Washington		
Established Negro Areas	5	1	...	1	4	...	...
Consolidation	55	29	70	19	41	35	25
Succession	29	19	44	11	9	17	4
Invasion	(6)	(2)	(2)	...	...	(4)	(7)
Growing	4(2)	2	12(2)	2	32(5)	6(3)	14(11)
Declining	16	6	12	6	...	8	...
Stable Interracial Areas	...	...	6	...	...	1	...
Displacement	9	7	29	5	17	...	...
"Pure"	...	1	2	...	2	...	...
Growing	1	...	3	...	14	...	...
Declining	8	6	24	5	1	...	...
Omitted°	...	...	6	1	1	...	...
Total	69	37	111	26	63	36	25

Note: Figures in parentheses indicate the number of tracts in the cell which had fewer than 250 non-whites in the initial year.

° Tracts omitted because the non-white population was primarily institutional.

SUPPLEMENTARY TABLES ON CLASS SEGREGATION

APPENDIX TABLE C-1

INDEXES OF DISSIMILARITY IN RESIDENTIAL DISTRIBUTION AMONG OCCUPATION GROUPS, FOR EMPLOYED NON-WHITE MALES, 1950 AND 1960

(VALUES FOR 1950 ABOVE DIAGONAL; CHANGE, 1950–60, BELOW DIAGONAL)

City and Occupation	Occupation							
	Professional	Manager	Clerical	Sales	Craft	Operative	Service	Labor
Detroit								
Professional, technical	.....	18.4	19.1	20.4	23.8	25.2	22.4	32.7
Managers, officials, proprietors	15.5	.....	17.5	16.2	17.4	18.4	15.1	22.5
Clerical workers	9.9	13.8	.....	18.0	15.9	17.4	18.5	27.1
Sales workers	14.5	15.8	11.7	.....	17.8	17.3	15.9	22.2
Craftsmen, foremen	8.4	15.8	5.2	7.5	.....	11.3	14.3	20.8
Operatives	12.3	15.7	4.7	9.2	2.5	.....	11.0	15.7
Service workers	14.7	19.9	6.1	14.3	5.3	5.2	.....	17.5
Laborers	10.8	14.0	1.2	8.5	1.7	−2.0	3.3	.....

APPENDIX TABLE C-1

INDEXES OF DISSIMILARITY IN RESIDENTIAL DISTRIBUTION AMONG OCCUPATION GROUPS, FOR EMPLOYED
NON-WHITE MALES, 1950 AND 1960 (CONT.)

(VALUES FOR 1950 ABOVE DIAGONAL; CHANGE, 1950–60, BELOW DIAGONAL)

City and Occupation	Professional	Manager	Clerical	Sales	Craft	Operative	Service	Labor
Cleveland								
Professional, technical	.....	23.1	20.9	25.5	29.8	31.2	26.2	43.6
Managers, officials, proprietors	7.6	.....	15.2	17.4	13.2	16.2	12.9	29.3
Clerical workers	10.8	10.1	.....	18.5	18.2	20.9	18.4	35.1
Sales workers	7.3	16.0	7.7	.....	15.6	13.3	12.1	23.9
Craftsmen, foremen	2.8	14.7	0.3	9.2	.....	6.7	11.7	19.8
Operatives	4.2	12.6	-3.2	12.7	3.7	.....	12.7	15.7
Service workers	7.0	16.4	1.4	15.2	0.3	-0.2	.....	22.8
Laborers	-1.7	4.3	-5.8	7.7	-0.7	1.3	-3.5	.....
Philadelphia								
Professional, technical	.....	19.2	15.1	18.0	18.4	24.0	17.4	27.3
Managers, officials, proprietors	9.9	.....	19.2	14.2	13.1	16.8	12.5	20.3
Clerical workers	12.5	2.2	.....	18.2	15.4	19.8	16.3	26.5
Sales workers	18.9	11.5	4.9	.....	11.0	14.5	11.5	18.6
Craftsmen, foremen	15.0	11.7	2.3	9.1	.....	9.9	11.4	16.4
Operatives	14.0	9.1	1.1	7.2	2.3	.....	16.0	12.0
Service workers	17.7	10.8	3.0	9.4	2.3	-1.2	.....	18.2
Laborers	16.2	7.9	0.7	6.8	0.6	2.9	-2.6	.....
St. Louis								
Professional, technical	.....	30.8	14.3	30.1	28.0	34.7	29.8	47.2
Managers, officials, proprietors	-6.5	.....	19.1	12.3	8.6	8.6	9.1	17.6
Clerical workers	9.2	3.6	.....	19.8	16.7	23.3	19.4	35.9
Sales workers	2.5	13.6	4.6	.....	8.9	9.6	10.8	19.5
Craftsmen, foremen	-0.8	16.1	1.0	14.5	.....	7.2	8.6	19.9
Operatives	-3.7	18.5	-4.7	13.4	5.3	.....	7.7	13.3
Service workers	-2.5	12.9	-1.4	7.6	4.4	3.3	.....	18.8
Laborers	-16.7	5.5	-15.8	-0.9	-4.4	-3.4	-10.8	.....

250

City and Occupation	Occupation							
	Professional	Manager	Clerical	Sales	Craft	Operative	Service	Labor
Washington								
Professional, technical	......	19.2	17.5	22.4	24.7	27.4	25.1	39.7
Managers, officials, proprietors	5.0	......	17.6	15.3	14.9	16.6	14.7	28.4
Clerical workers	2.1	8.4	......	19.1	16.1	19.3	20.5	32.3
Sales workers	7.0	9.7	1.6	......	13.3	14.1	13.3	24.5
Craftsmen, foremen	3.1	8.9	1.0	4.6	......	7.5	9.3	17.8
Operatives	6.0	12.3	2.2	6.0	2.7	......	11.0	14.9
Service workers	4.7	8.8	2.1	8.2	2.7	2.2	......	19.7
Laborers	-1.5	2.3	-1.6	0.5	0.0	-1.5	-4.5	......
Baltimore								
Professional, technical	......	30.9	16.7	26.5	26.3	31.3	22.8	38.0
Managers, officials, proprietors	1.1	......	24.2	18.3	16.1	15.1	17.8	21.4
Clerical workers	10.2	8.0	......	20.5	17.4	22.4	17.0	31.1
Sales workers	7.6	15.0	7.1	......	12.1	13.9	13.3	19.9
Craftsmen, foremen	7.7	18.6	2.6	16.4	......	8.7	10.0	17.9
Operatives	3.3	17.9	-0.8	12.6	2.0	......	14.7	13.6
Service workers	10.2	14.3	4.3	15.2	6.6	0.9	......	21.7
Laborers	1.0	10.2	-3.2	8.4	0.4	1.2	-5.0	......
New Orleans								
Professional, technical	......	22.8	22.0	22.8	21.4	22.9	21.9	29.7
Managers, officials, proprietors	11.5	......	25.6	22.4	16.5	16.1	18.1	21.0
Clerical workers	7.9	2.4	......	23.0	16.9	26.6	25.9	34.9
Sales workers	21.4	11.9	14.0	......	20.2	18.4	16.8	25.8
Craftsmen, foremen	10.6	6.1	4.2	13.3	......	15.4	19.3	22.5
Operatives	12.0	11.3	-0.2	14.2	3.3	......	11.0	13.3
Service workers	12.0	6.8	0.8	14.2	2.4	3.9	......	16.8
Laborers	10.6	7.4	-4.4	6.1	-1.5	0.6	0.9	......
Atlanta								
Professional, technical	......	23.8	16.7	26.8	27.0	31.9	28.6	37.6
Managers, officials, proprietors	12.3	......	14.4	18.7	17.3	18.4	16.4	22.6
Clerical workers	12.1	13.1	......	17.1	17.7	20.8	17.8	27.7
Sales workers	7.2	18.4	8.5	......	13.7	14.6	13.0	18.6
Craftsmen, foremen	18.4	19.0	10.8	19.7	......	11.2	11.9	16.2

APPENDIX TABLE C-1

INDEXES OF DISSIMILARITY IN RESIDENTIAL DISTRIBUTION AMONG OCCUPATION GROUPS, FOR EMPLOYED NON-WHITE MALES, 1950 AND 1960 (CONT.)

(VALUES FOR 1950 ABOVE DIAGONAL; CHANGE, 1950–60, BELOW DIAGONAL)

City and Occupation	Professional	Manager	Clerical	Sales	Craft	Operative	Service	Labor
Atlanta (Cont.)								
Operatives	14.7	20.1	8.0	21.1	7.4	.....	11.3	8.6
Service workers	18.7	22.1	12.1	19.7	6.2	1.2	.....	17.4
Laborers	17.8	19.0	8.1	21.0	4.5	7.4	-2.0	.....
Birmingham								
Professional, technical	.....	20.9	20.7	30.5	28.2	31.3	28.9	31.2
Managers, officials, proprietors	8.3	.....	19.7	25.6	23.3	25.2	23.7	25.8
Clerical workers	11.8	11.0	.....	21.8	19.2	25.6	18.2	25.8
Sales workers	10.5	7.7	17.4	.....	15.5	21.9	16.4	22.7
Craftsmen, foremen	7.2	8.4	6.7	18.4	.....	11.9	15.6	13.6
Operatives	8.9	9.5	0.3	10.3	0.1	.....	22.8	14.1
Service workers	6.4	9.0	2.7	15.2	0.2	-7.8	.....	18.6
Laborers	8.9	9.0	-1.0	1.5	2.7	-0.9	-4.6	.....
Memphis								
Professional, technical	.....	14.7	16.2	20.4	17.4	22.2	17.1	22.6
Managers, officials, proprietors	26.7	.....	16.0	19.4	13.4	18.2	14.5	18.0
Clerical workers	10.5	14.6	.....	20.0	13.6	14.2	17.2	18.1
Sales workers	19.7	15.9	10.8	.....	16.8	17.5	17.7	21.6
Craftsmen, foremen	11.3	15.1	5.5	12.9	.....	10.1	16.0	12.0
Operatives	9.9	10.1	3.5	10.7	2.5	.....	16.8	10.4
Service workers	18.3	14.5	6.5	12.1	4.4	0.8	.....	17.9
Laborers	11.5	13.0	3.6	10.8	2.9	1.9	4.5	.....

Source: Census Tract Bulletins for 1950 and 1960.

INDEXES OF DISSIMILARITY IN RESIDENTIAL DISTRIBUTION AMONG OCCUPATION GROUPS, FOR EMPLOYED NON-WHITE MALES, 1940 AND 1950

(VALUES FOR 1940 ABOVE DIAGONAL; CHANGE, 1940–50, BELOW DIAGONAL)

City and Occupation	Occupation						
	Professional	Manager	Clerical-Sales	Craft	Operative	Service	Labor
Washington							
Professional, semi-professional workers	.....	29.5	19.0	28.3	30.7	26.6	44.7
Proprietors, managers, officials	−10.3	.....	20.6	13.9	16.2	18.1	25.4
Clerical, sales workers	°	°	.....	19.2	19.7	19.2	34.0
Craftsmen, foremen	−3.6	1.0	°	.....	12.1	14.0	21.7
Operatives	−3.3	0.4	°	−4.6	.....	14.0	17.3
Service workers	−1.5	−3.4	°	−4.7	−3.0	.....	27.0
Laborers	−5.0	3.0	°	−3.9	−2.4	−7.3	.....
Baltimore							
Professional, semi-professional workers	.....	38.1	17.5	25.5	29.9	16.5	39.3
Proprietors, managers, officials	−7.2	.....	28.6	23.8	19.8	28.2	18.6
Clerical, sales workers	°	°	.....	15.8	18.4	11.7	27.5
Craftsmen, foremen	0.8	−7.7	°	.....	10.2	16.1	21.3
Operatives	1.4	−4.7	°	−1.5	.....	19.7	18.2
Service workers	6.3	−10.4	°	−6.1	−5.0	.....	30.9
Laborers	−1.3	2.8	°	−3.4	−4.6	−9.2	.....
New Orleans							
Professional, semi-professional workers	.....	28.9	21.3	23.5	20.5	22.2	30.3
Proprietors, managers, officials	−6.1	.....	28.9	27.7	21.7	25.2	21.3
Clerical, sales workers	°	°	.....	17.9	18.8	23.1	32.4
Craftsmen, foremen	−2.1	−11.2	°	.....	17.5	23.2	28.5
Operatives	2.4	−5.6	°	−2.1	.....	14.0	20.7
Service workers	−0.3	−7.1	°	−3.9	−3.0	.....	23.9
Laborers	−0.6	−0.3	°	−6.0	−7.4	−7.1	.....

APPENDIX TABLE C-2

INDEXES OF DISSIMILARITY IN RESIDENTIAL DISTRIBUTION AMONG OCCUPATION GROUPS, FOR EMPLOYED NON-WHITE MALES, 1940 AND 1950 (CONT.)

(VALUES FOR 1940 ABOVE DIAGONAL; CHANGE, 1940–50, BELOW DIAGONAL)

City and Occupation	Occupation						
	Professional	Manager	Clerical-Sales	Craft	Operative	Service	Labor
Atlanta							
Professional, semi-professional workers	……	30.0	19.5	26.0	30.8	30.2	37.2
Proprietors, managers, officials	-6.2	……	21.3	15.5	18.2	16.3	27.2
Clerical sales workers	°	°	……	17.1	19.8	20.0	28.3
Craftsmen, foremen	1.0	0.2	°	……	10.6	15.6	20.4
Operatives	1.1	0.1	°	0.6	……	15.5	15.3
Service workers	-1.6	1.8	°	-3.7	-4.2	……	26.1
Laborers	0.4	-4.6	°	-4.2	-6.7	-8.7	……
Birmingham							
Professional, semi-professional workers	……	26.5	22.8	31.0	30.8	34.0	32.9
Proprietors, managers, officials	-5.6	……	16.9	23.7	27.7	21.6	28.2
Clerical sales workers	°	°	……	22.4	26.2	18.0	27.0
Craftsmen, foremen	-2.8	-0.4	°	……	17.8	26.8	16.5
Operatives	0.5	-2.5	°	-5.9	……	32.3	13.4
Service workers	-5.1	2.1	°	-11.2	-9.5	……	31.1
Laborers	-1.7	-2.4	°	-2.9	0.7	-12.5	……
Memphis							
Professional, semi-professional workers	……	32.0	17.0	22.7	25.9	24.7	32.3
Proprietors, managers, officials	-17.3	……	23.5	25.3	22.6	24.5	25.0
Clerical sales workers	°	°	……	18.8	17.3	19.6	26.9
Craftsmen, foremen	-5.3	-11.9	°	……	13.6	22.8	22.8
Operatives	-3.7	-4.4	°	-3.5	……	20.0	18.5
Service workers	-7.6	-10.0	°	-6.8	-3.2	……	32.7
Laborers	-9.7	-7.0	°	-10.8	-8.1	-14.8	……

Source: Census Tract Bulletins for 1940 and 1950.

° Not comparable, since clerical and sales workers were treated as one group in 1940. The number of census tracts in 1940 upon which the index is based is as follows: Washington, 62; Baltimore, 52; New Orleans, 86; Atlanta, 44; Birmingham, 43; and Memphis, 53.

APPENDIX D

MAPS OF CENSUS TRACTS
IN TEN CITIES, CLASSIFIED
BY TYPE OF RACIAL CHANGE

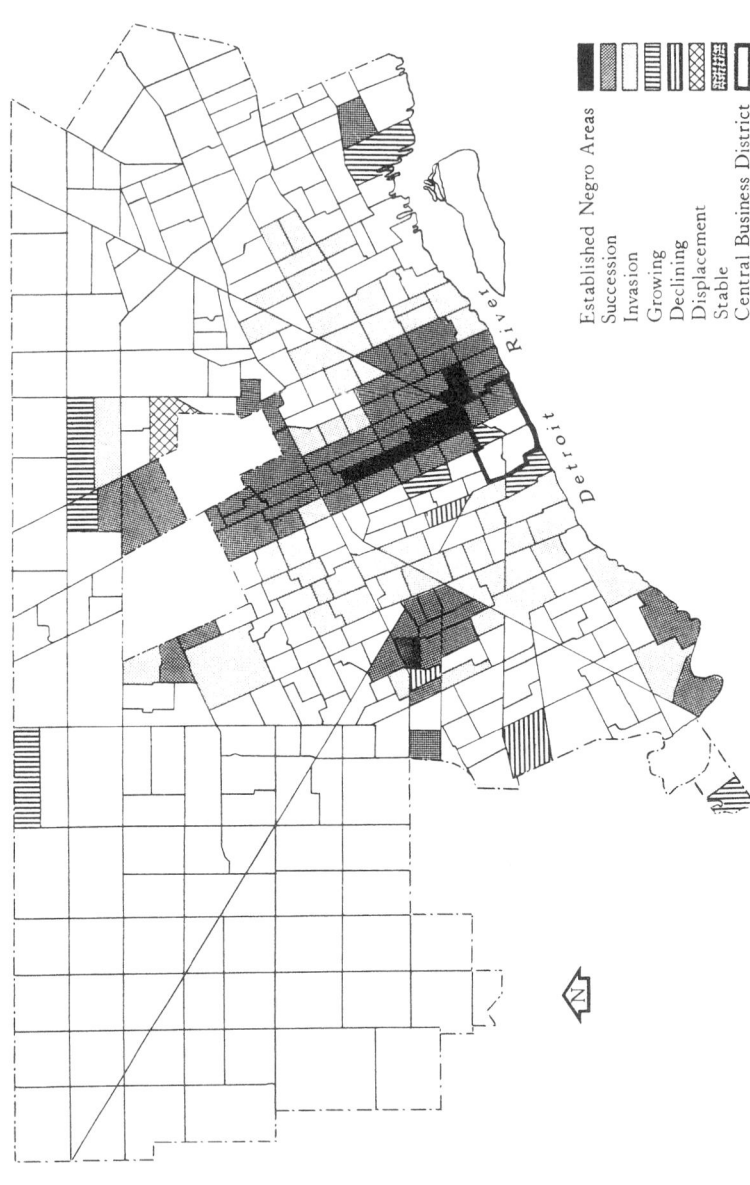

FIGURE D-1. – *Detroit: Census Tracts with 250 or More Non-whites in 1950, Classified by Type of Racial Change, 1940–50*

Legend:
Established Negro Areas
Succession
Invasion
Growing
Declining
Displacement
Stable
Central Business District

River
Detroit
N

FIGURE D-2.— *Detroit: Census Tracts with 250 or More Non-whites in 1960, Classified by Type of Racial Change, 1950–60*

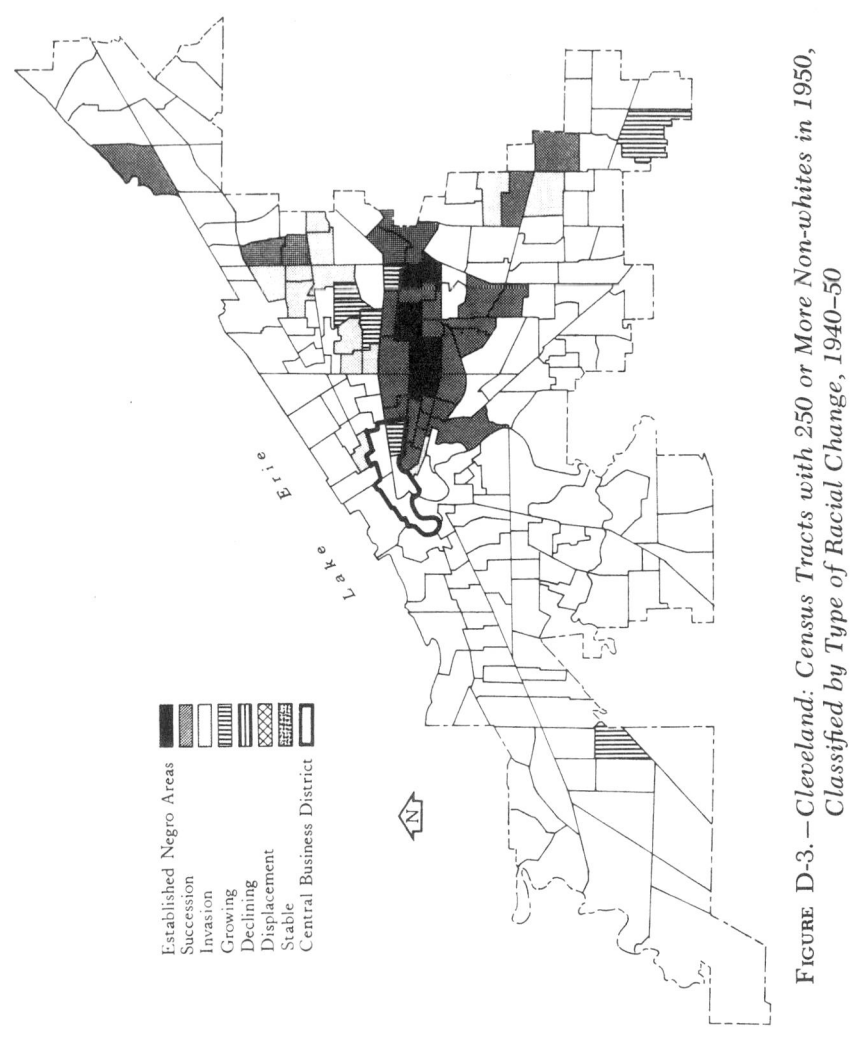

FIGURE D-3. — *Cleveland: Census Tracts with 250 or More Non-whites in 1950, Classified by Type of Racial Change, 1940–50*

Established Negro Areas
Succession
Invasion
Growing
Declining
Displacement
Stable
Central Business District

Lake Erie

N

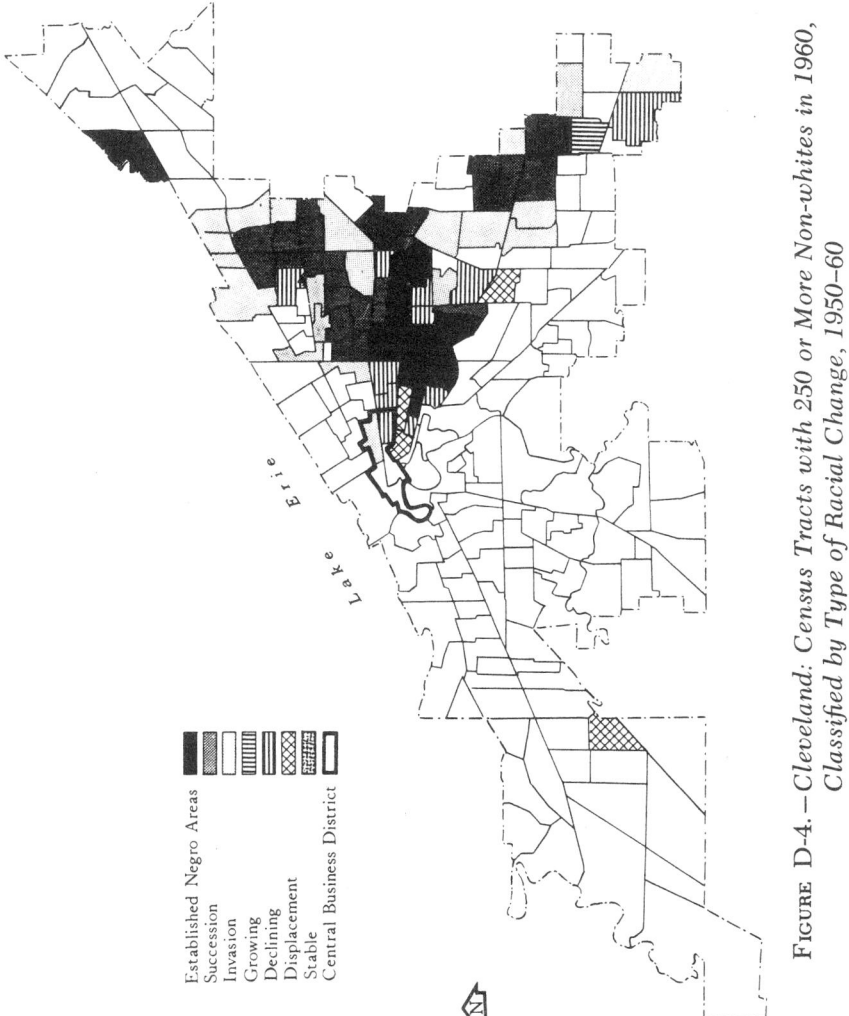

FIGURE D-4. — *Cleveland: Census Tracts with 250 or More Non-whites in 1960, Classified by Type of Racial Change, 1950–60*

259

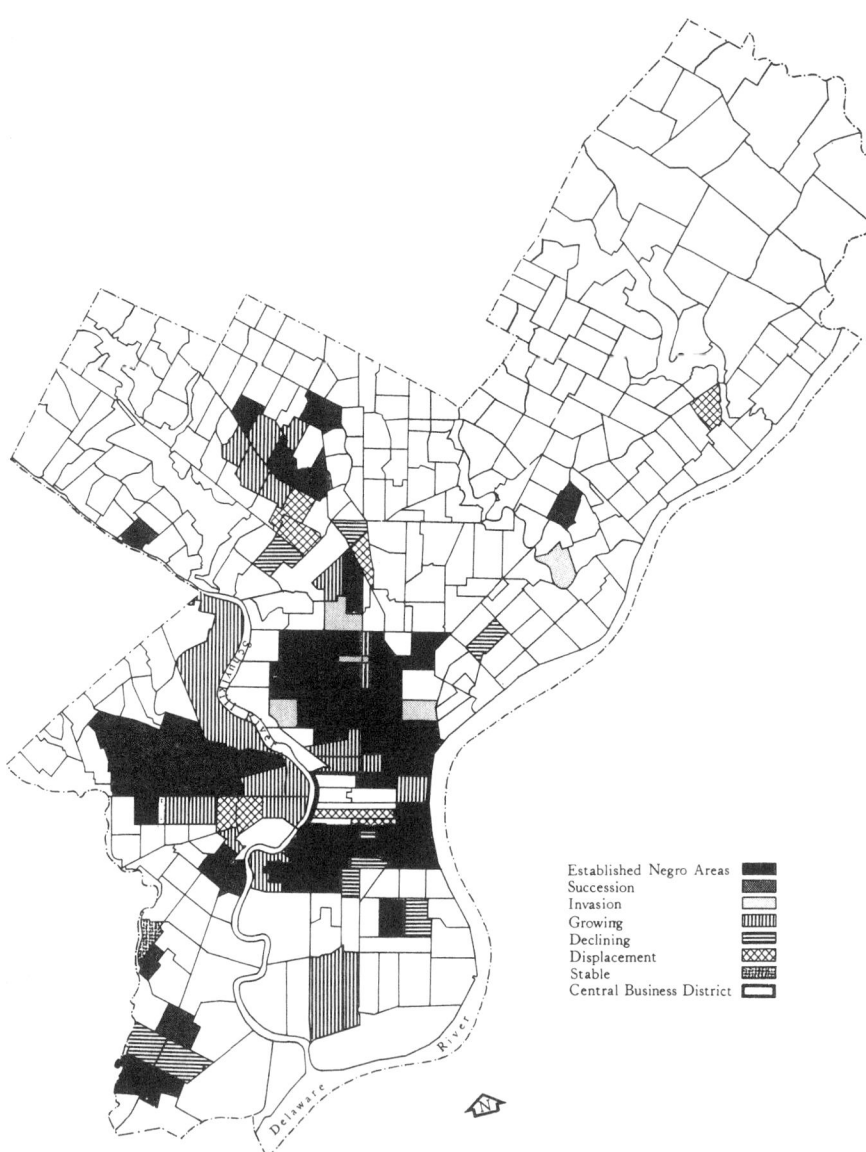

Established Negro Areas
Succession
Invasion
Growing
Declining
Displacement
Stable
Central Business District

FIGURE D-5.—*Philadelphia: Census Tracts with 250 or More Non-whites in 1950, Classified by Type of Racial Change, 1940–50*

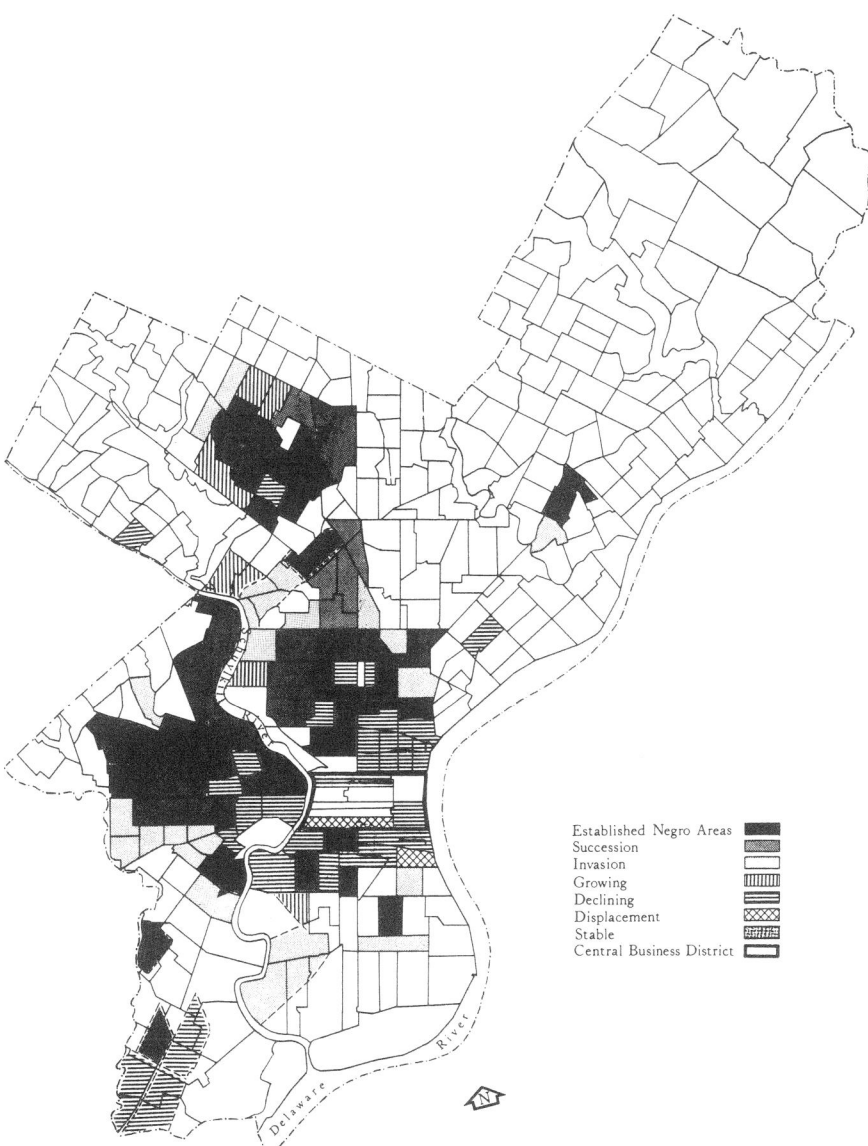

Established Negro Areas
Succession
Invasion
Growing
Declining
Displacement
Stable
Central Business District

FIGURE D-6.—*Philadelphia: Census Tracts with 250 or More Non-whites in 1960, Classified by Type of Racial Change, 1950–60*

Established Negro Areas
Succession
Invasion
Growing
Declining
Displacement
Stable
Central Business District

FIGURE D-7. — *St. Louis: Census Tracts with 250 or More Non-whites in 1950, Classified by Type of Racial Change, 1940–50*

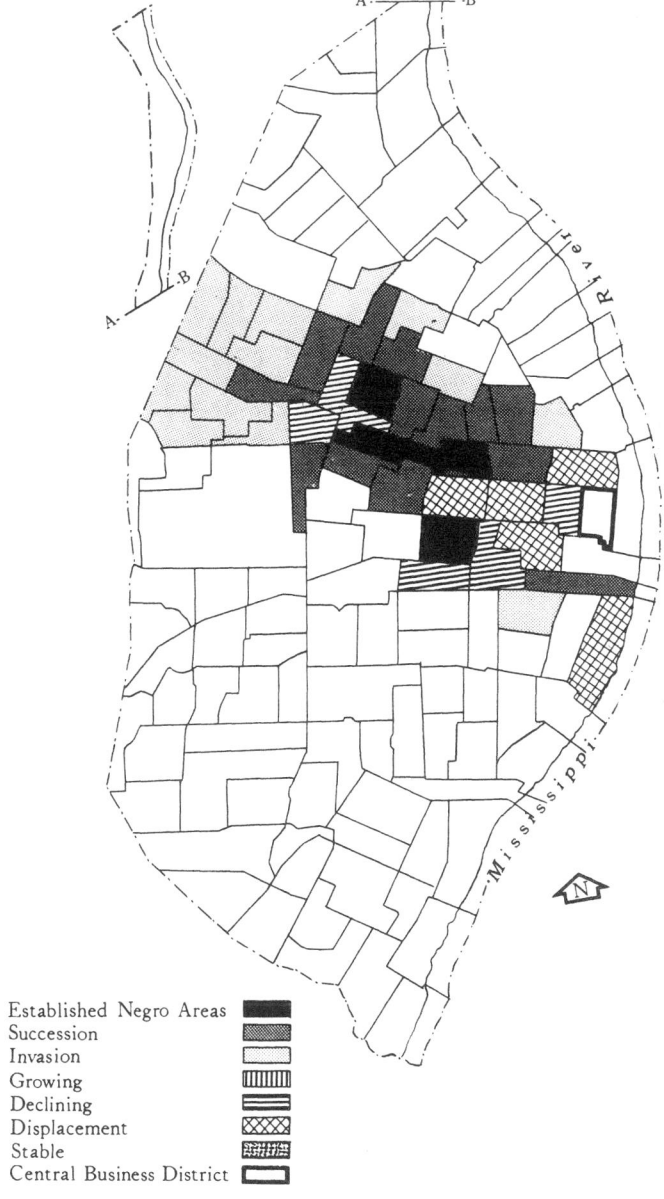

Established Negro Areas
Succession
Invasion
Growing
Declining
Displacement
Stable
Central Business District

FIGURE D-8. — *St. Louis: Census Tracts with 250 or More Non-whites in 1960, Classified by Type of Racial Change, 1950–60*

Established Negro Areas
Succession
Invasion
Growing
Declining
Displacement
Stable
Central Business District

FIGURE D-9.—*Washington, D.C.: Census Tracts with 250 or More Non-whites in 1950, Classified by Type of Racial Change, 1940–50*

Established Negro Areas
Succession
Invasion
Growing
Declining
Displacement
Stable
Central Business District

FIGURE D-10.—*Washington, D.C.: Census Tracts with 250 or More Non-whites in 1960, Classified by Type of Racial Change, 1950–60*

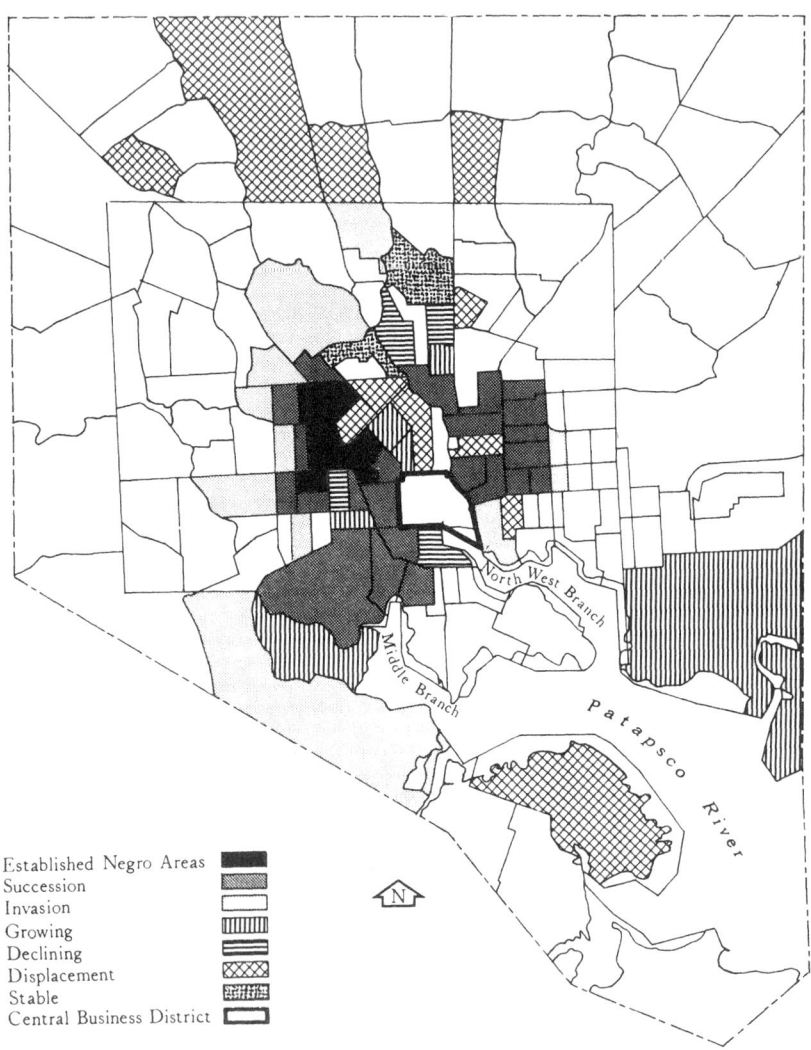

Established Negro Areas
Succession
Invasion
Growing
Declining
Displacement
Stable
Central Business District

FIGURE D-11. — *Baltimore: Census Tracts with 250 or More Non-whites in 1950, Classified by Type of Racial Change, 1940–50*

FIGURE D-12. — *Baltimore: Census Tracts with 250 or More Non-whites in 1960, Classified by Type of Racial Change, 1950–60*

Established Negro Areas
Succession
Invasion
Growing
Declining
Displacement
Stable
Central Business District

FIGURE D-13. — *New Orleans: Census Tracts with 250 or More Non-whites in 1950, Classified by Type of Racial Change, 1940–50*

Established Negro Areas
Succession
Invasion
Growing
Declining
Displacement
Stable
Central Business District

FIGURE D-14. — *New Orleans: Census Tracts with 250 or More Non-whites in 1960, Classified by Type of Racial Change, 1950–60*

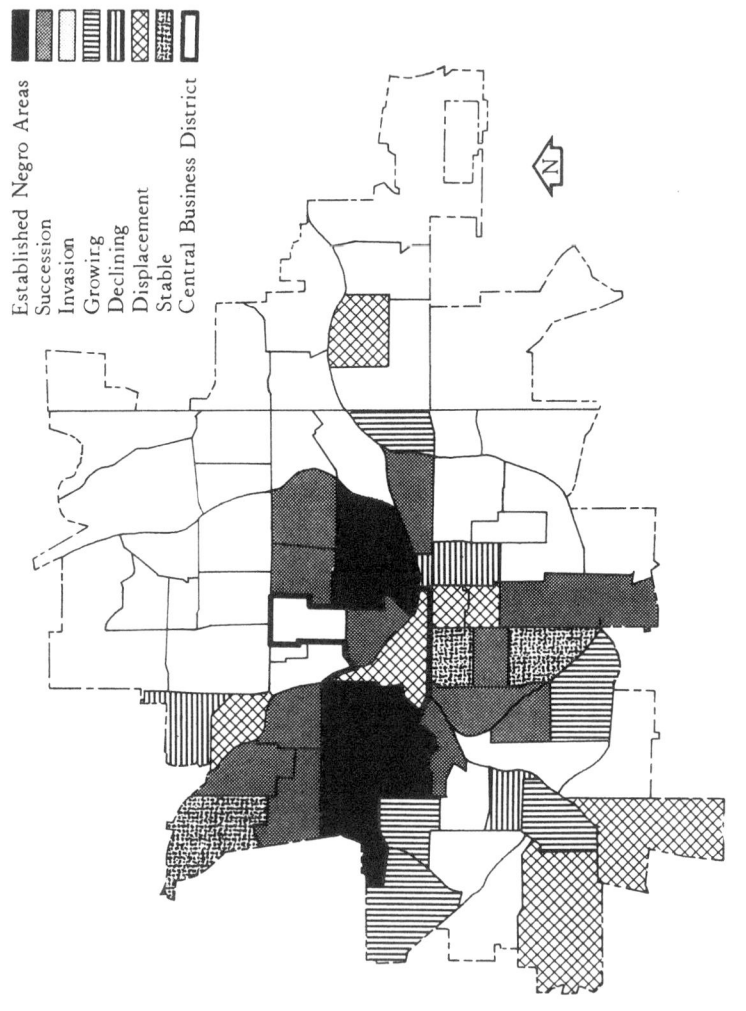

FIGURE D-15. – *Atlanta: Census Tracts with 250 or More Non-whites in 1950, Classified by Type of Racial Change, 1940–50*

Established Negro Areas
Succession
Invasion
Growing
Declining
Displacement
Stable
Central Business District

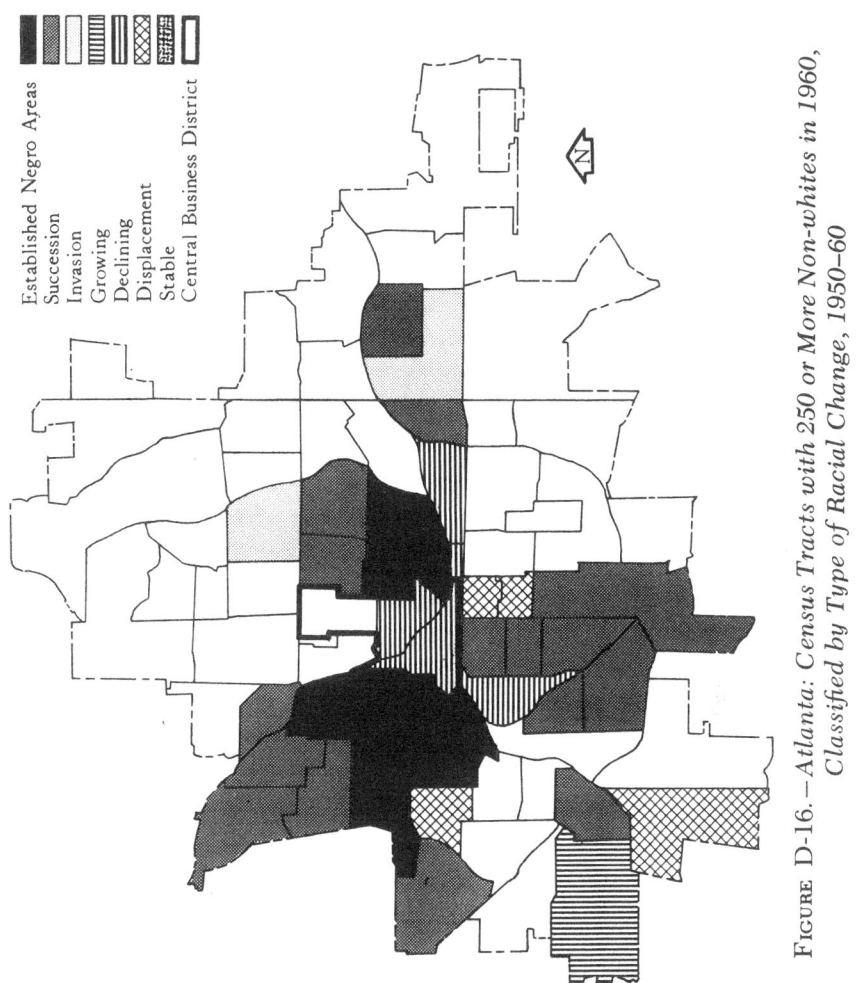

FIGURE D-16. – *Atlanta: Census Tracts with 250 or More Non-whites in 1960, Classified by Type of Racial Change, 1950–60*

Established Negro Areas
Succession
Invasion
Growing
Declining
Displacement
Stable
Central Business District

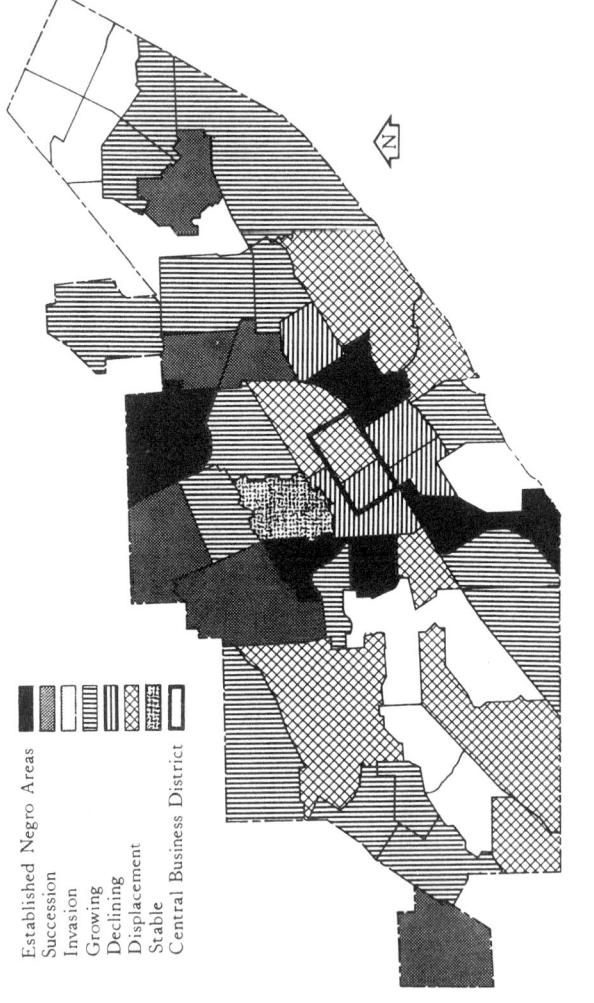

Established Negro Areas
Succession
Invasion
Growing
Declining
Displacement
Stable
Central Business District

N

FIGURE D-17. — *Birmingham: Census Tracts with 250 or More Non-whites in 1950, Classified by Type of Racial Change, 1940–50*

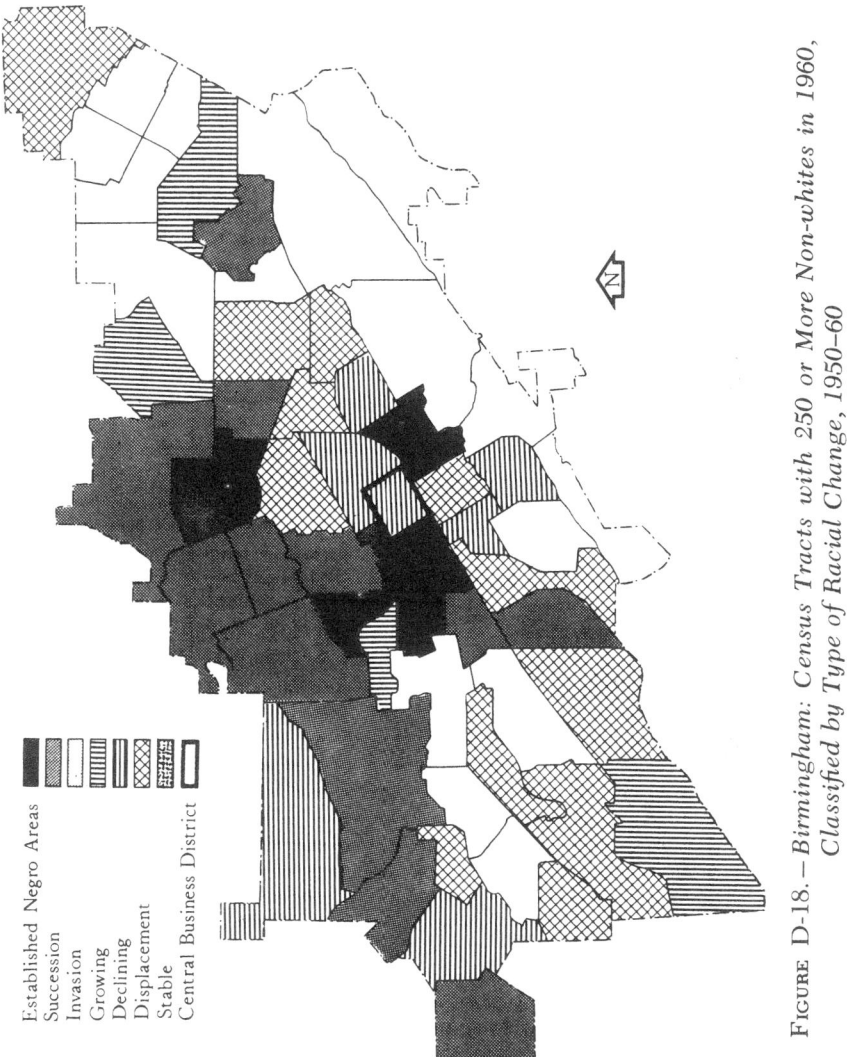

FIGURE D-18. – *Birmingham: Census Tracts with 250 or More Non-whites in 1960, Classified by Type of Racial Change, 1950–60*

Established Negro Areas
Succession
Invasion
Growing
Declining
Displacement
Stable
Central Business District

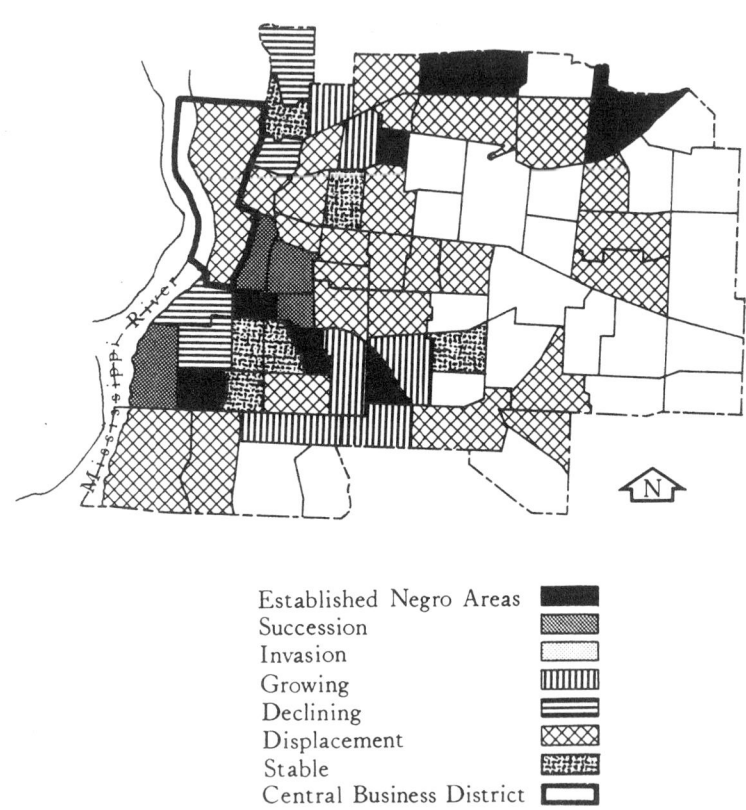

Established Negro Areas
Succession
Invasion
Growing
Declining
Displacement
Stable
Central Business District

FIGURE D-19. — *Memphis: Census Tracts with 250 or More Non-whites in 1950, Classified by Type of Racial Change, 1940–50*

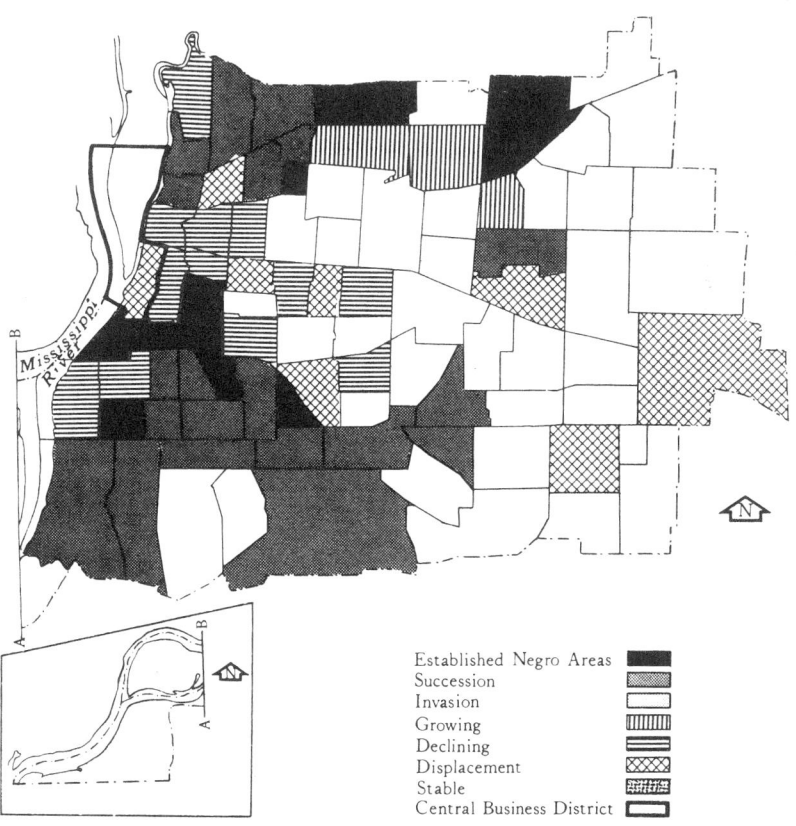

Established Negro Areas
Succession
Invasion
Growing
Declining
Displacement
Stable
Central Business District

FIGURE D-20. — *Memphis: Census Tracts with 250 or More Non-whites in 1960, Classified by Type of Racial Change, 1950–60*

SELECTED BIBLIOGRAPHY

ABRAMS, CHARLES. *Forbidden Neighbors: A Study of Prejudice in Housing.* New York: Harper & Brothers, 1955.

BURGESS, ERNEST W. "Residential Segregation in American Cities," *Annals of the American Academy of Political and Social Science,* Publication No. 2180 (November, 1928), 1–11.

CHICAGO COMMUNITY INVENTORY. *Chicago's Negro Population: Characteristics and Trends.* A Report to the Office of the Housing and Redevelopment Coordinator and the Chicago Plan Commission. Prepared by OTIS DUDLEY DUNCAN and BEVERLY DUNCAN. Chicago: Chicago Community Inventory, University of Chicago, 1956.

COMMISSION ON RACE AND HOUSING. *Where Shall We Live?* Berkeley: University of California Press, 1958.

DRAKE, ST. CLAIR and CAYTON, HORACE R. *Black Metropolis: A Study of Negro Life in a Northern City.* New York: Harcourt, Brace, 1945.

DuBOIS, W. E. B. *The Philadelphia Negro.* Philadelphia: Publications of the University of Pennsylvania, 1899.

_____ *The Souls of Black Folk.* Chicago: A. C. McClurg, 1904.

DUNCAN, BEVERLY and HAUSER, PHILIP M. *Housing a Metropolis—Chicago.* Glencoe, Ill.: The Free Press, 1960.

DUNCAN, OTIS DUDLEY and DUNCAN, BEVERLY. "A Methodological Analysis of Segregation Indexes," *American Sociological Review,* XX (April, 1955), 210–217.

_____ *The Negro Population of Chicago: A Study of Residential Succession.* Chicago: University of Chicago Press, 1957.

_____ "Residential Distribution and Occupational Stratification," *American Journal of Sociology,* LX (March, 1955), 493–503.

DUNCAN, OTIS DUDLEY, CUZZORT, RAY P., and DUNCAN, BEVERLY. *Statistical Geography.* Glencoe, Ill.: The Free Press, 1961.

FRAZIER, E. FRANKLIN. *The Negro in the United States.* Rev. ed. New York: The Macmillan Co., 1957.

FREEDMAN, RONALD. *Recent Migration to Chicago.* Chicago: University of Chicago Press, 1950.

GRIER, EUNICE and GRIER, GEORGE. *Privately Developed Interracial Housing: An Analysis of Experience.* Berkeley: University of California Press, 1960.

GRODZINS, MORTON. *The Metropolitan Area as a Racial Problem.* Pittsburgh: University of Pittsburgh Press, 1958.

HANDLIN, OSCAR. *The Newcomers: Negroes and Puerto Ricans in a Changing Metropolis.* Cambridge: Harvard University Press, 1959.

HAWLEY, AMOS H. *Human Ecology.* New York: The Ronald Press, 1950.

HEBERLE, RUDOLF. "Social Consequences of the Industrialization of Southern Cities," in *Cities and Society,* ed. Paul K. Hatt and Albert J. Reiss, Jr. Glencoe, Ill.: The Free Press, 1957.

HOYT, HOMER. *Structure and Growth of Residential Neighborhoods.* U. S. Federal Housing Administration. Washington: Government Printing Office, 1939.

JOHNSON, CHARLES S. *Patterns of Negro Segregation.* New York: Harper & Brothers, 1943.

KENNEDY, LOUISE V. *The Negro Peasant Turns Cityward.* New York: Columbia University Press, 1930.

LAURENTI, LUIGI. *Property Values and Race: Studies in Seven Cities.* Berkeley: University of California Press, 1960.

LIEBERSON, STANLEY. *Ethnic Patterns in American Cities.* New York: The Free Press of Glencoe, 1963.

MYRDAL, GUNNAR. *An American Dilemma.* 2 vols. New York: Harper & Brothers, 1944.

RODWIN, LLOYD. *Housing and Economic Progress: A Study of the Housing Experiences of Boston's Middle-Income Families.* Cambridge: Harvard University Press and The Technology Press, 1961.

TAEUBER, KARL E. AND TAEUBER, ALMA F. "The Negro Population in the United States," in *The American Negro Reference Book.* Englewood Cliffs, N.J.: Prentice-Hall, 1965.

——————"The Negro as an Immigrant Group: Recent Trends in Racial and Ethnic Segregation in Chicago," *American Journal of Sociology,* LXIX (January, 1964), 374–382.

U. S. COMMISSION ON CIVIL RIGHTS. *1961 Report.* Part VI, *Housing.* Washington: U. S. Government Printing Office, 1961.

WADE, RICHARD C. *Slavery in the Cities: The South, 1820–1860.* New York: Oxford University Press, 1964.

WALLACE, DAVID A. "Residential Concentration of Negroes in Chicago." Unpublished Ph.D. thesis. Harvard University, 1953.

WEAVER, ROBERT C. *The Negro Ghetto.* New York: Harcourt, Brace, 1948.

WIRTH, LOUIS. *The Ghetto.* Chicago: University of Chicago Press, 1928.

WOLF, ELEANOR. "Racial Transition in a Middle-Class Area," *Journal of Intergroup Relations,* I (Summer, 1960), 75–81.

WOODSON, CARTER G. *A Century of Negro Migration.* Washington: The Association for the Study of Negro Life and History, 1918.

WOOFTER, T. J., JR. *Negro Problems in Cities.* Garden City: Doubleday, Doran, 1928.

INDEX

Printed in Great Britain
by Amazon

54557388R00174